Merchant Congressman in the Young Republic
Samuel Smith of Maryland, 1752-1839

Merchant Congressman
in the Young Republic

Samuel Smith of Maryland, 1752-1839

FRANK A. CASSELL

The University of Wisconsin Press

MADISON, MILWAUKEE,
AND LONDON

PUBLISHED 1971
THE UNIVERSITY OF WISCONSIN PRESS
BOX 1379, MADISON, WISCONSIN 53701

THE UNIVERSITY OF WISCONSIN PRESS, LTD.
70 GREAT RUSSELL STREET, LONDON, WC1B 3BY

FIRST PRINTING

PRINTED IN THE UNITED STATES OF AMERICA
KINGSPORT PRESS, INC., KINGSPORT, TENNESSEE

ISBN 0-299-06000-4; LC 79-157390

For Beth

Contents

Illustrations

Preface

In April of 1911 a feature article appeared in the Baltimore *Sun* dealing with the history of Montebello, a magnificent old mansion that had been a landmark in the city for decades but had recently been torn down. Although the reporter described at length the architectural splendor of Montebello, he admitted that he was far more interested in the builder and first owner of the house, General Samuel Smith, who had died in 1839. In investigating Smith, the reporter discovered that this long-since forgotten man had not only been a major figure in Baltimore and Maryland during the early years of the Republic, but also had exercised significant influence in national affairs. A distinguished legislator, decorated soldier, and contributor to Baltimore's commercial prosperity, Samuel Smith had lived a long and exciting life, and the *Sun*'s reporter expressed amazement that "the gallant gentleman should so soon be forgotten."

The article in the *Sun* may well have stimulated renewed interest in Samuel Smith. A few years afterward the citizens of Baltimore tardily erected a statue to the man who had saved the city from invasion in 1814. Located near the harbor, the statue is a poor likeness, more reminiscent of Andrew Jackson than Samuel Smith. About the same time a descendant of Smith's, Mrs. Cary Nicholas Fink, compiled a family history which gave the general a prominent part. Mrs. Fink's work, however, never was published and still remains in typescript in the University of Virginia library. A few scholars, including Henry Adams, had pointed out Smith's significance as a political figure even before 1911, but it was not until 1949 that anyone seriously undertook a full-scale biography. In that year John Silas Pancake completed a dissertation for the University of Virginia that for the first time established the chronology of Smith's life and outlined his importance in state and national politics. In my own dissertation for Northwestern University in 1968 I undertook to analyze the first twenty years of Smith's career in Congress, concluding that his impact on public policy was greater than had been previously thought. While the present volume has benefited from these earlier works, it is mainly based on new and extensive research in manuscript materials.[1] I have also made use of the many scholarly studies on special aspects of the early national period that have appeared in recent years. My object has been to write a biography that not only relates the story of Samuel Smith, but also places him in the context of his times.

Although Smith's importance is most evident in national politics, his business and military careers cannot be neglected since each aspect of his life interacted with and reinforced the others. He was, for example, a powerful political figure in Washington because he was a popular military hero in Baltimore and a knowledgeable and successful merchant. But at the same token the fact that he was influential in Washington meant that his control over Baltimore's politics was buttressed by federal patronage and his problems as a military commander were eased by the support he received from his friends in the government. No one realized this interdependence more than Smith himself. It was part of his genius to skillfully blend his roles as politician, soldier, and merchant in such a way as to maximize his success in all three areas.

A biographer of Samuel Smith faces a difficult problem in his efforts to fully explore these intricate connections in his life. Despite the vast amount of available material either written by or about Smith, many vital documents are missing from the record. Some, especially political correspondence, were burned by Smith himself. By carefully checking the papers of those with whom he maintained contact, part of this information can be reconstructed. Much more serious is the absence of the bulk of Smith's business records. Aside from a few ledgers and letterbooks, little remains from which to judge the scope of S. Smith & Buchanan's operations. More precise knowledge of Smith's business interests at particular periods might well contribute to a better understanding of his political behavior. References to family and personal life are also very infrequent in the Smith papers, thus inhibiting judgment about the effects of domestic conditions on the general's conduct. Despite the scarcity of some types of information, I have yet pursued this topic in the belief that a scholarly biography

1. In quoting from primary sources, I have been faithful to the original texts except for a very few instances where I have silently made a minor correction in the punctuation or capitalization to avoid confusion.

of Samuel Smith was not only long overdue, but also potentially valuable in understanding the complex nature of American politics during the early national period.

In the research and writing of this book I have become indebted to more individuals than I can adequately acknowledge. I am particularly grateful for the courteous assistance given me by the staffs of the Manuscripts Division of the Library of Congress, the Maryland Historical Society, the New-York Historical Society, the Virginia Historical Society, and the libraries at Northwestern University, the University of Chicago, Columbia University, and the University of Wisconsin—Milwaukee. I owe a particular debt of gratitude to William G. Ray of the Manuscripts Division of the University of Virginia Library, who spent many hours pointing out useful materials. Professors Clarence Ver Steeg, Robert Wiebe, and George Daniels of Northwestern University, William Nisbet Chambers of Washington University in St. Louis, Daniel Crofts of New York University, and James Curtis of the University of Delaware either read the manuscript at an earlier stage or made useful suggestions. I reserve special thanks for my colleagues and friends, Professors Reginald Horsman and Keith Bryant of the University of Wisconsin—Milwaukee, who freely gave of their time and special knowledge. The labors of Mrs. Alice Schaus and Mrs. Hazel Kay in putting the manuscript into final form must also be acknowledged. Portions of chapters 7, 12, and 13 have previously appeared in the *Maryland Historical Magazine* 63, no. 4 (December 1968): 341–359, 66 (September 1971): 261–287, and *Military Affairs* 33, no. 3 (December 1969): 349–360. I am grateful to the publishers for permission to reprint this material. Above all I am deeply obligated to my wife, Elizabeth Weber Cassell, who typed many drafts, checked countless quotations, and corrected scores of punctuation errors, and who, in spite of herself, developed a sincere admiration for Samuel Smith.

Milwaukee, Wisconsin   FRANK A. CASSELL
October 1971

Merchant Congressman in the Young Republic
Samuel Smith of Maryland, 1752-1839

I

The Training of a
Merchant

SOMETIME IN the year 1750 a caravan of wagons carrying four
Scotch-Irish families reached the infant frontier settlement of Carlisle,
Pennsylvania. The families—Smiths, Buchanans, Sterrets, and Spears
—had migrated to America at the same time in the 1720s and
stayed together ever since. Before coming to Carlisle they had resided
in Lancaster County, Pennsylvania, where several of the families,
particularly the Smiths, had been numbered among the moderately
wealthy. The patriarch of the Smith clan was old Samuel Smith, who
was nearly seventy when the family arrived in Carlisle. Samuel had
been the first to make the journey from Ulster to America, coming
over in 1728 to fill a minor office in the proprietary government of
Pennsylvania. Partial to high living as a young man, Samuel also had
business ability and within a few years owned a considerable amount
of land as well as a flour mill. As his economic position improved,
his social stature increased, as shown by the fact that he served ten
years as the sheriff of Lancaster County. But by 1750 he was too
infirm to continue either in business or government and therefore
turned his affairs over to his son John.[1]

1. See the unfinished manuscript biography of Smith written by Cary Nicholas
Fink and located in the Smith-Carter Papers, University of Virginia Library;
Baltimore *Sun*, April 26, 1839; and Samuel Smith's Autobiography, 1834, [p. 1],
Samuel Smith Papers, Library of Congress.

John Smith was a remarkable man in his own right. Twenty-eight years old in 1750, he made the decision to liquidate the family's holdings in Lancaster and move west in search of greater opportunity. Once in Carlisle John wasted no time in establishing himself as a prominent citizen. With the funds earned from the sale of property in Lancaster he purchased land around Carlisle and opened a general store. The store was a shrewd investment. In it John stocked manufactured items needed or wanted by the local farmers. He took in payment the farmer's wheat crops, which he then shipped by wagon to another new town, Baltimore on Chesapeake Bay. There the wheat was purchased by merchants and sent to other parts of the sprawling British empire. Within a very few years John Smith's business enterprises had made him a rich man by contemporary standards. Like his father he accepted the public responsibilities that wealth entailed and served several terms in the lower house of the Pennsylvania legislature.

The same year he arrived in Carlisle John Smith wed Mary Buchanan, whom he had known since childhood. Less than two years later, on July 27, 1752, Mary gave birth to the first of five children, a boy, who was named Samuel in honor of John's father. Young Samuel Smith grew up in a commercial milieu; the sight of farmers exchanging their crops for plows, linens, and other goods at his father's store would have been familiar to him. The boy was also very much aware of the military activity around Carlisle, once recalling that he had seen elements of General Braddock's shattered army pass through the town after the disastrous ambush by the French and their Indian allies. Throughout the late 1750s Carlisle was an important military post often teeming with militia units. The scene of troops drilling might well have infused young Samuel with the taste for military life so evident in his later career.[2]

In 1758 John and Mary Smith enrolled their oldest son in a local school run by the Reverend William Suffield. The boy seems to have been an apt pupil, for in less than a year he had not only learned how to read, but also had mastered a great deal of classical Greek and Roman literature. His education was abruptly interrupted in 1759, when his father suddenly sold his store and moved the family to Baltimore. John Smith's decision to abandon the Pennsylvania frontier was due to the unsettled conditions caused by the prolonged war between France and England. After 1755 fierce fighting in the area

2. Smith's Autobiography, [p. 1], Smith Papers.

around Carlisle had adversely affected the fortunes of the family business. The demands on farmers to perform militia duties and the general fear of Indian attack drastically reduced the production of wheat. And, of course, there was always the possibility that Carlisle itself might be attacked. Influenced by these considerations, the Smiths (again accompanied by the Buchanans, Sterrets, and Spears) packed their belongings and resumed their trek, this time south and east toward the small but growing town on the Patapsco River.[3]

It was perhaps natural that John Smith should lead his family to Baltimore. For years he had done business with merchants there and could count on these friends to assist him in reestablishing himself commercially. As a successful entrepreneur he was aware that Baltimore showed signs of becoming a major port. Thirty years old, the city contained a few dozen houses, one inn, a shipyard, a brewery, and a population of less than a thousand. Because it was located farther inland than any other port there was every reason to believe that it would become a central entrepôt into which would flow the produce not only of Maryland but also of northern Virginia and central Pennsylvania. As these areas became more populated and agricultural productivity grew, the need for the kinds of services merchants offered would correspondingly increase. Men such as John Smith who were willing to risk their capital on the city's future when that future was still uncertain would be repaid many times over.[4]

The new citizens proved themselves assets to Baltimore's society and economy. With the forty thousand dollars he brought with him from Carlisle, John Smith soon formed a business partnership with his brother-in-law, William Buchanan. The new firm invested heavily in slaves and ships. The slaves were used to build several wharves in Baltimore harbor, one of them reputed to have been a thousand feet long. Since the wharves were the only ones in the town that reached as far as the ship channel, Smith & Buchanan enjoyed a definite advantage. While other merchants found it necessary to hire swarms of small barges to load or unload cargoes from sea-going ships, vessels dealing with Smith & Buchanan could tie up at the company's docks. The slaves were also assigned the task of constructing warehouses in which the firm stored wheat intended for export. As it had been in Carlisle, wheat was the basis of John Smith's fortune. Ships flying the blue and white flag of Smith &

3. Ibid.; S. Smith to Mrs. Mansfield, May 25, 1823, Smith Papers.
4. Hamilton Owens, *Baltimore on the Chesapeake* (Garden City, N.Y., 1941), p. 43; Smith's Autobiography, [p. 1], Smith Papers.

Buchanan carried Maryland and Pennsylvania wheat to Europe, South America, and, most frequently, to the West Indies, where food was chronically in short supply. Although details of Smith & Buchanan's business transactions are sketchy, there is no question that the partners made a great deal of money. They were able to buy several parcels of land in Baltimore on Gay and Water streets, and both men erected grand mansions that became centers of social life in the town. By the end of the 1760s John Smith and William Buchanan had emerged as leading commercial figures and had laid the groundwork for family dynasties destined to dominate Baltimore's economy and politics for decades to come.

While his father devoted his energies to business, Samuel Smith returned to school. Since Baltimore had no educational institution when the Smiths first arrived, Samuel spent several years in small private academies in Little Elk, Maryland, and Newark, Delaware, where he resumed his studies of classical literature. In 1762 he returned to Baltimore and entered the first school established in the town. After four more years of studying "the latin and some of the Greek classics," the young man, now fourteen, ended his formal education. Then, in expectation of one day joining his father's firm as a partner, Samuel began working as a clerk in the counting house of Smith & Buchanan. For the next five years, from 1766 to 1771, he labored over the firm's books, mastering the details of commercial transactions and imbibing the businessman's values of thrift, integrity, regularity, and shrewdness. While serving this rigorous apprenticeship Smith grew into manhood, and, despite the long hours spent peering at business ledgers, he somehow found time to develop a rugged physique. He was nearly six feet tall, with broad shoulders and a deep chest. The earliest portrait of the young man depicts a countenance that is pleasant, even handsome, but the nose is too prominent and the mouth too wide in proportion to the rest of the face. He also possessed black, unkempt hair that obviously resisted combing, and dark, intense eyes (see illustrations).

When Samuel Smith reached the age of nineteen his father decided to send him to England. John Smith apparently had several objects in view. For one thing he hoped to broaden his son's experience by having him work for several years in the offices of a large London mercantile establishment, Mildred, Roberts and Co. He also intended to reap a profit from his son's stay in the great center of world trade. Not only would Samuel be able to send back first-hand information on market conditions and opportunities for investment, but he would also act as a personal agent of Smith & Buchanan, seeking out business contacts among London's merchants. As it turned out John's faith in his son was not misplaced.[5]

Accompanied by two slaves, Samuel Smith traveled to Europe in the summer of 1771 aboard the *Carlisle*, a ship owned by Smith & Buchanan. Smith made the voyage not as a passenger but as supercargo; it was his responsibility to deliver safely to Havre de Grace the ship's cargo of flour, which had been purchased by the French government. He was then to cross the English Channel and take up his responsibilities in London. When the ship arrived in France, however, Smith found orders to sail immediately for Bristol and unload the *Carlisle*'s cargo at that port. Having completed this task Smith left the ship and journeyed by coach to London. There he spent a hectic few weeks becoming acquainted with the merchants his father had conducted business with for years but had never met. Despite his rusticity Smith evidently made a good impression on his hosts. Perhaps drawn by the extraordinary self-confidence in one so young or by his easy grace and good humor, several important businessmen took particular interest in the young American. For his part Smith eagerly cultivated these individuals and skillfully translated personal friendships into contracts for Smith & Buchanan.[6]

At some point during his stay in London Smith decided not to follow his father's instructions in regard to assuming a position with the commercial house. Reasoning that he could learn more about trade by touring Europe than as an obscure London clerk, Smith returned to Bristol in August 1772. There, on his own initiative, he rented the *Carlisle* to local merchants anxious to send a cargo of lead to Venice with the understanding that he would accompany the ship.[7] Several days before the vessel sailed Smith finally faced up to the delicate task of explaining to his father the reasons for embarking on a venture so different from what had been intended. Without mentioning why he had rejected the job in London, Smith stressed the possible economic benefits to Smith & Buchanan. "I may get some consignments from that part of the world," he noted, "if I don't I shall have the pleasure of seeing a fine country & learning a little of the trade of different places."[8] The young man apparently knew his father well since John Smith was only mildly critical of the

5. Ibid., [pp. 1–2]; Fink, "Smith," Smith-Carter Papers.

6. Fink, "Smith," Smith-Carter Papers; S. Smith to John Smith, August 15 and September 5, 1772, Smith Papers.

7. S. Smith to John Smith, October 22, 1772, Smith Letterbook, Library of Congress.

8. Ibid.

action. This tolerance may well have resulted from a growing confidence in his son's judgment. Already Samuel had brought a significant amount of new business to Smith & Buchanan, and there seemed little reason to doubt that he would be equally successful in Europe.

The journey to Italy was uneventful until the *Carlisle* approached Venice's harbor. A pilot who was supposedly knowledgeable about the treacherous tides and shoals that made entrance into the harbor extremely dangerous joined the ship. Smith was suspicious of the Italian from the first moment he boarded the ship, and his misgivings were confirmed when he spotted breakers directly ahead of the *Carlisle*. His shouted warning to the captain came too late to prevent a disaster as the *Carlisle* slammed into a sand bank and sharply keeled over to one side. The sailors could see that the damage was extensive; the rudder was useless and the sea poured into the ship through a gaping hole in the hull. With great difficulty the crew managed to refloat the *Carlisle*, but within minutes the ship began to sink and the crew abandoned it.[9]

Smith and the crew spent three days recuperating on the nearby island of Malamaco, after which he arranged for the men's pay and their trip back to America. For the next eight weeks the young American remained in Venice, settling the insurance and supervising the salvage operations on the *Carlisle*.[10] Despite its inauspicious beginning, his stay seems to have been profitable. Venice was in the midst of its famous carnival, a time of gaiety and parties. If Samuel partook of these pleasures, however, he certainly did not report the fact to his father. Indeed the young man's letters and notes reveal him as prudish and entirely disapproving of the local morals. "Honesty is entirely banished," he once wrote his father about the Venetians, "& the son will if possible cheat the Father & the Father tell you his son is not to be trusted, the women till they are married are coy & have very little liberty, afterwards they take every liberty. . . ."[11] If there were temptations, Smith appears to have successfully resisted them; his correspondence with his father shows that he conscientiously tended to business. In describing Venice he hardly spoke of the palaces and canals but provided great detail about the city's exports and imports, the geography of the area, the charges for using port facilities, and other information of commercial value.[12]

After fulfilling his responsibilities in Venice and finding himself "heartily tired of the Place & People," Smith left for Naples and

9. S. Smith to John Smith, December 16, 1772, Smith Letterbook.
10. S. Smith to John Smith, December 26, 1772, Smith Letterbook.
11. S. Smith to John Smith, December 30, 1772, Smith Letterbook.
12. Ibid.

Rome. He was now determined to make a complete tour of the western Mediterranean. Smith made good use of his time-consuming trip to Rome. Besides learning enough Italian to make himself understood he managed to compile an incredible array of facts on economic conditions in the places through which he passed. Nothing that might be helpful to Smith & Buchanan escaped his eye. If an area suffered from poor crops, he wrote the firm urging that a shipload of flour be sent immediately because a good price could be obtained. While visiting Leghorn, Samuel informed his father that Smith & Buchanan should channel its business with that city through the firm of Denham & Jenkins since Denham had the confidence of the Pope. Such a contact, Smith told his father, greatly assisted a man of business in Italy.[13]

In Rome Smith spent a fascinating month attending the theaters and, like any other tourist, eagerly taking in the historical sites. But once again matters of commerce took up most of his time. The youthful businessman adopted the form letter as one method to advertise the benefits Rome's merchants might derive from dealing with Smith & Buchanan. "We flatter ourselves," he asserted in one such letter, "we can supply cargoes of wheat & flour & Indian corn on the best terms."[14] To allay the idea prevalent in Europe that Philadelphia was the best source in America for grain, Smith explained that Baltimore's location permitted her merchants to purchase wheat and corn at lower prices than their northern rivals. Within a short time Smith's efforts began to yield a growing number of orders from Roman firms to Smith & Buchanan.[15]

In the spring of 1773 Samuel finally left Italy, traveling by ship first to Marseilles and then to Barcelona. There he found a letter in which his father praised his success and offered to make him a partner in the firm immediately. Exhilarated by this news, Smith increased his efforts to seek out commissions for the firm that he was soon to join. He visited every port in Spain and filled his notebook with information about the economic situation in each. Since the success or failure of any business transaction depended on the character of the men involved, he also carefully measured the honesty and capacity of every merchant he met. After seeing Valencia, Alicante, Granada, and Malaga, Smith journeyed to the imposing British fortress at Gibraltar. There he brought himself to the atten-

13. S. Smith to John Smith, January 17, 1773, S. Smith to Mildred & Roberts, January 17, 1773, and S. Smith to John Smith, February 4 and March 26, 1773, Smith Letterbook.

14. S. Smith to Wills & Leigh, March 26, 1773, Smith Letterbook.

15. S. Smith to Wills & Leigh, June 20, 1773, Smith Letterbook.

tion of the commanding general at the post, who assigned an officer to show him the fortifications.[16]

Continuing his trip, Smith resumed his investigations of Spanish and Portuguese ports. In Lisbon Smith made the curious decision not to include Paris on his itinerary. Part of his reluctance to visit a city famed for its sinfulness stemmed from the same provincial prudishness he had earlier manifested in Venice. "I was by no means fit to go there knowing too little of the world," he explained to his father.[17] In truth, however, Smith felt that for his purposes Paris was a waste of valuable time. Not only did he not have letters of introduction to smooth his path into Parisian society, but he also believed the city was not important enough commercially to warrant his attention. Besides, his travels around the Mediterranean had led him to conclude that the whole area was merely an economic appendage of London. London, Smith insisted to his relatives in America, was the "great foundation" of world commerce and only there could sizable profits be made. Therefore he informed Smith & Buchanan that he would spend the winter of 1774 in the British capital pursuing new business for the firm.[18] That a twenty-two-year-old man would pass up the pleasures of Paris to conduct business in London reveals, among other things, that Samuel Smith had to an unusual degree the qualities of ambition and self-discipline.

Sometime during his stay in Lisbon Smith was befriended by the captain of the British sloop of war *Alborough*, who offered to carry the American to England. After a long and difficult voyage the *Alborough* escaped the winter storms on the Atlantic and dropped anchor in Plymouth. By early January 1774 Smith had reached London and renewed the friendships made a year earlier.[19] If anything, Smith's sales ability had improved. Already inundated by offers for contracts generated by his son's journey through Italy, France, Spain, and Portugal, John Smith could not easily cope with the opportunities Samuel created in London. At one point young Smith complained of his father's failure to properly maintain some important business connections. "On our behaviour in this our first essay," he lectured his father, "greatly depends our future business."[20]

In the spring of 1774 Smith ended his European stay with an exten-

16. Ibid. The flyleaf of Smith's letterbook is filled with short, pungent descriptions of European merchants.
17. S. Smith to John Smith, October 9, 1773, Smith Letterbook.
18. Ibid.
19. Smith's Autobiography, [p. 3], Smith Papers.
20. S. Smith to John Smith, January 5, 1774, Smith Papers.

sive tour of England. In leisurely fashion he visited the manufacturing centers of Gloucester, Worcester, Coventry, and Birmingham. At each place he dutifully viewed important and historic places, but mainly he was interested in purchasing large amounts of locally produced goods, which he arranged to ship back to Baltimore for sale by Smith & Buchanan. Returning to London Samuel bought a few gifts for his numerous relatives, said goodbye to his friends, and boarded the *St. George,* whose destination was Philadelphia. After two years of constant traveling Samuel Smith was leaving Europe, never to return again.[21]

By almost any measure Smith's sojourn on the continent was valuable and successful. The young man had by his own efforts vastly increased Smith & Buchanan's business dealings in Europe. He personally had not only gained confidence in his abilities as a merchant but also had learned much about European economic conditions and the political factors that might influence them. He had met many of the important commercial figures of Europe, whose friendship and information contributed to his continuing prosperity as a merchant in the years to come. Finally, the young man had tasted the culture of the old world. He had acquired a passion for French literature and fine European furniture as well as a veneer of sophistication that partially compensated for his inadequate education. Samuel Smith was now prepared to take his place in the best society of Baltimore. With good health and some luck Smith could expect to grow both in riches and respectability.

This assumed, of course, that England and her American provinces would manage to settle their growing differences peacefully. During his European trip Smith had not written one word about the crisis threatening the British Empire. Entirely preoccupied with business affairs, he apparently took no notice of his countrymen's difficulties. But even as the *St. George* sailed slowly across the Atlantic, matters were coming to a climax. While Smith passed the voyage pleasantly chatting with a fellow passenger, Major John Andre of the British army, leaders of the American colonies assembled in Philadelphia. At the very moment Smith left the *St. George* and loaded his baggage aboard a coach bound for Baltimore and a happy family reunion, the First Continental Congress, meeting but a few blocks away in Carpenters' Hall, began debating measures that would eventually change his life.[22]

21. S. Smith to John Smith, April [?], 1774, and Smith's Autobiography, [p. 3], Smith Papers.
22. Smith's Autobiography, [p. 3], Smith Papers.

A Soldier in the Revolution

SAMUEL SMITH was only twenty-two years old when he returned to Baltimore, but he had already completed eight years of a rigorous apprenticeship. Now intimately acquainted with business practices on both sides of the Atlantic, he was prepared to take up his full burden as a partner in his father's firm, which had been reorganized and was now known as John Smith & Sons. While in Europe he had arranged many new business opportunities, and he now energetically exploited them to the fullest. The contracts for cargoes of wheat and flour he had so successfully solicited were promptly filled. Together with his father, Smith maintained a vast correspondence with virtually every business house he had visited in Europe. They wrote regularly to these associates, giving detailed descriptions of market conditions in America. In return the partners received information about the current European business situation that proved invaluable in profitably conducting John Smith & Sons' operations. Within a remarkably short time the firm's increasing affluence had made Samuel Smith a moderately wealthy man in his own right.[1]

The Smiths' prosperity appears all the more notable since it was achieved during a period of growing crisis between Great Britain and her American possessions. Relations had deteriorated over the

1. Samuel Smith's Autobiography, 1834, [p. 3], Samuel Smith Papers, Library of Congress; John Smith & Sons to Thomas Frank, September 20, 1774, and John Smith & Sons to John Noble, September 20, 1774, John Smith & Sons Letterbook, Maryland Historical Society.

issues of taxation and sovereignty in the empire, and commercial intercourse was adversely affected. The Boston Tea Party in December 1773 triggered the final series of events culminating in the War for Independence. Within a few months an angry Parliament reacted to the attack on the tea consignments by passing the aptly titled Coercive Acts, which sealed off Boston harbor and established a military government in Massachusetts. In September of 1774 representatives of twelve colonies met as a Continental Congress in Philadelphia to forge a common response to the British legislation. Among other measures, the Congress approved the Continental Association, a plan to force concessions from Parliament by depriving England of American markets and raw materials. As they had before in other confrontations with the mother country, the merchants in every American city agreed among themselves to observe the trade restrictions. Those businessmen who attempted to avoid the ban were systematically and publicly exposed by local revolutionary committees. In Baltimore, for example, newspapers periodically printed lists of those merchants accused of breaking the nonintercourse agreements, but the firm of John Smith & Sons never appeared.[2]

From the very beginning the Smiths, father and son, had committed themselves professionally and personally to the American cause. When John Smith & Sons ceased doing business with London, the firm managed to maintain profits by expanding trade with the Mediterranean area and in the West Indies. By the end of 1775 the Smiths were trading cargoes of flour for arms and ammunition, which they then resold to the Council of Safety, a revolutionary committee that had emerged as the real government of Maryland. John Smith himself sat as a member of the Baltimore Committee of Safety and assisted that group in enforcing the commercial nonintercourse decrees of Congress. His son expressed his feelings in 1775 by enlisting in the Baltimore Independent Cadets, a militia unit made up of young and socially prominent Baltimoreans.[3]

Primarily a man of action, Samuel Smith did not bother to philosophize about his decision to become a rebel against the authority of the British Empire; instead he threw himself into the world of soldier-

2. Edmund Cody Burnett, *The Continental Congress* (New York, 1964), pp. 55–59.

3. John Smith & Sons to the Maryland Council of Safety, December 4, 1775, John Smith & Sons Letterbook; Cary Nicholas Fink, "Smith," Smith-Carter Papers, University of Virginia Library; Roll of the Baltimore Independent Cadets, December 3, 1774, Gist Papers, Maryland Historical Society; J. Thomas Scharf, *Chronicles of Baltimore* (Baltimore, 1874), p. 138.

ing. Although lacking any prior experience, Smith quickly mastered the necessary military skills. With his quick intelligence, his flair for organization, and his youthful zeal, he won rapid promotion first to sergeant and then to adjutant of his company. In January 1776 he managed to secure a captaincy in Colonel William Smallwood's regiment, which had recently been formed. Three of Smallwood's companies were stationed in Baltimore and became Captain Smith's particular responsibility. During the long winter months he drilled the untrained recruits until they at least gave the appearance of soldiers.[4]

Perhaps because his military competence had impressed his superiors, Smith was selected in the spring of 1776 to carry out a delicate and politically dangerous mission involving Robert Eden, the last proprietary governor of Maryland. Despite the beginning of hostilities Eden had remained at his post in Annapolis and exercised what little influence he had to keep Maryland from drifting into open rebellion. It was his misfortune, however, to have one of his letters to the government in London intercepted and turned over to an American general, Charles Lee, who was then supervising defensive preparations in Charleston. Eden's letter asked that a single regiment of British troops be sent to Maryland. With that small force, he bragged, the colony's loyalty could be insured. Offended by both the tone and contents of Eden's message, Lee personally urged Samuel Purviance, chairman of the Baltimore Committee of Safety, to arrest Eden and hold him until he could be exchanged for some high-ranking American prisoner. At almost the same time he received Lee's information, Purviance learned from other sources that Eden planned to leave for England in the near future.[5]

Acting with dispatch the Committee of Safety asked Major Mordacai Gist, the top American military official in Baltimore, to recommend an officer capable of leading an expedition to prevent Governor Eden's escape. Without hesitation Gist named Captain Samuel Smith, who was then summoned before the committee. Smith's instructions were explicit: he was to stop Eden from sailing and then present a letter of explanation to Thomas Johnson, chairman of the Maryland Council of Safety.

Captain Smith handled the first part of his mission with creditable skill and daring. After leaving the Committee of Safety, Smith marched a company of men down to the harbor and boarded a sloop.

4. Smith's Autobiography, [p. 3], Smith Papers.
5. Ibid.; Samuel Purviance to the Maryland Council of Safety, April 22, 1776, in B. C. Steiner et al., eds., *Archives of Maryland—Journal and Correspondence of the State Council of Maryland,* 63 vols. (Baltimore, 1884–1946), 11: 364.

Proceeding to Annapolis he positioned the ship in such a way as to prevent any vessel from escaping into Chesapeake Bay. Then, with a small body of men, the captain rowed to a ship that looked suspiciously ready to sail. The small force quickly scrambled aboard and conducted a thorough search which failed to turn up Eden but did uncover a large quantity of port and claret wines, known to be Governor Eden's favorites. Ignoring the objections of the ship's outraged owner, Smith detailed two men to remain on board and seize Eden should he appear.[6]

Having taken all possible precautions to keep Eden from fleeing, the young commander went ashore and reported to the Council of Safety as he had been ordered. Smith now found himself in the middle of a most embarrassing situation. Instead of praising him for his bold actions, the council attacked him bitterly for usurping powers that rightfully belonged to it. After a memorable tongue-lashing, Smith was told to take his men back to Baltimore. The council's anger stemmed from a belief that a subordinate body, the Baltimore Committee of Safety, had brazenly tried to establish its authority above that of the council. The members of the council were also personally disturbed that General Lee had chosen not to communicate with them in the first place, for the implication was that he believed them untrustworthy or unpatriotic. In late April 1776 the Council of Safety summoned Smith and Samuel Purviance to Annapolis and conducted an investigation of the whole affair. After an intensive interrogation both men were released and Smith was exonerated from all responsibility since he had merely obeyed orders. As for Eden, he was permitted to leave peacefully for England. Samuel Smith had been most fortunate. If the Council of Safety had chosen to be vindictive, he might well have ended his military career in disgrace. Instead his reputation prospered because of the adventure. He had shown himself able to handle difficult assignments with verve and imagination, and in the coming years his commanding officers would recognize these qualities and put them to good use.[7]

In July 1776, shortly after word reached Baltimore that Congress had issued the Declaration of Independence, Smallwood's regiment received orders to join General Washington and the Continental

6. S. Smith's account of the Eden Affair, April 1776, in Steiner et al., eds., *Archives of Maryland*, 11: 391.

7. Smith's Autobiography, [p. 4], Smith Papers; see the Council of Safety records of April 22, 1776, in Steiner et al., eds., *Archives of Maryland*, 11: 365–375; S. Smith to Thomas W. Griffith, December 31, 1821, *Maryland Historical Magazine* 5 (June 1910): 151.

army at New York City. By the third week in August the Maryland troops, accompanied by the Delaware Brigade, arrived at the American camp on Long Island, shortly before the British army attacked. Well-armed and disciplined, the southern troops impressed the predominantly Yankee army. Together with a contingent of Pennsylvanians, the Maryland and Delaware units were put under the command of Major General Lord Stirling and rushed into position at the extreme right of the American line next to Gowanus Bay and the perilous swamps of Gowanus Creek. Having quickly formed his men into a battle line, Smith surveyed the situation. He could plainly see that in the impending contest Stirling's seventeen hundred men would be facing superior numbers. In fact, the enemy had committed over five thousand troops against Stirling, and they were led by Major General James Grant, who as a member of Parliament had once boasted that with such a force he could march from one end of America to the other.[8]

The Battle of Long Island, fought on August 27, nearly ended as a total American disaster. New to large-scale military operations, Washington and his chief lieutenant, General Israel Putnam, allowed themselves to be easily out-maneuvered by the British commander, General Sir William Howe. As Smith and his fellow Marylanders nervously awaited Grant's attack, the major British thrust took place against the poorly defended American left wing. Within hours the British had managed to get behind the entire American line and then opened a coordinated attack from front and rear that soon crushed opposition. Trusting to flight, the survivors of the rout managed to reach the fortifications on Brooklyn Heights.[9]

Lord Stirling and his men, isolated from the main area of action, were slow to realize what had happened or to perceive their danger. Occupied with periodic skirmishes they did not learn until too late that they were surrounded by a force many times their own strength. Stirling's first reaction was to stand and fight despite the odds. His troops, only two weeks in the field, performed bravely and maintained their formation until forced to retreat. The only possible avenue of escape, however, was through the swamps and across Gowanus Creek, an area believed to be virtually impassable. Nevertheless Stirling ordered the bulk of his command to attempt the

8. Smith's Autobiography, [p. 5], Smith Papers.

9. John R. Alden, *A History of the American Revolution* (New York, 1969), pp. 66–68; James Thomas Flexner, *George Washington in the American Revolution* (Boston, 1967), pp. 106–118; Christopher Ward, *The War of the Revolution*, 2 vols. (New York, 1952), 1: 211–230.

crossing while he and two hundred fifty Maryland troops, among them Samuel Smith, acted as a rear guard.[10]

In desperation Stirling led his small band against the encircling British in an effort to cut his way through to safety. But the American general had no sooner begun his march than he was ambushed by several enemy companies, and the first units in the American column fell back in disorder. Smith quickly wheeled his company into platoons and with perfect discipline charged the concealed British troops, but inexplicably a direct order from Stirling halted the advance. All too soon British reinforcements arrived and succeeded in repelling Stirling's efforts to escape. The magnificent courage of the Marylanders was one of the few redeeming features of the battle from the American point of view. Unfortunately, only a handful lived to receive their comrades' praise; most died from Hessian bayonet thrusts and Stirling himself was captured.

The remaining few fled into the Gowanus swamps. Among the lucky ones were Smith and the remnants of his company. Although he and his men were worn out and cut off from assistance, the young officer never lost his poise nor his command of the situation. After picking his way through the marshes, Smith reached Gowanus Creek, which he discovered was far too deep and swift to cross for those who were wounded or unable to swim. Without hesitation Smith and one of his sergeants stripped to the waist and jumped into the stream. Pushing logs in front of them to which the soldiers clung, the two men swam back and forth until every member of the company was safely ferried across. Exhausted, Smith and his men managed to reach Brooklyn Heights and rejoin the American army.[11]

Smith's ordeal, however, had not ended. The American position on Long Island was hopeless. Washington's army, thoroughly defeated, faced extinction when the sun rose the next day. In a gamble to save the army and his country's future the American general ordered his twelve thousand troops to leave their positions and march to Brooklyn Ferry, where a host of small boats had been collected to carry them to Manhattan. The retreat proved a great success, partly because the subterfuge of keeping the abandoned camp fires burning temporarily fooled the British into believing the American army had maintained its position.[12]

Perhaps because of the secrecy with which the operation was carried

10. Ward, *Revolution,* 2: 226–227.

11. Smith's Autobiography, [p. 5], Smith Papers.

12. Douglas Southall Freeman, *George Washington: Leader of the Revolution* (New York, 1951), pp. 174–175.

out and the necessary confusion that accompanied it, Smith's company received no orders to embark. Even as the last elements of the army were leaving for New York City, Smith learned from one of his corporals that there were no other soldiers in the American fortifications. Reasoning that he had been left behind to act as a rear guard, he marched his men into the main redoubt and prepared to resist to the end.

Throughout the long hours Smith and his companions leaned over their muskets, listening to the eery stillness of the night, and awaited their fate. In the early hours of the morning, however, an officer looking for stragglers galloped up and told Smith to remove his men at once to the boats. Fatigued after twenty-four hours without sleep, Smith's company staggered to the landing, one of the last units to leave Long Island. General Washington, who had personally overseen the troop transferral, stopped Smith and inquired why he was so late, to which the young officer replied that he had received no orders. The brief talk on the wharf was Smith's first contact with the commander-in-chief, and it proved to be the beginning of a relationship that continued until Washington's death. Smith and Washington left Long Island aboard the last boats, barely ahead of swarms of British dragoons who had discovered the Americans' ruse; musket balls hit the water nearby, narrowly missing a future president and a future senator of the United States.[13]

In extricating the army from Long Island Washington had acted brilliantly, but he had not yet insured his safety. In attempting to defend New York City the American leader suffered more reverses. Outflanked and outfought, he retreated first to Harlem Heights then to White Plains. Smallwood's regiment, now sadly depleted by sickness and battle losses, yet trusted because of its stand on Long Island, was assigned the vital duty of rear guard. At White Plains the regiment received reinforcements in the form of fresh companies from Maryland, and General Howe's leisurely movement gave all the men time to rest. Strengthened and refreshed, the Marylanders were once again ready to fight and once again they were assigned the most hazardous duty.

When Howe finally attacked the Americans at White Plains on October 28, Smallwood's regiment was part of a force of sixteen hundred men stationed on Chatterton's Hill, located across the Bronx River and a mile to the south and west of the main American positions. The hill commanded a complete view of the American de-

13. Smith's Autobiography, [p. 6], Smith Papers.

fences across the river, and, if the enemy succeeded in capturing it, Washington would be forced to retreat. Although not protected by fortifications, the American position on the hill appeared strong. To assault the hill the British would have to ford the river, climb a steep slope nearly two hundred feet high, and do all of this under the continuous fire of American cannons and muskets. Yet Howe decided to make the attempt and designated four thousand British and Hessian infantrymen for the task.[14]

Samuel Smith vividly remembered the battle for Chatterton's Hill. It began with a prolonged artillery duel that took a heavy toll of the unprotected Americans. Smith and his company, situated at the rear of the American artillery, were especially hard hit since much of the British cannonade was aimed at silencing the American guns. In one terrifying instant a cannon ball struck the ground in front of Smith and bounced over his shoulder, beheading a sergeant standing directly behind him. The Marylander maintained his composure and kept his men in formation.

Despite their best efforts the Americans could not prevent the British engineers from constructing crude log bridges across the Bronx. With their usual discipline the elite British grenadiers ignored American fire as they crossed the bridge and deployed swiftly. Within minutes the British and their Hessian allies had easily dispersed the right wing of the American forces. The British pushed their attack with such speed that Smith's company found itself nearly surrounded. To save his men, Smith gave the order to break and run. As the men fled, their captain conducted a rear-guard action with two other soldiers. At one point the three men turned to fire at their pursuers and Smith was hit by a spent musket ball that rendered his arm temporarily useless. Seeing that they would be overtaken, the Americans took cover behind a stone wall and fired a volley at their pursuers, wounding or killing at least two. The rest turned back. Although injured and in pain, Smith set about restoring order and discipline among the retreating troops. Within a few miles he gathered over a hundred members of the regiment and found Colonel Smallwood badly wounded. After seeing that the colonel was attended, Smith formed the troops into ranks and marched them back to the main army. As on Long Island, Smallwood's Marylanders had borne the brunt of the fighting; their casualty lists showed that one-fifth of the men were dead or missing.[15]

14. Freeman, *George Washington*, pp. 227–231.
15. Smith's Autobiography, [pp. 6–7], Smith Papers.

Soon after the Battle of White Plains, General Washington moved a large part of his force, including Smallwood's regiment, to New Jersey. As the great retreat toward Philadelphia got under way, the Marylanders resumed their familiar position as the rear guard of the American army, often marching as much as sixteen miles behind the baggage train. Not only did Smallwood's men have the job of fending off the advance units of the pursuing British army, but they also were responsible for destroying everything that might be of value to the enemy. At Hackensack they burned military supplies in danger of being captured and then blew up an important bridge that delayed the British advance, gaining time for Washington's limping army to escape. The discomfort and danger of being the rear guard increased as the days went by. Because of the necessity of traveling light, the men and their officers lacked tents and cooking utensils. The cold, wet weather caused many to sicken and fall out. The heavy wagons and cannon turned the roads into rivers of mud through which the rear guard slogged, frequently sinking up to their knees. And then, of course, there were the ever-present bands of British dragoons who harassed the tired men and captured or killed those who straggled. Smith himself nearly fell into the hands of one such maurauding party. While washing a shirt in a stream the captain was surprised by enemy horsemen and forced to run for his life. In the process he necessarily had to abandon the garment, a serious blow to a man who had only two shirts to begin with.

Given such conditions it was not surprising to find that the regiment, now reduced to less than a hundred men, sought relief. Acting under orders, Smith and another captain from the regiment rode to Washington's temporary headquarters at Newark and requested that another regiment be sent to the rear as a replacement. The commander-in-chief refused, explaining that he could not find another unit "in which I could place the same confidence." On returning to his company Smith called his men together and told them of the general's remarks, to which they responded with cheers and vowed to continue their duty.[16]

War weariness was certainly not confined to the rear guard. Throughout the army desertion rates rose while militia scattered as soon as their terms of enlistment expired. With the army beaten, demoralized, and dwindling in numbers the war seemed practically at an end, and many whose commitment to the American cause was less than total edged toward Toryism. Among them were several

16. Ibid., [pp. 8–9].

officers in the Continental army, including Colonel William Allen, a wealthy Philadelphian and an acquaintance of Smith's. As Small-wood's regiment lay encamped at Amboy, Allen appeared and asked to speak privately with Smith. After revealing that he disagreed with the Declaration of Independence, Allen said he intended to resign immediately and left the unmistakable impression that he hoped Smith would join him. If the young Marylander felt tempted by Allen's proposal, he hid his thoughts well. He coolly replied that he had not wanted independence when he joined the army, but his loyalty was unshakable, and, he added, "whatever Congress deter-mines I will obey." Smith also told Allen that on reflection he thor-oughly agreed with the Declaration and its principles. The two men then parted, one for exile in England and the other for a long career of public service in the nation he was helping to create.[17]

Throughout November and into December 1776 the American army pushed across New Jersey toward the relative security of the west bank of the Delaware River. For the rear guard, now made up of Smallwood's company-sized regiment and the Delaware Battalion, the last stages of the retreat consisted of grueling day-long marches and constant skirmishing. Around December 7 the rear guard finally reached and crossed the Delaware, only hours ahead of the British. The campaign of 1776 had ended for Smith. Although he preferred to stay with the troops, he obeyed orders to leave at once for Balti-more.

It was Smith's misfortune to miss the American victories at Trenton and Princeton, but the task he had been assigned in Baltimore was vital: to help recruit men for a regiment that the Second Continental Congress had authorized be raised in Maryland. As an experienced officer of proven courage Smith was promoted to lieutenant-colonel and made second-in-command of the new Fourth Maryland regiment. Through the winter months Smith enrolled men to fill the ranks of the unit and saw to their training. When not involved in military duties he attended to his business affairs, finding to his dismay that inflation and the British blockade were causing his fortune to evaporate. But his stay in Baltimore was not entirely devoted to work, since he found time to become engaged to the beautiful and high-spirited Margaret Spear. The match was a natural one, for the two families had been closely associated for generations. Furthermore, Margaret's father was also a successful merchant, and her dowry would strengthen the young

17. Freeman, *George Washington*, p. 297; Alden, *American Revolution*, p. 276; Smith's Autobiography, [p. 10], Smith Papers.

man's financial position. Marriage, however, was temporarily out of the question since the prospective groom was soon to rejoin the army. In the spring of 1777 Smith left Margaret, his family, and his business to march with the Fourth Maryland to Morristown, Pennsylvania, where the Continental army had spent the winter.[18]

The campaign of 1777 opened with a series of maneuvers by General Howe aimed at drawing Washington into a pitched battle on unfavorable terrain. Though tempted, the American leader wisely declined to fight. For Smith's regiment and the rest of the army these weeks were filled with the endless marches and counter-marches across New Jersey that made up the American part of this military minuet. By the end of June, Howe had moved his entire army out of New Jersey and back to Staten Island, the very place he had landed a year earlier. Then, in early July, the British general put his men aboard transports and sailed for an unknown destination. Washington could only guess whether Howe intended to sail up the Hudson to Albany (there to meet General Burgoyne), up the Delaware to Philadelphia, or perhaps even to Charleston or New England.

Eventually intelligence reports made clear that the British had entered Chesapeake Bay and their aim was to capture Philadelphia. Washington immediately put his army in motion, placing it between Howe and the capital of the nation. On September 11 the American army had established itself along Brandywine Creek, and, with the enemy rapidly approaching, a major confrontation appeared imminent. On the day of battle Lieutenant Colonel Smith and the Fourth Maryland were assigned to General John Sullivan's division, which was posted on the left wing of the American line.

For Colonel Smith and his Maryland troops September 11 was to be a day of terror and defeat. It began with a brisk skirmish between the Americans and a large body of Hessian troops across Brandywine Creek. But Howe had once again fooled Washington. While the Hessians were distracting the Americans, the British general crossed the Brandywine above Washington's positions and threatened to destroy the army. Sullivan's division was rapidly shifted from the left to the right wing in an effort to halt the British advance but arrived too late to save the situation. Before the Fourth Maryland and the other regiments of Sullivan's command could form ranks, Howe's men struck. British artillery killed many and grenadiers using bayonets added to the casualties.[19]

18. Smith's Autobiography, [p. 11], Smith Papers.
19. Ibid., [pp. 12–13]; Ward, *Revolution*, 2: 325–333.

The suddenness of the rout surprised Smith. Frantically he tried to rally the panicked troops, but to no avail. Only one lieutenant and thirty soldiers remained and these he marched in good order away from the approaching enemy. The battle had now broken up into isolated skirmishes and British detachments seemed to be everywhere. While passing through a corn field Smith and his men ran into a party of enemy soldiers. Forming his men, Smith directed several volleys at the British, who rapidly withdrew. Toward the middle of the afternoon Smith reached the top of a prominent hill, where he established a crude headquarters. All about him he could see scattered groups of leaderless American soldiers. Attracting their attention, he ordered all he could find to join him and eventually collected a force of over a thousand men. As night approached Smith pondered what his next move should be. The area was unfamiliar and he had no idea where either army was located. Finally his men found a Quaker farmer whom Smith requested to point out the road to Chester, where it was hoped the American army lay encamped. Either because of his Tory sentiments or religious principles the man at first refused but soon changed his mind when Smith placed a gun to his chest. In the early evening Smith led his column of weary men safely inside the American lines, where each rejoined his own unit.[20]

Following Brandywine, Smith and his regiment participated with the rest of the American army in a series of maneuvers designed to keep Howe out of Philadelphia. On September 22, however, the British succeeded in crossing the Schuylkill River, where no significant force stood between them and the American capital. With the fall of the city certain, Washington turned his attention to formulating a strategy that would force the enemy to relinquish their prize. On September 23 the general dashed off a series of orders directing that the American defenses on the Delaware River below Philadelphia be improved and fully manned. Washington hoped to prevent the British navy, which was expected any day, from linking up with the army within the city. He reasoned that if Howe could be cut off from his supplies and transport, he would necessarily have to leave Philadelphia. The American commander-in-chief considered the maintenance of the river fortifications so important that he personally took charge of their preparation.[21]

20. Smith's Autobiography, [pp. 13–14], Smith Papers.
21. George Washington to the President of the Second Continental Congress, September 23, 1777, in John C. Fitzpatrick, ed., *The Writings of George Washington*, 39 vols. (Washington, D.C., 1931–1944), 9: 257–259.

On September 24 an officer from General Washington's staff instructed Colonel Smith to report to headquarters at eight o'clock that night where he was to be given "an honorable command which might keep him from his Regiment some time."²² Curious and perplexed Smith arrived at the appointed hour to discover that Washington had nominated him temporarily to command Fort Mifflin located on Mud Island in the Delaware River. "The keeping of the fort is of the greatest importance," Washington's orders read, "and I rely strongly on your prudence, spirit and bravery for a vigorous and persevering defence."²³ Smith was told to prepare the fort for a seige by strengthening the fortifications and laying in a supply of food. Washington's instructions specified that a Prussian officer, the Baron D'Arendt, was to take over command of the fort as soon as he could get there. Smith was then to be second-in-command.²⁴

Guided by a Pennsylvania farmer loyal to the cause, Smith led his two-hundred-man force to Bristol on the Delaware River and crossed to the Jersey shore. The next morning he cautiously proceeded south along the river's bank to Gloucester, where he directed his troops to build a large log raft. Taking advantage of the ebbtide, Smith loaded the soldiers aboard the raft and allowed it to drift down the river until it reached Mud Island and Fort Mifflin. Only twenty-five years old and with no experience in building or defending fortifications, Samuel Smith now had the primary responsibility for holding a post that the British had to destroy in order to retain their control of Philadelphia.²⁵

Located a few miles below Philadelphia near the mouth of the Schuylkill, Fort Mifflin was part of the defensive system designed to close the Delaware to enemy shipping. The heart of the system was two lines of chevaux-de-frise—metal-tipped beams firmly anchored to the river bottom and rising to within a few feet of the surface. These sturdily built barriers could rip holes in the hulls of ships passing over them, and as long as they remained in place the British navy could not reach Philadelphia. To keep the British from removing the chevaux-de-frise the Americans had constructed three fortified positions: a redoubt at Billingsport, Fort Mifflin, and Fort Mercer. The fortification at Billingsport guarded the first line of chevaux-de-frise; but, being poorly constructed and undermanned, its garrison aban-

22. Smith's Autobiography, [p. 14], Smith Papers.
23. Washington to S. Smith, September 23, 1777, in Fitzpatrick, ed., *Writings of Washington,* 9: 260–261.
24. Ibid.
25. Smith's Autobiography, [pp. 14–15], Smith Papers.

doned it before the British fleet had even appeared. Fort Mifflin protected the second line of chevaux-de-frise, while Fort Mercer, on the Jersey shore, was intended to keep the British away from a strategic point from which they could easily have destroyed Fort Mifflin.

In addition to the forts, a fleet of galleys, small gunboats, and floating batteries patrolled the river, ready to resist any efforts to pass the barriers. This small flotilla belonged to the state of Pennsylvania. Its commander, Commodore John Hazelwood, took his orders from the state government and not the Continental Congress. Since Hazelwood was independent of the Continental army, there was no way for Washington to force his cooperation with the commanders at Forts Mifflin and Mercer. A division of authority existed that could imperil the whole plan to keep the river closed.[26]

Even Smith's untrained eye could see that an attack of any size would easily capture Fort Mifflin in the condition he found it. In the first place its design was imperfect. To be sure, the south and east sides of the fort facing the river boasted thick stone walls fitted with apertures through which muskets might be fired. Most of the fort's heavy batteries were located on these walls. But the defenses on the west and north consisted of only some ditches, a palisade, and three wooden blockhouses mounting a few cannon. Less than five hundred yards away from the vulnerable west wall, across a narrow channel, lay Province Island, unguarded and unfortified by the Americans. In British hands Province Island might prove fatal to Fort Mifflin. From it large-caliber cannons could knock down the wooden walls and flatten the barracks inside. Once this happened no part of the fort would provide shelter, and surrender would be inevitable. Furthermore Province Island provided a handy staging area from which the British might launch an amphibious assault against the all-but-exposed rear of the fort.[27]

Smith found matters inside the fort even less encouraging. At least a thousand men were required to man the fortifications properly, yet Smith had only two hundred Continentals and a few score militia. The latter were so unfit for service that he evacuated them immediately. His own men lacked shoes, coats, and blankets; and he soon discovered that the fort's magazines were practically empty of powder and shot. There were no substantial supplies of food and medicine,

26. Ibid.; Ward, *Revolution*, 2: 372–373; Henry B. Carrington, *Battles of the American Revolution* (New York, 1877), pp. 392–393; Washington to Commodore John Hazelwood, September 23, 1777, in Fitzpatrick, ed., *Writings of Washington*, 9: 255.

27. Carrington, *Battles*, p. 393; Smith's Autobiography, [p. 15], Smith Papers.

and very few of the soldiers had any experience in operating artillery pieces. Understandably the colonel began to feel that Washington intended he merely delay the fleet's progress up the Delaware as long as possible and then retreat. Washington, however, insisted that he meant to hold the river defenses until the Delaware froze and ended any hope of the fleet reaching Philadelphia before spring. Smith's requests for ammunition, food, clothes, and gunnery officers were promptly filled by direct order of the commander-in-chief.[28]

Smith had little more than a week to prepare his post before the British fleet arrived and efforts were made to open the river. Working almost without sleep the Marylander supervised the building of additional fortifications that gave better protection to both men and guns. He also assigned sixty men to receive instruction from the artillery officers on how to operate the cannons. By the first week in October, when over eighty British warships sailed into Delaware Bay and began to ascend the river, Fort Mifflin was prepared to meet them.

The first moves in the British campaign to gain control of the river were easily accomplished. Redcoats occupied the deserted post at Billingsport, and units of the British fleet cleared a path through the first line of chevaux-de-frise. At the same time, on the Pennsylvania side of the Delaware, engineers from Howe's army began constructing batteries near the mouth of the Schuylkill River that could fire on the American flotilla. The British strategy was systematically if slowly to put the Americans into an untenable position, one in which the only way to escape sure destruction would be to abandon their posts.[29]

The British were shaken, however, by the results of the engagement at Germantown on October 4 in which Washington narrowly missed annihilating Howe's army. The near disaster underlined the importance to Howe of achieving free communication with the fleet. With winter approaching and his stocks of ammunition and food depleted, the British commander made the opening of the river his first priority. Washington too agreed that the struggle now centered on the river defenses, and he dispatched large reinforcements to both Fort Mifflin and Fort Mercer. Howe's decision to clear the river immediately became apparent to Smith on the afternoon of October 10, when he observed a party of British soldiers cross to Province Island and begin

28. S. Smith to Washington, September 27, 1777, in "Defense of Fort Mifflin," *Maryland Historical Magazine* 5 (September 1910): 207–208; Washington to S. Smith, October 1, 1777, in Fitzpatrick, ed., *Writings of Washington*, 9: 292–293.

29. Ward, *Revolution*, 2: 372–373; S. Smith to Washington, October 3 and 6, 1777, in "Defense of Fort Mifflin," pp. 210, 211.

the construction of batteries. Every gun the American forts and flotilla could bring to bear fired on the British positions, and the survivors soon surrendered. Smith then sent troops to seize the prisoners and destroy the fortifications, but before the work had been completed British reinforcements arrived and drove off his men. The Americans resumed their cannonade but could not again dislodge the British, who managed to strengthen their works and mount several small-caliber cannon.[30]

The Province Island batteries and Fort Mifflin engaged in an uninterrupted artillery duel for the next six weeks. The British cannon were too light to force the garrison to withdraw, but the fort sustained extensive damage; one blockhouse was destroyed, the barracks caught fire several times, two cannon were ruined, and a few men were killed or wounded. But on balance the British on Province Island were more an annoyance than a serious threat. Now in a state of seige, Smith's soldiers spent their days huddled in shelters and their nights repairing the damage. Smith himself took to sleeping as best he could during the daylight hours. At night he endlessly paced about the fort and along the dikes that kept the tide from inundating Mud Island. As he passed along the west wall of the fort he could hear the sound of muffled oars as small British boats ferried supplies from the fleet to the army in Philadelphia. Despite pleas from both Washington and Smith, Commodore Hazelwood had refused to blockade the channel between Mud and Province Islands to prevent this movement. Night was also the time when Smith received reinforcements from Fort Mercer and evacuated those men who had been wounded or who had taken sick with the swamp fever. As he watched each night the procession of boats carrying away sick or injured soldiers who had become comrades in the stress of battle, the young colonel must have acutely felt the loneliness and the burden of leadership.[31]

On October 20, some three weeks after receiving orders to do so, Colonel the Baron D'Arendt arrived to take command of Fort Mifflin. Tall and distinguished, D'Arendt looked the part of a competent Prussian officer, but in battle showed himself to be less than brave. D'Arendt's presence angered Smith, who had come to view Fort Mifflin as his personal responsibility, and he wrote Washington asking

30. Washington to Brigadier General James Mitchill Varnum, October 7, 1777, in Fitzpatrick, ed., *Writings of Washington*, 9: 326–327; Smith's Autobiography, [p. 17], Smith Papers; S. Smith to Washington, October 10 and 11, 1777, in "Defense of Fort Mifflin," pp. 213–214.

31. Smith's Autobiography, [pp. 18–19], Smith Papers; S. Smith to Washington, October 18 and 19, 1777, in "Defense of Fort Mifflin," pp. 217–223.

that he be allowed to return to his own regiment. But even before Washington received the letter events totally changed the circumstances, and Smith once again found himself in charge of Fort Mifflin.[32]

Baron D'Arendt's cowardice became apparent on October 22, when the British launched a coordinated assault against both Fort Mifflin and Fort Mercer. The action began with two thousand Hessians ferociously storming Fort Mercer only to be repulsed after suffering staggering casualties. While the Hessians were attacking, the Province Island batteries opened up on Fort Mifflin and four British men-of-war approached the second line of chevaux-de-frise in an attempt to break through. Amidst a scene of exploding shells and the unremitting thunder of cannon, the baron's nerve broke and after hastily turning over command of the fort to Smith he hid in the nearest shelter.

Fort Mifflin's position might have become critical save for the fact that the British ship captains were ignorant of the location of sand bars in the river and ran their vessels aground. Instantly the fort's guns opened fire on the stranded vessels and Hazelwood's galleys and gunboats soon added their fire power. Two of the British ships managed to free themselves and escape down the river, but the *Augusta,* a ship-of-the-line carrying sixty-four guns, caught fire and exploded. Shortly thereafter the crew of the frigate *Merlin* abandoned ship after lighting fuses in the powder magazines. Fifty years later Smith could still visualize the blasted hulk of the *Merlin* sinking while a column of smoke rose "beyond human vision." After the battle had ended Baron D'Arendt reported that even though he had spent the battle in the deepest shelter in the fort he had somehow sustained a groin injury. Although the man was obviously unhurt, Smith told the doctor to treat him as if there actually had been some injury. Within hours D'Arendt left Fort Mifflin for the Jersey shore and never returned again.[33]

The events of October 22 encouraged Washington to believe that the river forts would indeed be able to hold out until winter. The commanding general enthusiastically congratulated his officers in the river posts and urged them to continue their resistance. His report of the action to the Continental Congress led that body on November 4, 1777, to highly commend Smith, Hazelwood, and Colonel Christopher Greene, the commander at Fort Mercer, for their success. Congress

32. S. Smith to Washington, October 19, 1777, in "Defense of Fort Mifflin," p. 223; Washington to S. Smith, October 27, 1777, in Fitzpatrick, ed., *Writings of Washington,* 9: 416.

33. Ward, *Revolution,* 2: 374–375; Freeman, *George Washington,* pp. 528–529; Smith's Autobiography, [pp. 21–24], Smith Papers.

ordered that each of the men be given an "elegant sword" as a testimony to their gallantry.[34]

The British had by no means decided to abandon their efforts to
overcome the American river defenses. Each day that passed made
Howe's position more difficult. While the British general gathered men
and cannon for another assault, the batteries on Province Island resumed their pounding of Fort Mifflin. But the same bad luck that had
caused four men-of-war to run aground continued to thwart British
designs. For some time Smith had sent out nightly raiding parties to
Province Island with the object of cutting the dikes. Despite British
efforts to repair the damage, most of the island usually lay under
water. Regrettably for the Americans Mud Island also suffered from
flooding thanks to D'Arendt, who during his brief stay had ordered
the dikes around the fort broken in order to frustrate any ground
attack. Several days after the battles of October 22 a strong wind
helped flood both islands to a depth of two or three feet. The American garrison at Fort Mifflin was thoroughly soaked and a great deal of
water damage occurred, but the British gunners on Province Island
suffered far more. The tide swept across their works, ruining much of
their powder and rendering all but one of their guns unusable. Seeing
an opportunity to capture the British positions, Smith sent word to
Commodore Hazelwood asking him to bring the flotilla and launch an
attack. Hazelwood complied by sending a few vessels but ordered
them to avoid serious combat. The ships sailed no closer to Province
Island than Fort Mifflin, where they commenced firing at the nearly
defenseless enemy. They were answered by the single British gun.
Unable to contain his anger at this stupidity, Smith left the barracks,
the only dry place within the fort, and waded in waist-deep water out
to the American ships. He yelled at the squadron commander that he
should immediately move toward the British battery since its gun
could fire but once before the fleet's cannons would be close enough
to silence it. The naval officer refused and while the cannonade continued the two men carried on a verbal battle of their own. At one
point a British ball splashed into the water next to Smith, which
caused the naval commander to complain that Smith's presence had
drawn the enemy's fire and endangered the ship. Losing his temper

34. Washington to the President of the Second Continental Congress, October
24, 1777, and Washington to S. Smith, October 28, 1777, in Fitzpatrick, ed.,
Writings of Washington, 9: 422, 459; Congressional resolution of November 4,
1777, in Worthington Chauncey Ford, ed., *Journal of the Continental Congress*,
34 vols. (Washington, D.C., 1907), 9: 862. Smith's sword was not presented to
him until 1786.

entirely, Smith replied that unless the officer took his vessels and left immediately he would order the cannon at Fort Mifflin to fire on *them!* The lack of coordination between Smith and Hazelwood allowed the British to maintain their control of Province Island—from which place Howe had already decided to mount the next major attack on Fort Mifflin.[35]

Through his spies Washington knew that the British intended to attack Fort Mifflin at almost any moment, but the agents had not learned when or how they planned to act. On November 9, however, Smith alerted Washington that large numbers of British soldiers had arrived on Province Island and were employed in vastly expanding the fortifications. What Smith did not know was that by incredible industry the British had stripped their fleet of ten large-caliber guns and moved them into the newly enlarged works on Province Island. In addition the enemy had constructed a floating battery within range of the fort and added more cannon to the batteries at the mouth of the Schuylkill. Altogether the British armament far exceeded in destructive power anything that Fort Mifflin had yet experienced.[36]

At 7 A.M. on November 10 the British commenced their grand cannonade. By the end of the day over fifteen hundred shells had hit the fort, tearing apart its vulnerable wooden walls and damaging many of the buildings inside. On the afternoon of November 11, when an opportunity presented itself to get a message to Washington, Smith went to the barracks building, which had miraculously remained intact, and scribbled out a pessimistic report. He told the general that the north and west walls of the fort had been knocked down, that the blockhouses were destroyed, and that many of the fort's guns were out of commission. Though casualties were yet light, Smith warned that they could not be expected to hold out more than a few days. As Smith handed the letter to a messenger a cannon ball crashed through the wall of the barracks, collapsed two chimneys, and then, nearly spent, struck him on the left hip. The wounded officer fell, covered by bricks. He was nearly unconscious and his wrist was badly dislocated. The other men in the room were stunned and reacted slowly. Unable to walk and severely bruised Smith managed to roll over and over until he reached the door and fresh air. The doctor set his wrist and following standard practice bled him. Smith's injuries were serious

35. S. Smith to Washington, October 30, 1777, in "Defense of Fort Mifflin," pp. 224–225; Smith's Autobiography, [pp. 24–25], Smith Papers.

36. Washington to General Varnum, November 8, 1777, in Fitzpatrick, ed., *Writings of Washington*, 10: 25; S. Smith to Washington, November 9, 1777, in "Defense of Fort Mifflin," p. 227.

enough to require evacuation, and that evening he was transferred to Fort Mercer.[37]

For the next five days Smith recuperated and watched from a distance as the British relentlessly smashed Fort Mifflin into rubble. Even though he was hardly able to move, the young colonel tried to help the garrison by forcefully arguing that supplies and reinforcements should be sent at once to the fort. Commodore Hazelwood, in one final act of petulance, refused to use his ships in such an enterprise. By November 16 the British had managed to maneuver several men-of-war into the channel between Province and Mud Islands. Smith could see the marine sharpshooters high atop the masts of the enemy vessels firing down into the fort, killing anyone who strayed into the open. That night the garrison blew up what remained of the works at the fort and rowed to Fort Mercer, somehow managing to save most of their cannon.[38] The next morning, his arm in a sling, Smith bought a horse and rode painfully to Washington's headquarters at White Marsh to report what had happened. Arriving just as the general and his principal officers finished dinner, he received a hero's welcome. In his report to Congress Washington expressed disappointment that Fort Mifflin had fallen, but called its defense a "credit to the American arms, [which] will ever reflect the highest honor upon the officers and men of the garrison."[39] The commander-in-chief also informed the legislators that Hazelwood's conduct would be investigated.[40]

Soon after Fort Mifflin surrendered, the British fleet reached Philadelphia and secured British control of the city. The American army slowly withdrew toward Valley Forge, which had been selected as its winter quarters. Smith, although still in agony from his wounds, joined his regiment on this melancholy march but soon received orders to return home to Baltimore. He spent the next few months again recruiting soldiers for the Continental army and, it may be supposed, being comforted by Margaret Spear.

37. Smith's Autobiography, [pp. 26–28], Smith Papers; S. Smith to Washington, November 11, 1777, in "Defense of Fort Mifflin," pp. 227–228.

38. Washington to Patrick Henry, November 13, 1777, and Washington to the President of the Second Continental Congress, November 17, 1777, in Fitzpatrick, ed., *Writings of Washington*, 10: 54, 73–74; Smith's Autobiography, [p. 28], Smith Papers.

39. Washington to the President of the Second Continental Congress, November 17, 1777, in Fitzpatrick, ed., *Writings of Washington*, 10: 73–74.

40. Ibid.

3

Rising Merchant
of Baltimore

IN THE late spring of 1778 Samuel Smith led his newly recruited
Baltimore troops into the American encampment at Valley Forge.
There he found the army in a far different condition than when he
had left it. Although the soldiers had been obliged to endure a bitter
winter in the most primitive circumstances, a vigorous training program had successfully transformed them into a tough and disciplined
force. There was every reason to hope that the American army, reinforced by thousands of militia, would be more successful in the coming
campaign.

By the middle of June it was apparent that General Henry Clinton,
who had replaced Howe in February, was preparing to evacuate
Philadelphia and return to New York. On June 16 the withdrawal
began as three thousand Tories who chose not to face their countrymen stowed their belongings aboard the British fleet and sailed away.
Two days later Clinton's ten thousand redcoats and their twelve-mile-
long baggage train crossed the Delaware and began a slow march
back across New Jersey. For his part, Washington determined to do
battle with the British and so put his army in motion, hoping to place
it between Clinton and New York.[1]

1. Christopher Ward, *The War of the Revolution*, 2 vols. (New York, 1952),
2: 571–572; James Thomas Flexner, *George Washington in the American Revolution* (Boston, 1967), pp. 296–297.

As the Americans broke camp and prepared to march, Smith received orders detaching him from the main army. He was instructed to join a special unit, a light brigade led by General Charles Scott, assigned to follow the British army and observe its movements. For most of a week Scott's men dogged the enemy's rear-guard. So close were the Americans that on many mornings they extinguished the still-smouldering British cooking fires and arrested camp followers who had remained to plunder anything the English troops had left behind. On June 26 the British army encamped at Monmouth court house. A day later Washington ordered General Charles Lee to attack and gave him five thousand soldiers—including Scott's brigade—to do the job.[2]

The day of the battle, June 28, Smith and his unit were stationed on the right wing of the American army. Lee had planned to cut off and destroy the British rear guard, but General Clinton frustrated the Americans by sending timely reinforcements. In the face of this unexpected resistance Lee lost control of his troops. By regiments, by companies, or simply in disorganized bunches Lee's soldiers turned and fled back toward Washington and the main army. This precipitous movement left two regiments of Scott's brigade vulnerable on the right flank. General Scott was not present and it was uncertain who was now in command. The officers of the two regiments quickly gathered to decide on a plan. Arguing persuasively, Smith convinced the group that the troops had to be turned around and marched away immediately if they were to escape.

Smith's coolness under pressure was never more apparent than in the retreat from Monmouth. The two regiments Smith now virtually commanded had to move along a narrow path with a steep sand hill on one side and an impassible marsh on the other. The Americans were spread out and exposed to attack. To make matters worse, units of the British army pursuing Lee's troops were marching parallel to Smith on the other side of the sand ridge. Although the enemy was unaware of Smith's men, the Americans might have been discovered at any moment and annihilated. Riding at the very rear of the American column, Smith anxiously directed small groups of skirmishers to climb the hill and give warning should any British soldiers approach. At one point a troop of British cavalrymen fired on an American flanking party; Smith hastily sent reinforcements, who managed to drive the enemy off. Before the British could attack in force, Smith's men had passed through the ravine and rejoined Washington.

2. Samuel Smith's Autobiography, 1834, [p. 29], Samuel Smith Papers, Library of Congress; Ward, *Revolution,* 2: 576.

Even though exhausted by the heat, Smith and his soldiers were not allowed to rest, for they no sooner had reached the American positions than the entire British army struck. Under Washington's leadership the American line held and repulsed the attack. Heat and fatigue kept the Americans from following up their victory, but at Smith's orders several companies pursued the British, capturing or killing many stragglers. For Smith Monmouth proved to be the last battle of the Revolution. While he remained with the army until the end of the 1778 campaign, he saw no more action because the British barricaded themselves inside New York City and refused to fight.[3]

During the long summer months of 1778 the Marylander chafed at the army's inactivity. He was so anxious for more combat that he twice refused the honor of becoming a staff officer. General Washington, who had taken a special interest in Smith ever since the Delaware River campaign of the year before, was the first to ask the young colonel to join his illustrious entourage. Most officers would have seized such an opportunity, but Smith told the commander-in-chief that he preferred to stay with his men in the field. A short while later General Lafayette invited Smith to accept a position as aide-de-camp at his headquarters. Once more the colonel declined, giving the Frenchman the same reasons as he had Washington. That the two most famous leaders of the Continental army thought him worthy of recognition understandably pleased Smith. Like his decision not to visit Paris while touring Europe, his insistence on being a fighter rather than an administrator marked the Marylander as an unusual young man. But his dreams of achieving additional military glory never materialized. The war remained stalemated and with cold weather approaching, Washington sent his army into winter quarters. For the third time Smith was ordered to superintend the recruiting service in Baltimore.[4]

Perhaps before he had even left the army but certainly within a few weeks after he arrived home, Samuel Smith decided to resign. Such an act was not easy for the young soldier, who was fiercely loyal to his comrades-in-arms, yet he believed he had no alternative. One essential problem was money. Continental army officers received little compensation, certainly not enough to cover living costs, and what little they were given was eroded away by inflation. It had taken, for example, six months of Smith's salary as a lieutenant colonel to pay

3. Smith's Autobiography, [pp. 30–33], Smith Papers; Ward, *Revolution*, 2: 580–585.

4. Smith's Autobiography, [p. 33], Smith Papers.

for his trip from New York to Baltimore. He and most other officers had from the beginning of the war depended on their personal fortunes to make up the difference between salary and costs. By the end of 1778, however, the firm of John Smith & Sons, hard hit by inflation and the disruption of trade, was having difficulty providing Smith with the necessary funds. The deplorable condition of the firm suggested to Smith that he could not continue his military career without suffering a financial disaster. Another motive for Smith's retirement, one he spoke of only to intimate friends, involved his pride. Always acutely aware of rank, the Hero of Mud Island, as his admirers dubbed him, resented the fact that he had not been promoted and given a regiment of his own.[5]

Smith delayed submitting his letter of resignation until the spring of 1779. In part his hesitation was caused by a desire to perform one last service for Washington by completing his recruiting assignment. Mainly, however, he desperately hoped that he might somehow manage to obtain a promotion from the Maryland government. "I want a Regiment," he wrote to a fellow officer, "which cannot be without a settlement of Rank."[6] In the end his efforts to sway the state legislature accomplished nothing. Torn between a desire to rejoin the army and his personal ambitions and responsibilities, the young man suffered through several months of intense emotional strain. The one immediate benefit Smith derived from his decision involved Margaret Spear, to whom he had been engaged for nearly two years. Despite his shortage of funds, Smith apparently felt that marriage was feasible since he would now remain in Baltimore, where he could devote his full attention to rebuilding the business. And so, on December 31, 1778, the marriage took place in the First Presbyterian Church of Baltimore. It proved a durable match, lasting sixty years.[7]

In May 1779 Smith reluctantly took pen in hand and wrote George Washington, resigning his commission. The commander-in-chief responded graciously and complimented the Marylander on his conduct as a soldier.[8] Perhaps because he was relieved that Washington had not condemned him or because he felt guilty about leaving the army

---

5. S. Smith to James McHenry, December 10, 1778, in Bernard C. Steiner, ed., *The Life and Correspondence of James McHenry* (Cleveland, 1907), pp. 2–21; S. Smith to Otho Holland Williams, March 10, July 2, and October 23, 1779, O. H. Williams Papers, Maryland Historical Society.

6. S. Smith to Williams, March 10, 1779, O. H. Williams Papers.

7. S. Smith to Williams, February 16, 1779, O. H. Williams Papers; Smith's Autobiography, [p. 33], Smith Papers.

8. Smith's Autobiography, [p. 33], Smith Papers.

while the war continued, Smith addressed another letter to the general in July 1779. "I ever shall regret having been obliged to leave the service, to which I had devoted my life," he wrote, "and shall esteem myself happy, when I have it in my power to do an obliging thing to those who remain in it."[9] Smith's pledge was not taken lightly, for only a few weeks before he had led a mob of Baltimoreans into the print shop of William Goddard, whose newspaper had printed an article considered unpatriotic. The future Jeffersonian Republican assisted in the vandalism of Goddard's property and the terrorizing of Goddard himself. One of Goddard's associates, Eleazer Oswald, promptly charged Smith with infringing on the freedom of the press and challenged him to a duel with pistols. Obviously chagrined, Smith tried to persuade Oswald to withdraw his challenge. Finally he refused to fight on the grounds that the challenge was not justified; Oswald replied by publicly calling him a coward.[10] The affair certainly did Smith no credit, but it was not the last time he would use violent means to repress those with whom he disagreed.

Although retired from the army, Samuel Smith continued to promote the interests of the new nation in several different ways. He was, for one thing, named a colonel in the Maryland militia and given command of the Baltimore Town Battalion. Charged with the responsibility of protecting Baltimore from attack, Smith rigorously trained and disciplined his eight-hundred-man force. In April of 1781 a British fleet blockaded the city, forcing Smith to keep the militia on duty for several days. Eventually the enemy ships sailed away, having given Smith a scare and some valuable experience on the problems of defending Baltimore from assault. A few months later rumors that Lord Cornwallis and his rampaging army were determined to complete their sweep through the southern states by capturing Baltimore again forced Smith to call out the militia and prepare for battle. That threat ended with the capitulation of the British at Yorktown.[11]

The less glamorous occupation of the Baltimore Battalion and its colonel was the investigation and arrest of Tories. The Tory danger

9. S. Smith to George Washington, July 2, 1779, copy of letter in Cary Nicholas Fink, "Smith," Smith-Carter Papers, University of Virginia Library.

10. See J. Thomas Scharf, *Chronicles of Baltimore* (Baltimore, 1874), pp. 176–181, which includes a letter from Oswald to Smith, July 11, 1779.

11. Ibid., p. 172; Benjamin Nicholson to Governor Thomas Lee, August 5, 1780, and S. Smith to Governor Lee, April 12, 22, 23, 25, and August 5, 1781, in B. C. Steiner et al., eds., *Archives of Maryland—Journal and Correspondence of the State Council of Maryland*, 63 vols. (Baltimore, 1884–1946), 45: 42, 47: 183, 200, 203, 213, 391–392.

could not be taken lightly. During the brief British blockade of Balti-more in 1781 Smith had told the governor of Maryland there were so many British sympathizers in the city that many militiamen were reluctant to leave their homes for fear the Loyalists would burn them. The colonel had then suggested that the governor order all suspected Tories in Baltimore rounded up and moved thirty miles away. As military commander of the city Smith was vested with unusually broad powers, which he used against alleged Loyalists, often with a callous disregard for due process and common decency. On one oc-casion, Smith, at the head of a raiding party, burst into the home of John Parks in the middle of the night. After searching the house and confiscating Parks' personal papers, Smith ordered the unfortunate man locked in jail even though nothing incriminating had been found. Sometime afterward Smith and a magistrate interrogated Parks, once again failing to turn up any evidence of wrong-doing. Three months later Parks was still in jail and was released only after his wife tear-fully pleaded with the governor for mercy and a number of leading citizens in Baltimore testified to his loyal and peaceful character: even Smith conceded there was no good reason to keep Parks in prison.[12]

Smith's business activities contributed much more to the American war effort and incidentally to his own financial recovery than did his services in the militia. On his return to Baltimore Smith had found John Smith & Sons, once the most successful mercantile establishment in the city, nearly moribund. Growing British naval power off the American coast had increasingly restricted trade, thus depriving mer-chants of their foreign markets and sources of supplies. And currency depreciation had totally deranged the system of economic relations through which John Smith & Sons and other Baltimore merchants distributed goods into the back country of western Maryland and central Pennsylvania. Retail merchants, such as John Smith had once been in Carlisle, paid their debts in practically valueless paper money. Caught between the British navy and American economic conditions, many firms, including John Smith & Sons, were in jeopardy of being driven out of business. But to some extent John Smith was himself the author of his company's unhealthy state. Barred by age from join-ing his son on the battlefield, John had served the cause in other ways. He had been a member of the constitutional convention that drafted a new instrument of government for Maryland and then had served several terms in the lower house of the state legislature. These activi-

12. Memorial of John Parks to S. Smith, June 1781, Alexander McFadon to Governor Lee, August 13, 1781, and S. Smith to Governor Lee, August 17, 1781, in Steiner et al., eds., *Archives of Maryland,* 47: 330, 414, 426.

ties had consumed much of his time and prevented him from exercising the close supervision a business house required. Whether because of his years or his public commitments, John Smith readily surrendered active control of the firm to his son as soon as Samuel had retired from the army. Twenty-seven years old, with a new bride, and the grand sum of one hundred dollars in his pocket, Samuel Smith was now responsible for preserving himself and his family from bankruptcy. After surveying the economic situation in Baltimore and seeking out his relatives for help in financing, the young merchant moved aggressively and successfully into two areas of enterprise: privateering and government supply contracts.[13]

Privateering, or legal piracy, was the rock upon which Samuel Smith and many other American businessmen rebuilt their fortunes. For all practical purposes the United States had no navy. Its only naval weapons were the hordes of privately owned but publicly commissioned vessels that swarmed out of American ports to harass and disrupt the British merchant marine. These swift raiders often brought wealth to their owners while forcing the enemy to divert large numbers of warships to convoy duty. Inevitably Smith's instincts for profits and his robust patriotism attracted him to a business that promised to satiate both. By the end of the war Smith owned all or part of perhaps a dozen privateers. His biggest profits came not from the capture of prizes but from the sale of the wheat or flour cargoes that many Baltimore privateers carried in addition to their cannon; in the summer of 1779, for example, Smith made over $12,000 as his portion of a cargo carried to the French West Indies aboard a privateer. Smith and another merchant tripled their investment by the sale of the cargo from a voyage in 1782. Yet privateering, despite its glamor and extravagant profits, was a risky affair. In 1781 and 1782 five vessels in which Smith had an interest were captured or disappeared, thus costing him thousands of dollars. Even losses such as these, however, failed to match the sums earned by more successful privateering ventures.[14]

Like privateering, fulfilling government contracts for food and other kinds of supplies allowed Smith an opportunity to help himself while helping the war effort. Lacking big bureaucracies, state governments relied on private contractors to purchase and deliver food and military goods. During the war years Smith was a contractor for both

13. S. Smith to Williams, July 2, 1779, O. H. Williams Papers.

14. Minutes of the Maryland Council of Safety, December 11, 1779, June 19, August 28, September 5, and December 30, 1780, in Steiner et al., eds., *Archives of Maryland*, 43: 35, 199, 267, 276, 257; S. Smith to Williams, November 10, 1779, and March 14, 1781, O. H. Williams Papers.

Virginia and Maryland. The Virginia contract involved bread, flour, and wheat of which Virginia had a shortage and Maryland an abundance. The Virginia Board of War in 1779 arranged with the Maryland government to purchase unlimited supplies of wheat and wheat products. It then named Samuel Smith, who had journeyed to Williamsburg to solicit the job, as its sole purchasing agent in Maryland. Operating on a healthy commission, Smith not only bought the supplies but rented the vessels that carried them along the coastline from Maryland to Virginia. The lucrative arrangement between Smith and the Virginia Board of War ended abruptly in 1781, when Maryland passed a law prohibiting the shipment of wheat or flour outside the state without special permission. Although Smith had received a permit, an over-zealous port official in Baltimore seized large quantities of Smith's flour destined for Virginia. Not until eight months passed did Smith manage to regain his property. By then Virginia had lost interest and the contract was terminated.[15]

Most of Smith's war-time contracts were with the Maryland government. In late 1780 a number of Baltimore merchants approached the legislature to propose that a subsidy be granted to the businessmen enabling them to purchase cargoes of wheat and flour for shipment to the Spanish West Indies. The merchants, among them Samuel Smith, argued that inflation had destroyed their capacity to procure cargoes for their ships. By supporting the merchants the state could earn money from the increased import duties. Eventually the state government agreed to supply the merchants on the condition that the state treasury be paid 50 percent of the profits of voyages it helped finance. Smith was named as the state's purchasing agent responsible for buying the wheat and flour. For his trouble he received a commission of 5 percent. In the ensuing months other valuable contracts flowed from Annapolis into the Baltimore office of John Smith & Sons. Early in 1781 the company became the state's representative charged with the supply and repair of the gun boats that regularly engaged the British vessels operating in Chesapeake Bay. Four months later the government of Maryland appointed Smith's firm as its agent for the procurement of military supplies for those Maryland troops serving in the Continental army.[16]

15. S. Smith to Governor Johnson, October 31 and November 9, 1779, S. Smith to Governor Lee, November 23, 1779, January 8, and February 4, 1780, Maryland Council to S. Smith, May 24 and September 28, 1780, and Minutes of Maryland Council, November 8, 1780, in Steiner et al., eds., *Archives of Maryland,* 43: 181, 360, 362, 371–372, 400, 416, 507, 353.

16. Maryland Council to S. Smith, November 30, 1780, ibid., 45: 230.

By shrewdly exploiting his opportunities Smith emerged from the war a wealthy man. His privateering ventures and government contract work generated immense profits, most of which he apparently reinvested in his firm. He did use some funds to purchase Tory property that had been seized by the state, eventually acquiring six lots in the city of Baltimore and nearly five hundred acres in Baltimore County. In addition, Smith established a distillery in the city before the war ended. In short, the American War for Independence had turned out to be a boon to Samuel Smith's career. Because of the war he was a military hero, twice wounded, and honored by both George Washington and the Continental Congress. Also because of the war Smith had become a highly successful businessman who had investments in many areas and who had developed contacts throughout the middle Atlantic states. This combination of business and military success resulted in Smith's emergence in the post-war years as a leading merchant and politician.[17]

At the end of the hostilities Smith could be optimistic that he and the other merchants of Baltimore would continue to enjoy material good fortune. The rapid economic growth of Baltimore that had begun in the 1760s had not been seriously retarded by the war and in the 1780s it continued unabated. John Smith had predicted when he first came to the city that its unique location, farther to the west than any other port, would eventually make Baltimore one of the principal market places of the middle Atlantic region. The old merchant had lived to see his prophecy fulfilled as the agricultural riches of central Pennsylvania and western Maryland poured into Baltimore along natural waterways and a network of fine roads authorized by the Maryland legislature but largely paid for by Baltimore businessmen. Without question wheat was the basis of the city's prosperity. The whole economy of Baltimore was geared to process, store, transport, and sell the grain. As the population on the frontier grew and wheat production increased, Baltimore's capitalists responded by building more flour mills, wharves, warehouses, and ships. The boom economy generated an insatiable demand for manpower. Men were needed as sailors, carpenters, iron workers, millers, clerks, and for hundreds of other occupations. Baltimore's population, a mere five thousand before the war, nearly tripled by 1790. Whereas there had been only a few houses in the town when the Smiths arrived, Baltimore boasted twenty-five hundred dwellings by the end of the 1780s. Everywhere

17. See list of property owned by Samuel Smith in 1800, and land survey dated February 15, 1785, Smith Papers.

there were signs of affluence. They could be seen in the busy harbor where the ships of many nations rode at anchor, or at the crowded, frantic market on Fell's Point, or along the broad, newly paved avenues besides which the successful built spacious red brick mansions. There was hardly a foreign visitor who did not comment on Baltimore's impressive public buildings, particularly the court house, which had been constructed over a vault-like passageway which carriages could roll through. Already a rival of New York and Philadelphia, Baltimore was a vital and exciting city on the verge of a great future.[18]

While the end of the Revolutionary War opened new opportunities for the merchants of Baltimore, it also confronted them with perplexing problems. Although the British no longer blockaded the coast of the United States, both the English and the French imposed restrictive and discriminatory controls on American trade. England and France allowed the importation of only those goods that were noncompetitive with similar domestic products and even then stipulated that with a few exceptions their own and not American ships must carry the cargoes. At the same time European merchants exploited the political weakness of the United States by flooding American markets with manufactured goods that easily undersold the same products made by less efficient and legislatively unprotected American industry. As a consequence the new nation suffered a severe if short-lived post-war depression. The economic uncertainties of the 1780s seriously threatened the prosperity of Smith and other American merchants. It took skill, courage, energy, and a touch of larceny to survive, qualities the Marylander seems to have had in abundance.

Although they inhibited American trade, the French and English laws did not entirely eliminate all channels of legitimate commercial intercourse. John Smith & Sons, renamed Samuel and John Smith Company in 1784 after John formally retired, once more opened their old routes to the Mediterranean that Samuel Smith had established during his European tour. The firm shipped large quantities of lumber, wheat, and flour to Italy and Spain in return for wine. Smith also engaged in shipping tobacco to Britain, a trade permitted and even encouraged by English law. But in addition to legal commerce the Smiths initiated a number of voyages that were expressly prohibited. In order to make a profit the company did not scruple at bribery,

18. Stuart Weems Bruchey, *Robert Oliver, Merchant of Baltimore, 1783–1819* (Baltimore, 1956), pp. 29–32; Fillmore Norfleet, ed., "Baltimore as seen by Moreau De Saint-Méry in 1794," *Maryland Historical Magazine* 35 (September 1940): 221–240; Scharf, *Chronicles of Baltimore*, pp. 213–234.

forged papers, and cleverly disguised cargoes. Using such methods Smith's vessels were able to do business both in France and in the French West Indies.[19]

Throughout the 1780s Smith continued to seek new ways of making money. In 1787 his representatives in London arranged to buy safe-conduct papers from the Barbary powers. Smith's vessels were now free to operate in the eastern Mediterranean without fear of capture by the North African pirates, a significant advantage over his American competitors. A year earlier Smith had struck a bargain with the powerful and influential Robert Morris of Philadelphia. Morris had managed to obtain from the French government a contract as the sole purchasing agent of American tobacco for France. On March 7, 1786, Smith wrote Morris, offering to act as a subcontractor for the financier in Maryland. Morris agreed and sent money with which Smith purchased Maryland tobacco and hired ships to carry the cargoes to France. For his trouble he received a commission of 2.5 percent. Within a few years Smith had gotten involved in yet another money-making venture: the Bank of Maryland. Along with other Baltimore businessmen he obtained a charter for the new financial institution so necessary to the city's expanding economy. Smith bought a number of shares of stock in the bank and sat as a member of its first board of directors. By the end of the decade Samuel Smith presided over an extensive economic empire. Among his assets were twenty ships, a distillery, a retail store in Baltimore that sold some of the goods he imported, substantial landholdings in Maryland, warehouses, wharves, houses, some domestic slaves, and investments in a number of local businesses. He had done very well indeed in the ten years since he had returned from the army with only a few dollars to his name.[20]

One indication of Smith's prestige within Baltimore during the 1780s was the large number of civic responsibilities the city government heaped upon him. Baltimore, like all eighteenth-century American cities, existed because of and for trade. Owing to their wealth and economic power, merchants dominated almost every aspect of urban life. The more prominent a merchant became the more responsibility

19. Samuel and John Smith to Francis LeMee, December 8, 1784, Samuel and John Smith to Captain Dean, June 9, 1786, and Samuel and John Smith to Captain Stran, December 18, 1787, Smith & Company Letterbook, Maryland Historical Society.

20. Samuel and John Smith to M. V. T. Gregory, April 30, 1787, Smith & Company Letterbook; Robert Morris to Samuel and John Smith, March 16, March 25, April 23, June 25, July 9, August 27, October 7, and November 26, 1786, and February 15, 1787, Smith Papers; Thomas W. Griffith, *Annals of Baltimore* (Baltimore, 1833), p. 129.

he was expected to assume. Some of Smith's civic tasks, such as serving on committees welcoming important visitors to Baltimore, were merely honorary. In 1782, for example, he joined other leading citizens in greeting the French army commander, Count de Rochambeau. A year later he was part of another group that welcomed the popular American general, Nathaniel Greene. Of more substantive importance was Smith's appointment as one of the wardens of the port of Baltimore in 1783. Only the most respected merchants of the city were named to these posts. Collectively the port wardens supervised the upkeep of the harbor, making sure that the ship channel was clearly marked and kept free of obstructions. As if these duties were not enough to exhaust Smith's time, the governor of Maryland added yet another by designating him as brigadier general of the Maryland militia, the highest military post in the state. Henceforth, in the title-conscious society of early America, he would be known as General Samuel Smith.[21]

Smith's private life seems to have been as happy as his business and public careers were successful. By 1783 Margaret had presented her husband with three children, Louis, St. John, and Elizabeth. During the 1780s the family lived in a large two-story brick mansion on Gay Street near the homes of many relatives. Although Samuel was not a fervently religious man, he and Margaret regularly attended services at the First Presbyterian Church, where they had been married. John Smith, William Buchanan, and William Spear had been part of the group that had founded the church in 1760, and Samuel was now counted among its leading members. Smith and his wife do not appear to have been very active socially, but on occasion they did hold gracious dinner parties attended by the city's elite. In 1785 Robert Hunter, a young Englishman, joined one such gathering at the Gay Street house. The party, he remembered, began at three in the afternoon in a second-floor drawing room. There Samuel and Margaret, "a genteel and elegant woman," presided over a "most agreeable company." In the early evening the guests were treated to violin music, and at ten o'clock they were finally led downstairs to the dining room and offered an "elegant" dinner.[22]

One area that had not attracted Smith's attention in the 1780s was

21. Scharf, *Chronicles of Baltimore*, pp. 199–200, 207–208; Griffith, *Annals of Baltimore*, p. 100; Fink, "Smith," Smith-Carter Papers.

22. Wilson Miles Cary to "Polly," February 28, 1897, Smith-Carter Papers; John H. Gardner, "Presbyterians of Old Baltimore," *Maryland Historical Magazine* 35 (September 1940): 244–255; Robert Hunter, Jr., *Quebec to Carolina, in 1785–1786*, ed. Louis B. Wright and Marion Tinling (San Marino, Calif., 1943), p. 180.

politics. Unlike his father, who had served in both the Pennsylvania and Maryland assemblies and was currently in the Maryland senate, Samuel neither sought nor seemed interested in elective office. Even the great debates over ratifying the Constitution failed to stimulate his interest, although there can be no question that he, like most merchants, supported the Constitution because it would benefit the business community. Most likely Smith's obligations to his business, the militia, the port wardens, and his growing family had kept him completely occupied. By 1790, however, Smith may have felt himself able to try his hand at something new. Besides being financially and socially secure, he had recently reorganized his business firm by taking on a new partner, his cousin James Buchanan, son of John Smith's first partner and brother-in-law, William Buchanan. In the new house of S. Smith & Buchanan, the younger partner took over much of the burden, thus giving Samuel Smith more leisure time than he was used to enjoying.[23]

Whatever his reasons, Smith allowed his name to be entered as a candidate for a seat in the lower house of the Maryland legislature in the fall elections of 1790. Probably because of his position in the social and economic hierarchy of Baltimore, no one chose to oppose him. A year later he won reelection, again without challenge. During his two rather undistinguished years in the House of Delegates, Smith displayed little of the legislative ability that characterized his later career. What little is known of his record in the legislature would seem to indicate that he faithfully represented the views of his wealthy and conservative merchant colleagues. On one occasion he vigorously opposed the efforts of Samuel Chase, a future Supreme Court justice, to secure relief for insolvent debtors in the state. If Smith knew of the desperate plight of these individuals, some of whom were in debtor's prisons, he did not let his sympathy deter him from voting in defense of his interest and that of his fellow creditors. While conservative on financial matters, Smith outspokenly supported state-subsidized improvements in Maryland's road system. Again the key to his political position was the interest of Baltimore merchants as he perceived it. Businessmen in Philadelphia had recently begun to challenge Baltimore's monopoly of the trade of central Pennsylvania by convincing the Pennsylvania legislature to underwrite the construction of a turnpike from Philadelphia to the west. To counter the Philadelphians' ambitions, Baltimore merchants, through their friend Samuel Smith, pressed hard for the improvement of old roads and the construction

23. Fink, "Smith," Smith-Carter Papers.

of new ones. Although Smith's tenure as a state legislator was lacklus-
ter, his record did him no harm in Baltimore. On the contrary, his
political stock steadily rose in value. A military hero, commander of
the Baltimore militia, and accepted member of the city's merchant
elite, Smith now had the added prestige of winning two successive
elections. When the seat in the fifth Congressional district—comprised
of Baltimore city and county—fell vacant, it was only natural that his
friends would nominate him for the position.[24]

24. Ibid.; Scharf, *Chronicles of Baltimore,* p. 261; Griffith, *Annals of Baltimore,*
pp. 133–137; John Silas Pancake, "The General from Baltimore" (Ph.D. diss.,
University of Virginia, 1949), p. 95.

4

Merchant Congressman

As IN most elections in 1792, the outcome of the congressional contest in Baltimore was determined by personal loyalties rather than by the activities of disciplined parties. In the months before the election two others joined Smith in announcing their candidacies. Charles Ridgely, the most serious challenger, represented the nonurban portions of Baltimore County that traditionally feared the growth and political power of the city. John O'Donnell, the third contestant, was a merchant who had held several minor political offices during the 1780s. None of the three candidates waged a vigorous campaign, and no significant issues were raised. Instead, each man relied on his friends to solicit support. The results of the election, held in early October, showed that Samuel Smith had lost none of the popularity and respect that had twice sent him to the House of Delegates. Although only a small percentage of the eligible voters in the city and county went to the polls, Smith easily defeated his two opponents. Now forty years old, Smith prepared to begin a new career in national government, one that would last another forty years.[1]

Shortly before the election, James McHenry, a future secretary of war and one of the leaders in the emerging Federalist party in Maryland, wrote to Secretary of the Treasury Alexander Hamilton assur-

1. James McHenry to William Tilghman, October 4, 1792, James McHenry Papers, Library of Congress; *Maryland Journal and Baltimore Advertiser*, July 27, August 14, August 17, and October 5, 1792.

ing him that Smith would be a supporter of administration measures in Congress. McHenry described Smith as a "good federalist" who was "without skill in public affairs."[2] Acting on this information Hamilton opened a correspondence with Smith in the summer of 1793. Soon Smith began dispatching intelligence to the secretary concerning the political situation in Baltimore. In August of 1793, for instance, he told Hamilton that Baltimore was loyal to the administration and "except [for] half a dozen fools of no consequence will act right."[3] Even before he had taken his seat in Congress, Smith felt that his relations with Hamilton were such that he could request patronage. On August 27, 1793, he asked the secretary to appoint either Daniel Delozier or John Purviance to fill the vacant post of surveyor of the port of Baltimore.[4]

Toward the end of November Smith bid his family goodby and boarded a ship that took him from Baltimore to Elkton, Maryland, located at the extreme north end of Chesapeake Bay. From there he traveled by coach to Philadelphia and took lodgings in one of the city's many boarding houses. Early on the morning of December 2, the day appointed for the opening of Congress, Smith made his way to the red brick building, located adjacent to Independence Hall, where the national legislature held its sessions. The House of Representatives' chamber on the first floor was dimly lit and heated only by a few stoves spaced along the walls. The congressmen sat on long, red-felt-covered benches arranged in a semicircle to the front of the Speaker's platform. As a new member Smith was probably required to sit near the center aisle that ran from the main entrance down to the podium, since those seats were farthest from the sources of heat and exposed to wintry drafts every time someone opened or closed the door. The established leaders of the House, men such as James Madison of Virginia, were given the privilege of selecting their seats as near as possible to the stoves. Probably chilled and perhaps a bit awed, the Marylander took the oath of office along with the other representatives and prepared to consider the business before the House.

The first session of the Third Congress assembled in Philadelphia against a somber background of a European conflict that threatened American security and prosperity. In February 1793 England and France had gone to war. Despite treaty obligations to France, Presi-

2. McHenry to Alexander Hamilton, August 16, 1792, in Bernard C. Steiner, ed., *The Life and Correspondence of James McHenry* (Cleveland, 1907), p. 137.
3. S. Smith to Hamilton, August 20, 1793, Alexander Hamilton Papers, Library of Congress.
4. S. Smith to Hamilton, August 27, 1793, Hamilton Papers.

dent Washington had issued his famous Neutrality Proclamation on April 22. The exigencies of war and American weakness, however, invited the two belligerents to interfere with the commerce and shipping of the United States. Britain especially contested the doctrine of "free ships make free goods" and with its overwhelming naval power forced American ships to submit to search and frequent seizure for carrying whatever the English government chose to define as contraband. As one of the very few merchants in Congress, Smith paid close attention to the developing crisis that so intimately affected his interests.

The freshman congressman from Maryland could take heart from the tough words in Washington's annual address delivered to Congress on December 3, 1793. After detailing the restrictions imposed on neutral commerce by France and England as well as revealing that Algerian pirates had attacked American vessels in the Mediterranean, the president solemnly warned Congress not to allow those outrages to go unchallenged. "If we desire to avoid insult, we must be able to repel it," Washington declared; "if we desire to secure peace, . . . it must be known that we are at all times ready for war."[5] Along with his message the president submitted to Congress several measures intended to improve the nation's defenses. Samuel Smith's procommerce and promilitary biases were clearly revealed in the House debates over the administration proposals.[6]

The first defense bill came before the House on December 17 and provided for a large increase in the army. Immediately it became the center of a bitter partisan struggle. While Smith and other adherents of the administration backed the measure, it was disapproved by a small but growing group of antiadministration congressmen, who consistently opposed the centralization of power in the national government. A few years earlier this group had unsuccessfully fought Hamilton's plans for a national bank and the assumption of the states' war debts by the central government. Now they opposed expanding the size of the military not only as unnecessary and expensive, but also as a serious threat to the rights of the states and individual citizens. As a new congressman, Smith took little part in the discussions on the army bill. When one of the opponents of the administration objected to the great difference in pay between officers and soldiers called for in the measure as being undemocratic, Smith replied that

5. U.S., Congress, *The Debates and Proceedings in the Congress of the United States . . . 1789–1824*, 42 vols. (Washington, D.C., 1834–1856), 3d Cong., 1st sess., 1793, p. 7; hereafter cited as *Annals of Congress*.
6. Ibid.

such incentives were necessary. He pointed out that officers would leave the army if they were not paid enough and rejected the idea that officers and recruits should be paid the same amount.[7] "Gentlemen might speak of equality," he added sarcastically, "but in practice the thing was impossible."[8] On January 23, 1794, the army bill finally passed the House, with Smith voting in the affirmative.[9]

The Marylander was more active in his support of another administration bill asking for the construction of four frigates and several smaller vessels. James Madison, the leading antiadministration figure in the House, assailed the proposed fleet, charging that it was too small, too costly, and that it would take too long to build. The Virginian correctly surmised that so few ships were not intended to overawe France and Britain but to protect American merchant vessels in the Mediterranean from North African pirates. Still fighting to keep down the size and expense of the military, Madison suggested that instead of building warships the United States should follow the practice of other nations and bribe the Barbary powers not to attack American vessels. Smith made two extemporaneous replies to Madison. In the first, delivered on February 6, he argued that the proposed fleet would be more than adequate to the task of defending American commerce in the Mediterranean. Furthermore, he told his colleagues, his extensive travels through the Mediterranean lands as a young man convinced him that adequate harbors and supply facilities existed in Spain and Italy to maintain an American squadron permanently on station. As a clinching argument Smith warned that failure to build the naval vessels might expose the coast of the United States to raids by Algerian corsairs.[10]

A few days later the Maryland congressman again spoke on the naval bill, this time addressing his remarks to the issues raised by Madison's bribery scheme. "Who would join this country," he asked, "when we declared that we could do nothing?" He called such a situation "disgraceful" and with little generosity or logic labeled opponents of the naval bill as "friends to Monarchy."[11] Smith's intemperate attack on Madison and the other antiadministration representatives seems all the more remarkable because Smith himself had been

7. Ibid., p. 252.
8. Ibid.
9. Ibid., p. 272.
10. S. Smith to Otho Holland Williams, December 18, 1793, O. H. Williams Papers, Maryland Historical Society; *Annals of Congress*, 3d Cong., 1st sess., 1794, pp. 250, 433–436.
11. *Annals of Congress*, 3d Cong., 1st sess., 1794, p. 448.

bribing the North African pirates for some years to protect his own ships. But if the Marylander's tactics were crude, his sense of what benefited commerce was highly sophisticated. By marshalling numerous statistics, a characteristic feature of all of his speeches, Smith showed that the cost of the proposed fleet would be less than the cost of the higher insurance rates merchants would be forced to pay in the absence of a navy. At every opportunity Smith championed the naval bill and was even able to amend it to increase the armaments of the smaller ships. On February 21 the House passed the measure by a vote of 43 to 41, with Smith again voting in the majority.[12]

While Smith and other supporters of the president's program moved to build up American military capacity, opposition congressmen were preparing a legislative program that they promised would achieve peace without war or the sacrifice of national honor. Madison and his allies in the House felt the need to contest Britain's high-handed treatment of American ships and sailors as much as their opponents. They feared massive defense appropriations, however, because they believed that a large military establishment and an executive department swollen in power by vast patronage presented a clear danger to republican government. It was far better, they argued, to make England respect American rights by means other than war or threats of war. Their alternative was economic coercion, a tactic employed successfully against Britain during the decade preceding the Revolutionary War. The antiadministration congressmen contended that America was still economically indispensable to England both as a market for its manufactures and as a supplier of food to the British West Indies. Such being the case, James Madison concluded that "the readiest expedient for stopping [England's] career of depradation on those parts of our trade which thwart her plans, will be to make her feel for those which she cannot do without."[13]

In January 1794 Madison introduced in the House seven resolutions that, under the guise of commercial regulation, aimed at retaliation against Britain. The key resolution demanded that additional duties be placed on certain categories of imports "manufactured by European nations having no commercial treaty with the United States." The products listed were those made of iron, steel, tin, pewter, and wool. These were precisely the articles that made up the bulk of British exports to the United States, and Britain was the only major trading nation with which America had no commercial treaty. The last of

12. Ibid., p. 459.
13. James Madison to Horatio Gates, March 24, 1794, in Gaillard Hunt, ed., *The Writings of James Madison*, 9 vols. (New York, 1900–1910), 6: 208.

Madison's resolutions proposed that any money raised from the new duties should be given to Americans who had suffered losses because of Britain's illegal orders-in-council. Smith, always sensitive to matters concerning commerce, reacted negatively to placing "new impositions on trade" and led the fight to defeat Madison's program.[14]

After several days of research and contemplation Smith rose on January 15 to deliver his first major speech as a congressman. Concentrating his attack on Madison's plan for discriminatory duties, Smith opened his remarks with a thorough analysis of American trade relations with both treaty and nontreaty powers. He noted that France and other nations with whom the United States did have commercial treaties had flagrantly restricted American commerce when it suited their purposes. In other words, Madison's distinction between treaty and nontreaty nations was irrelevant since both trampled upon American rights. On the other hand, the United States imported seventeen million dollars in goods annually from nontreaty powers, mainly England, and this trade brought in revenues to the government totaling $850,000. The question, Smith said, was whether England had so abused the United States that it should sacrifice this important income simply to gain revenge. The Marylander's answer was most definitely negative. Again resorting to statistics he demonstrated that despite the orders-in-council, the British had treated American commerce tolerably well. As an example he pointed out that England admitted many raw materials produced in the United States duty-free. Only the regulation prohibiting American shipping from carrying domestic produce to the British West Indies constituted a serious curb on trade. Yet even this imposition, he added, had not kept American merchants from exporting forty-five hundred barrels of flour to the West Indies aboard British ships. "Shall we risk this advantage," he asked, "because they will not let us employ 12 brigs to carry it?"[15]

Smith's speech perfectly reflected his prejudices. His concern, at least at this point, was less in preserving America's honor than in protecting the profits of the merchants. "It is not what Britain may suffer by the system proposed," the Marylander lectured his colleagues, "but the disadvantage which will be the consequence to the United

14. Ibid., p. 204; Dumas Malone, *Jefferson and the Ordeal of Liberty* (Boston, 1962), p. 159; Irving Brant, *James Madison; Father of the Constitution* (New York, 1950), p. 389; Nathan Schachner, *Alexander Hamilton* (New York, 1946), p. 327; *Annals of Congress*, 3d Cong., 1st sess., 1794, p. 159; Libero Marx Renzulli, "Maryland Federalism, 1787–1819" (Ph.D. diss., University of Virginia, 1962), p. 209.

15. *Annals of Congress*, 3d Cong., 1st sess., 1794, pp. 231–232.

States, that ought to be taken into consideration."[16] A short while later he returned to the same theme: "Our duty is not to injure others but to protect our own interest."[17] In his mind commerce was of paramount importance and national policy should be directed toward insuring its well-being. Thus he could support the army and navy bills as tools which might be used diplomatically to force Britain to relax her controls over American trade. But Madison's resolutions, even though directed against the British, were unacceptable to Smith because their immediate impact on American commerce would be adverse. Smith shared with most American merchants a determination to put up with violations of American rights if a reasonable profit could still be made. He differed from many of them in his willingness to fight a war with Britain if the means were at hand and the commercial losses great enough.[18]

Through the last two weeks of January the House wrestled with Madison's resolutions. Almost daily Smith participated in the debates. On January 16, 1794, he spoke in rebuttal to an attack on his loyalty and that of merchants in general. The day before, an antiadministration member had asserted that American merchants who did business with England on a credit basis were probably under foreign influence and certainly could not be trusted. In a panegyric to the virtues of his business associates, Smith praised merchants as "men of liberal sentiments," who were not swayed "by the petty motives of interest." As far as he was personally concerned, the Marylander bluntly told his antagonist that he was far too rich to need English credit. Then with a fine touch of patrician arrogance he added that the British had seized as much of his property "as the gentlemen to whom [I] reply would think a tolerable fortune for dividing among his sons."[19] A week later Smith embarrassed the antiadministration faction by suggesting that Madison's resolutions should be rewritten so as to frankly accuse Britain of violating not only the 1783 Treaty of Paris by clinging to military posts in the American northwest, but also international law by unjustifiably interfering with neutral commerce. Suspecting that so bald a statement of their purpose would frighten off potential supporters of Madison's plan, antiadministration representatives denounced the Marylander's proposal.[20] "They got angry,"

16. Ibid., p. 231.
17. Ibid.
18. S. Smith to Williams, January 26 and March 20, 1794, O. H. Williams Papers.
19. *Annals of Congress*, 3d Cong., 1st sess., 1794, p. 247.
20. S. Smith to Williams, January 26, 1794, O. H. Williams Papers.

Smith confided to a friend, "but I persisted that we could not answer them if they flew from one ground to another."[21] The rising tide of opposition led Smith and other administration congressmen to predict that the resolutions would not pass.[22]

In early February Congress finally began acting on Madison's resolutions, and preliminary votes indicated that they would be rejected. Samuel Smith could rightfully take some of the credit for Madison's impending defeat. His comprehensive knowledge of commerce and the conditions under which American trade operated had made him a valuable ally for the administration. In an assembly made up mainly of lawyers and planters who necessarily had to deal with complex financial and commercial matters of which they were often ignorant, Smith's expertise could not but influence political decision-making.[23]

Before the House had time to pass final judgment on Madison's program, news arrived that rendered it superfluous. On November 6, 1793, the British government had issued a new order-in-council declaring all neutral ships found carrying produce or goods belonging to France or her colonies liable to seizure. The new law had not been publicized in order to allow English naval vessels and privateers to reach the West Indies and surprise unsuspecting American ships trading with the French islands. The deception succeeded and over two hundred fifty American ships were captured. British policy, however, had now brought the two nations to the very brink of war.[24]

The debacle in the West Indies left Smith shaken and angry. "I do believe that the temperate will not be able to keep peace with G. B.," he wrote to his friend Otho Holland Williams in Baltimore, "her insolence & her cruel depradation on our property would Influence any the most moderate."[25] He seriously contemplated supporting a declaration of war but soon discarded the possibility since the nation stood virtually unarmed.[26]

Despite Washington's message urging congressional action on defense measures, the British annihilation of American shipping in the West Indies caught the nation unprepared. The strong measures passed by the House of Representatives had stalled in the Senate.

21. Ibid.

22. Fisher Ames to Christopher Gore, January 28, 1794, in Seth Ames, ed., *Works of Fisher Ames*, 2 vols. (Boston, 1854), 2: 133.

23. *Annals of Congress*, 3d Cong., 1st sess., 1794, pp. 421, 430–431.

24. Samuel Flagg Bemis, *Jay's Treaty*, rev. ed. (New Haven, 1962), pp. 212–215.

25. S. Smith to Williams, February 25, 1794, O. H. Williams Papers.

26. Ibid.

Smith blamed "Maddison's party" for preventing the passage of the army and navy bills in the upper chamber, something they had been unable to do in the House. The more he thought about the behavior of Madison and his friends the more furious Smith became. In private letters he claimed that the Virginian had deliberately delayed many important bills from reaching the House floor by prolonging debate on his resolutions.[27]

While Smith fumed, Alexander Hamilton and other leaders of the administration party held a secret meeting at which they hammered out a new legislative program calling for a temporary embargo to get American ships off the ocean, increased taxes, and the construction of harbor fortifications. They also agreed that a special diplomatic mission should be sent to England in an effort to settle the crisis peacefully. Without hesitation Smith supported all of the bills including the embargo just as he had voted for every major administration measure of the first session of the Third Congress. Nevertheless he had reached a significant turning point in his political career. He was beginning to drift away from his earlier attachment to Hamilton. The Marylander considered British attacks on American commerce intolerable and suspected that the administration's zeal to protect mercantile interests did not match his own.[28]

On March 27, 1794, his anti-British sentiments led Smith for the first time to challenge the administration party in the House. The issue involved a motion made by an antiadministration representative to sequester all debts owed to British citizens by Americans. Madison's faction hoped that the House would accept their measure as a substitute for military preparations. Administration congressmen generally expressed opposition to the idea, but Smith eagerly backed the plan as a useful addition to other military measures. The Marylander urged the House to approve confiscation of the debts since they totaled more than $20,000,000, a sum that would easily reimburse those Americans whose ships had been captured in the West Indies. He reminded the representatives that the president was about to dispatch a special emissary to London, and that the debt-seizure plan would provide a valuable bargaining counter in the negotiations.[29]

The last point was central to Smith's reasoning. He sincerely hoped that Chief Justice John Jay's mission to England would be successful

27. S. Smith to Williams, March 20, 1794, O. H. Williams Papers.

28. Hamilton's Journal, March 10, 1794, Hamilton Papers; *Annals of Congress,* 3d Cong., 1st sess., 1794, pp. 500, 530–531, 536; S. Smith to Williams, March 6, 1794, O. H. Williams Papers.

29. *Annals of Congress,* 3d Cong., 1st sess., 1794, pp. 536–537.

and that the "King of Sea Robbers," as Smith now called Britain in his speeches, would stop attacking American ships. But he realized that American military preparations were not yet sizable enough to influence England. Lacking an army and navy, the United States might hope to force concessions from England in exchange for the $20,000,-000 in debts. If the negotiations proved unsatisfactory, then the government could use the funds to recompense citizens wronged by England. In reply, administration congressmen claimed that sequestration of the debts would actually interfere with Jay's negotiations and might even be considered "a declaration of war." Never before had Smith and the followers of Madison found themselves on the same side of a question. Despite this they were not able to bring the debt-seizure bill to a vote.[30]

Continuing his efforts to strengthen Jay's hand in London, Smith again abandoned the administration to support bills calling for nonintercourse and nonimportation sponsored by Madison's faction. He explained to Otho Holland Williams that "all exports to & Imports from G. B. shall cease, until they give us full satisfaction for the Depredation on our property."[31] By backing measures that would close off all trade with Britain, Smith obviously contradicted his earlier stand against Madison's proposal for a much milder form of economic warfare. The same logic, however, that caused him to approve the plan to confiscate British debts in America forced him to reverse his position on economic coercion. The November 6 order-in-council had changed everything. Although a later decree issued in January 1794 moderated some aspects of the November order, it did not halt British aggression against American commerce. In this new context Smith found the larger interests of American trade could only be served by a temporary self-imposed restriction. If approved by Congress and effectively enforced, the trade stoppage would severely affect the English economy. By holding out the possibility that nonintercourse and nonimportation might be repealed, the United States could reasonably expect the British to make reciprocal concessions. Rejecting this rationale, the administration supporters in the House attacked both measures on the same grounds they had fought seizure of the debts: that such actions would only antagonize the British and hamper negotiations. Despite their efforts, both bills passed by almost identical margins.[32]

Although Congress did not adjourn until June, no other important

30. Ibid., pp. 537, 543–544, 554.
31. S. Smith to Williams, March 6, 1794, O. H. Williams Papers.
32. *Annals of Congress*, 3d Cong., 1st sess., 1794, pp. 567–605.

measures were debated. Indeed, little could be done until Chief Justice Jay had concluded his mission. Tired and embittered, Samuel Smith returned to Baltimore in early May. His business correspondence during the next several months indicated that the virulent Anglophobia he had displayed in Congress resulted partly from his personal losses to British cruisers enforcing the orders-in-council. To one merchant he complained that a cargo of coffee owned by S. Smith & Buchanan had been condemned by a British Admiralty Court. He regarded a legal appeal useless because Americans could "expect nothing" from the English judicial system. At the end of May Smith informed a business associate that the danger of seizure was so great that he had ordered his own vessels kept in port. Proclaiming anti-British sentiments to one and all, he predicted that if Jay's mission failed, war must ensue.[33]

Although an active participant in Congress during his first session, Samuel Smith had not been among the leading figures. Neither Hamilton nor Madison had asked him to help formulate legislative strategies, nor had the president invited him to dinner in order to solicit his support for an important bill. Inexperienced and politically naive, Smith entered Congress as an adherent of Washington and Hamilton. By the end of the session, however, he was veering toward a course of political independence. His every action had reflected his allegiance to the merchant and shipping interests, particularly those in Baltimore. Indeed, his uncompromising attitude on matters relating to commerce explains the rift between Smith and the administration party, soon to be known as the Federalists. The Marylander, stung by his own business losses, felt that British assaults on American commerce were so ruinous that any response, including war, was justified if it promised to restore the free flow of trade. Thus he supported Washington and Hamilton in their program of arming the nation as well as the antiadministration schemes for economic coercion. Although Hamilton, Fisher Ames of Massachusetts, and other leaders of the government faction also resented British policies, they thought negotiations backed by defense preparations were the only remedy available to the United States. They scoffed at the plans for economic retaliation and believed war to be an unrealistic option. As Fisher Ames put it when told of British seizures in the West Indies: "Peace, peace, to the last day that it can be maintained."[34]

33. S. Smith to Daniel Steel, May 26, 1794, S. Smith to William Gibbons & Co., May 31, 1794, and S. Smith to Sebastian de Aldana, June 24, 1794, Smith & Company Letterbook, Maryland Historical Society.

34. Ames to Gore, February 25, 1794, in Ames, ed., *Works of Fisher Ames,* 2: 136.

Smith had even greater differences with the group opposing the administration party. While he shared with them a favorable attitude toward France and a distrust of England, he disagreed with them on such issues as defense and foreign policy. Moreover, the chief leaders of the slowly evolving opposition party represented agrarian America; though they smiled on certain types of trade, they generally regarded commerce as an occupation subservient to agriculture. They were also suspicious of merchants as a group, believing them to be closely aligned with England. Smith, of course, was first and foremost a merchant. If nothing else his speeches in Congress had established him as one of the preeminent spokesmen for commerce in the House of Representatives. Nevertheless, the tortuous trail that led him to become a Jeffersonian Republican began in the spring of 1794.[35]

35. Thomas Jefferson frequently voiced such sentiments. See Jefferson to Edmund Pendleton, April 22, 1799, Jefferson to Thomas Leiper, January 21, 1809, and Jefferson to Benjamin Stoddert, February 18, 1800, in Paul Leicester Ford, ed., *The Writings of Thomas Jefferson*, 10 vols. (New York, 1892–1899), 7: 376, 9: 239, 245.

5

The Maturing Politician

BEFORE RETURNING to Philadelphia to attend the second session of the Third Congress, Smith was called into action in his capacity as commander of the Baltimore militia. In the summer and fall of 1794 a widespread revolt in western Pennsylvania and Maryland tested the stability and strength of the new national government. Financially hurt by the excise tax placed on corn whiskey, a major product of those isolated areas, large numbers of western farmers challenged the national government's authority by abusing tax collectors, interfering with the operation of local courts, and seizing United States mail. At the height of the movement the whiskey rebels composed a sizable army, but federal troops accompanied by President Washington and Alexander Hamilton were soon on their way to the troubled areas. Although the excise taxes were also unpopular in Baltimore, the constitutional question of whether federal laws were binding was paramount as far as the city's leaders were concerned, and they fully supported the forceful measures initiated by the administration.[1]

Smith, recently promoted to major general of the Maryland militia, was attending a service with Margaret at the First Presbyterian Church when he received word that a large body of the rebels was supposedly marching on the state arsenal at Frederick.[2] At his order

1. See Leland D. Baldwin, *Whiskey Rebels* (Pittsburgh, 1939); Libero Marx Renzulli, "Maryland Federalism, 1787–1819" (Ph.D. diss., University of Virginia, 1962), p. 215; *Maryland Journal and Baltimore Advertiser*, September 5, 1794.

2. J. Thomas Scharf, *History of Maryland from the Earliest Period to the Present Day*, 3 vols. (Baltimore, 1879), 2: 585.

on September 17, the Baltimore militia hastily assembled at the city's parade ground. One exuberant newspaper editor, after viewing the formations of colorfully attired soldiers, reported that the city had not exhibited a more "warlike appearance" since the early days of the Revolutionary War. While thousands of Baltimoreans looked on, General Smith addressed his troops. He described the whisky rebels as "a lawless banditti, who set themselves up to govern." The general asked: "shall we permit them to seize our arms and give us laws, or shall we keep them and give laws to ourselves?"[3] After a brief pause Smith called for three hundred volunteers to go with him to Frederick; nearly three times that number stepped forward. Nine days later the general arrived in Frederick with his tired men only to find that no attack threatened the arsenal, nor, apparently, had one ever been planned.[4]

Although the march to Frederick served no military purpose, it revealed glaring weaknesses in the militia system. It was not that the Baltimore troops were badly organized or trained; Smith had commanded the city militia for fourteen years and made them into one of the best fighting units in the middle Atlantic states. The real problem lay with the state government in Annapolis, whose niggardliness and inefficiency left many of Smith's men without shoes, arms, or adequate clothing. By the time the Baltimore troops reached Frederick, most of them were in no condition to fight, and the general's pleas for assistance from the state government drew no response. All in all Smith could consider himself fortunate that the rebels did not attack.[5]

By late December 1794 the uprising had been entirely suppressed, and Smith, who in the midst of the recent turmoil had been reelected without opposition to a second term in the House, journeyed to Philadelphia for the opening of Congress. The memory of the ill-equipped militia was still fresh in his mind when a special report on the militia system reached the House floor on January 9, 1795. Smith related to his colleagues the pathetic story of the Maryland militia, revealing that some of the citizen-soldiers from outside Baltimore had not even known how to load a gun, let alone fire it. When the House referred the militia report to a select committee it was only natural that as a war hero and long-time militia commander Smith should be named

3. Annapolis *Maryland Gazette,* September 18, 1794, quoted in Scharf, *History of Maryland,* 2: 586.

4. *Maryland Journal and Baltimore Advertiser,* September 26, 1794.

5. John Davidson to Samuel Smith, September 18, 1794, Smith-Carter Papers, University of Virginia Library.

chairman.[6] On February 12 the Maryland congressman presented the committee's recommendations in the form of a bill that provided for an elite force of one hundred thousand militia directly controlled by the national government rather than by the states. Such an arrangement, he felt, insured that at least part of the nation's militia would be properly prepared for combat. The general defended the bill as vital to the security of America's frontiers with Canada and Florida. "The Government must either have a good militia or a standing army," Smith declared, "for the present militia at least in the Southern states, do not deserve that name; and a militia is more agreeable to Republican principles."[7] Since many congressmen felt it gave too much power to the federal government, however, the bill failed to pass.[8]

The excise taxes that had caused the western unrest also attracted Smith's attention. The tax on distilled whisky became the best known of these levies, but a number of other domestically manufactured items were affected, including snuff, sugar, wine, and carriages. Not only western farmers but also urban businessmen, of whom Samuel Smith was one, suffered from the excise taxes. Disregarding this discontent, the Federalists brought forward in January 1795 a bill to continue the excise taxes in order to reduce the public debt. Already a leading spokesman for the mercantile community, Smith now stepped forward as a defender of manufacturing in America. In a significant speech he attacked the excise tax bill and all but declared his open opposition to the administration. Smith told the House that the taxes could be repealed and the national debt still reduced because of the rapidly increasing revenues collected from duties on imports. He then accused the administration of falsifying budget requests. Smith cited certain "single-shot" expenses, such as those incurred in suppressing the Whisky Rebellion, that had been listed as if they were annual costs. By such juggling of the books the administration had built a case for the excise tax system unjustified by the real facts.[9]

The second half of his speech showed that Smith's opposition to continuing the excise taxes was a matter of economics and not ideology. The general emphasized that the taxes adversely affected all areas of the country and not merely the West. He charged that, if continued, they would "extirpate" manufacturing in America. Citing his own

6. U.S., Congress, *The Debates and Proceedings in the Congress of the United States . . . 1789–1824,* 42 vols. (Washington, D.C., 1834–1856), 3d Cong., 2d sess., 1795, p. 1071; hereafter cited as *Annals of Congress.*

7. Ibid., pp. 1214–1215.

8. Ibid., p. 1215.

9. Ibid., pp. 1091–1092.

industrial enterprise in Baltimore, Smith claimed that because of the excise, his distillery had "not made five shillings." Besides being harmful the taxes were also "unfair." Before imposing the taxes the government had followed a policy of encouraging manufacturing enterprise by placing extra duties on many imported articles. This had induced "gentlemen of capital" to invest heavily in plants, labor, and machinery. Now that investment was being destroyed by the new and contradictory policy of taxing industry. The government, he asserted, was guilty of bad faith.[10]

Once started the general could not contain himself. Turning to the Federalists he inquired of them why they persisted in favoring excise taxes when there was no longer any reason for them. To continue the excise system when the import duties produced enough money was "a deception upon the public," but, added the excited congressman, "there was deception upon deception in the management of this business."[11] Smith had, as he would many times in the future, gone too far. His analysis of the excise system was devastating, but his personal attack on his opponents vitiated his effectiveness. The fact that he apologized a day later to the House "for the warmth of his observations" did little to smooth ruffled feelings. Eventually the excise tax bill passed, with Smith and the antiadministration representatives voting against it.[12] Once more on an important measure the Marylander had turned away from the Federalists. This time he not only had disagreed with their policy, but also had questioned their motives.

Left to himself Smith might have continued pursuing a political course based entirely on economic interest rather than party loyalty. But the volatile political situation of the mid-1790s made such a role more and more difficult.[13] Thomas Jefferson best expressed the feelings of many ardent party men when he condemned those who followed a "middle line" in politics, especially when "the principle of difference is as substantial and as strongly pronounced as between the Republicans & the Monocrats of our country . . . ."[14] The Virginian's remarks came amidst the controversy over Jay's Treaty, perhaps the most

10. Ibid., p. 1091.

11. Ibid.

12. Ibid., p. 1100.

13. Noble Cunningham, *The Jeffersonian Republicans; The Formation of Party Organization, 1789–1801* (Chapel Hill, N.C., 1957), p. 97.

14. Thomas Jefferson to William Branch Giles, December 31, 1795, in Paul Leicester Ford, ed., *The Writings of Thomas Jefferson*, 10 vols. (New York, 1892–1899), 7: 43.

important issue the new nation had yet faced. The emotions aroused in the public mind over the treaty virtually created two national political parties in the United States. Although Congress had long been loosely divided between those who generally favored administration policies and those who opposed them, local political factions integrated with a national party structure had not previously existed. Such political organizations first appeared in 1795 and 1796 as a result of the Jay Treaty controversy. Party affiliation began to emerge as an important factor in national and local elections.[15]

When the treaty Jay had concluded with Great Britain in November 1794 finally reached the United States, even many Federalists expressed astonishment at its terms. The British had agreed to evacuate the military posts in the northwest and to make a few concessions to American commerce. Nothing, however, was said about the impressment of American seamen, the problem of the western Indians who attacked American settlements with British arms, or the return of slaves seized during the Revolutionary War. Nearly everyone could find a clause in the treaty to disagree with. "I expect," wrote Hamilton, "the treaty will labor." The New Yorker had masterfully understated the problem—as the angry public reaction following publication of the treaty showed. In Philadelphia mobs burned an effigy of the unfortunate chief justice, while in Baltimore the newspapers announced that antitreaty petitions were "available for signatures" at the Courthouse. On July 28, 1795, a large public meeting in Baltimore approved resolutions denouncing the treaty and authorizing an address to the president expressing "disapprobation of said treaty, and requesting that it not be ratified." Despite similar protests from Philadelphia and New York as well as his own misgivings, President Washington proclaimed the treaty as law as soon as the Senate voted its acceptance.[16]

Samuel Smith had hoped that Jay's negotiations would end the dispute with Britain. His major concern had been and continued to be an end to the harassment of American commerce. On studying the

15. Jefferson to James Monroe, September 6, 1795, ibid., p. 27; Broadus Mitchell, *Heritage from Hamilton* (New York, 1957), p. 79; Irving Brant, *James Madison; Father of the Constitution* (New York, 1950), p. 426; Cunningham, *Jeffersonian Republicans*, pp. 74–85; Dumas Malone, *Jefferson and the Ordeal of Liberty* (Boston, 1962), p. 248.

16. Alexander Hamilton to William Bradford, May 1795, in Henry Cabot Lodge, ed., *The Works of Alexander Hamilton*, Federal ed., 12 vols. (New York, 1903), 10: 99; *Federal Intelligencer and Baltimore Daily Advertiser*, July 1, 25, and 28, 1795.

terms of the treaty, however, he was dismayed by the unfavorable nature of many of the articles relating to trade. On January 11, 1796, before the bills providing funds to implement the treaty were presented in the House of Representatives, Smith submitted an important resolution. In brief the resolution stated that it should be the policy of the United States not to allow foreign ships to bring into the country goods or produce not grown or produced by the nation to which the ships belonged. The obvious and intended result of this policy would be to benefit the American shipping industry at the expense of the British. British ships would be allowed to bring British goods into American ports but no one else's—as they were now doing in competition with the domestic carrying trade. The Marylander did not disguise the fact that his resolution was aimed at countering certain provisions of Jay's Treaty he considered detrimental to the interests of the mercantile community.[17]

The House debate on Smith's resolution began on January 15. The general moved that his proposal be discussed immediately by the Committee of the Whole House, but the Federalists insisted that proper procedures be observed and the resolution directed to the Federalist-controlled Committee on Commerce and Manufactures. Fearing that Smith's plan was an attempt to attack the treaty and embarrass those who made it, the Federalists wanted either to kill the resolution in committee or delay its consideration by the House. For two days the Federalist and antiadministration factions contended over which agency of the House should be granted jurisdiction. The Marylander spoke frequently, urging on the congressmen the vital importance of his scheme as the "only provision which was left us by that Treaty to save our Commerce from prostration." Eventually the antiadministration forces won the skirmish but lost the battle; for while Smith's resolution was put on the calendar of the House for debate, the Federalists kept it from being officially considered.[18] The general was frankly surprised by the intensity and source of the resistance to his resolution. "Strange as it will appear to you," Smith observed to a Baltimore banker, "it will be opposed by the N.[ew] E.[ngland] members & supported by the Southern members."[19] In the same letter he predicted that even if the House passed the resolution the Federalist majority in the Senate would defeat it. The

17. S. Smith to Daniel Steel, May 26, 1794, Smith & Company Letterbook, Maryland Historical Society; *Annals of Congress*, 4th Cong., 1st sess., 1796, p. 195.

18. *Annals of Congress*, 4th Cong., 1st sess., 1796, pp. 245–249.

19. S. Smith to William Patterson, January 17, 1796, Personal Papers Miscellaneous, Library of Congress.

explanation of why commercially minded New Englanders would oppose Smith's resolution and anticommerce Southerners back it was simply that both groups were looking beyond the immediate question to the larger issue: whether the House of Representatives would appropriate funds needed to put the Jay Treaty into effect. While Smith was attempting to assist American commerce, the two parties in Congress were engaged in a political game where the stakes were nothing less than the prestige of the president and ultimately control of the government.

On January 26 Smith again tried to moderate the effects of the Jay Treaty on American trade by suggesting that the United States abolish its discriminating duties. These extra taxes on foreign tonnage amounted to a government subsidy for shipowners. Because of them foreign exporters had found it cheaper to use American vessels when sending their goods to the United States. Smith had in mind one article in the treaty that prevented the American government from making further increases in these import duties while allowing England to "countervail," or raise its own duties without restriction.[20] "I fear this countervail," he told the House, "it will be made at [British] discretion, and may or may not be just."[21] Quoting from British and French law as well as from letters he had received from Europe, Smith built a convincing case that failure to repeal the discriminating duties could lead to decimation of the American carrying trade by Great Britain. By simply placing excessively high import rates on goods carried by American ships entering its ports, England could effectively keep out those vessels while the Jay Treaty prevented Congress from retaliating. Smith argued that if all import duties discriminating against England were dropped, then that country might be persuaded to reciprocate. Trade between England and America would then grow immensely and everyone concerned would profit. This second resolution of Smith's shared the fate of the first; it was referred to the Committee of the Whole but never acted upon.[22]

Early in March the two factions in the House stopped sparring over subsidiary issues and began to consider the Jay Treaty itself. Edward Livingston, an antiadministration congressman from New York, opened the contest with a resolution calling upon the president to submit to the House all papers he possessed concerning the treaty.

20. *Annals of Congress*, 4th Cong., 1st sess., 1796, p. 268. This was article fifteen. The entire text of the treaty can be found in Samuel Flagg Bemis, *Jay's Treaty*, rev. ed. (New Haven, 1962), pp. 453–489.

21. *Annals of Congress*, 4th Cong., 1st sess., 1796, p. 269.

22. Ibid., pp. 269, 428.

Such papers had in the past been routinely handed over on request, but the Federalists chose to resist on this occasion for two reasons. The first was constitutional: neither Washington nor his party were willing to admit Livingston's assertion that "the House were vested with a discretionary power of carrying the Treaty into effect, or refusing it their sanction."[23] According to the Federalists, the Constitution vested the treaty-making power with the president and the Senate, and the House had no choice but to comply with what was officially the law of the land. The second reason was frankly political. The treaty had been negotiated by a Federalist emissary, approved by a Federalist majority in the Senate, and proclaimed by a Federalist president. Without question it constituted the keystone of the Federalist foreign policy. If the administration's opponents managed to keep the treaty from going into effect or could seriously discredit it, they would deal the Federalists a crippling political blow. And with good cause the administration party anticipated that Jay's instructions and correspondence concerning the treaty would damage the chances of the appropriations bills passing the House should the enemies of the agreement get hold of them. Hamilton went so far as to describe the papers as a "crude mass" which would "do no credit to the administration."[24]

Smith spoke before the House of Representatives on March 17 and supported Livingston's resolution. He insisted the House could not accept the Federalists' definition of the treaty-making power, which he sarcastically paraphrased as saying that the president and two-thirds of the Senate can do anything they choose by negotiating a treaty, and the House "have only to be informed thereof, and to obey." If this view became the accepted one, said Smith, then the balance of government would have shifted dangerously toward tyranny. The Marylander also charged that certain provisions of the Jay Treaty were unconstitutional. Citing the third article of the treaty that allowed British ships to pay less duties in the Great Lakes harbors than in other ports, Smith reminded his fellow congressmen that the Constitution specifically required that all commercial regulations must be uniform. In his opinion such a discrepancy justified the House in conducting a thorough investigation of the treaty.[25] Even though he had made plain his dislike of certain aspects of Jay's Treaty, the general refused to commit himself on how he would

23. Ibid., pp. 401, 428.
24. Hamilton to George Washington, March 28, 1796, in Lodge, ed., *Works of Hamilton*, 10: 152.
25. *Annals of Congress*, 4th Cong., 1st sess., 1796, pp. 624–626.

finally vote on the question of appropriations. He asserted he was "entirely open to conviction," but at the present time he "did not think [the treaty] good."[26]

The House approved Livingston's resolution on March 24, and Smith cast his vote with the antiadministration faction. Six days later President Washington refused the request for papers on the grounds that the House constitutionally had no right to interfere in the treaty-making process. The only legitimate reason for the House to demand such papers, Washington continued, was if they contemplated his impeachment, and that had not been stated in the resolution. Surprised by Washington's vehemence and his unthinkable suggestion about impeachment, opponents of the treaty managed to maintain their composure and, with Smith's support, committed the president's message to the Committee of the Whole over strong Federalist protests. The several ballots taken on Livingston's resolution showed that party organization and discipline had improved substantially in the House. Smith's consistent alliance with the antiadministration faction indicated that he now identified himself with that group as against the Federalists. Identification, however, did not imply total conformity with every position the opposition party took. The only continuous thread in Smith's political career was a commitment to protecting commercial interests over which he never allowed party affiliation to take precedence. This central facet of Smith's politics was perfectly illustrated by his approach to the Jay Treaty. Smith could with clear conscience join other antiadministration representatives in passing Livingston's resolution, for it did not affect mercantile interests and at the same time promised to promote the political fortunes of the nascent Republican party at the expense of their opponents. But his position on the Jay Treaty appropriations was a far different matter since the trading community would be crucially affected when the treaty went into effect. Smith's problem was to decide whether American trade would be better off with or without the treaty. His dilemma was complicated by political developments in Baltimore, where the friends and enemies of the Jay Treaty mobilized their forces to influence their congressman's vote.[27]

Smith's association with the opponents of the administration in Philadelphia had not gone unnoticed in Maryland. A Federalist congressman from the Eastern Shore of Maryland, William Vans Mur-

26. Ibid., p. 626.

27. Ibid., pp. 759–760; the outline of the message had been sent to Washington by Hamilton on March 7, 1796; see Lodge, ed., *Works of Hamilton*, 10: 145.

ray, had described Smith's resolution calling for repeal of the discriminating duties "strange work" and cautioned Secretary of War James McHenry, another Marylander, that the general might vote against the Jay Treaty appropriations bill. Acting on Hamilton's suggestion, McHenry made an effort to build local political pressures in Baltimore that he expected would compel Smith to vote with the Federalists. On April 12 the secretary dispatched a letter to Federalist merchant Robert Oliver urging him to take the lead in organizing protreaty sentiment in Baltimore. McHenry warned Oliver that unless the House approved the appropriations the treaty would be lost and the British would resume their depredations on American shipping. "A great deal," McHenry said, "if not everything rests upon Baltimore." Choosing his words carefully, the secretary hinted that Oliver should convene a meeting of all Baltimore Federalists and encourage them to send an "instruction" to Smith. McHenry went so far as to enclose a draft of the petition which he said should be carried around for signatures in every ward of the city at exactly the same time. Speed and secrecy was essential if "a certain party" was to be prevented from taking steps to neutralize the scheme. McHenry stressed the need for haste and told Oliver that as soon as the signatures were collected the petition should be given to Smith.[28]

The Baltimore Federalists moved immediately to carry out McHenry's plan. Instead of circulating the petitions by hand, however, they chose to advertise in the public prints. On April 18 a Baltimore newspaper published a notice that citizens might sign petitions favorable to the Jay Treaty in the offices of the Baltimore and Maryland Insurance Company. Less than a week later nearly six hundred individuals had signed. Meanwhile, a large group of merchants had met on April 20 and formed a corresponding committee which sent an appeal to Smith asking him to vote for the treaty funds.[29]

The political enemies of the merchants in Baltimore, small businessmen, laborers, and skilled artisans, immediately linked them-

28. William Vans Murray to James McHenry, January 28, 1796, in Bernard C. Steiner, ed., *The Life and Correspondence of James McHenry* (Cleveland, 1907), p. 167; McHenry to Robert Oliver, April 12, 1796, James McHenry Papers, Library of Congress. See also Hamilton to Rufus King, April 15, 1796, in Lodge, ed., *Works of Hamilton*, 10: 157.

29. *Federal Gazette & Baltimore Daily Advertiser,* April 18, 20, and 22, 1796; King to Hamilton, April 20, 1796, Alexander Hamilton Papers, Library of Congress; Peggy Caldwell McHenry to James McHenry, April 21, 1796, McHenry Papers.

selves to the antiadministration, antitreaty party and moved to counteract the effects of the petitions. On April 21 the Mechanical Society, a labor organization, sponsored a public meeting attended by the "Manufacturers and Mechanics" of Baltimore. Claimed by its organizers to be the largest gathering in the city's history, the rally passed a resolution applauding the antitreaty posture of the House of Representatives. A few days later the president of the Mechanical Society sent Smith a letter endorsing his conduct in the Livingston resolution debates.[30] It soon became evident, however, that the opposition's efforts had not been successful. The Mechanical Society's mass meeting was exposed as a minor affair made up of less than three hundred people, "five sixths of whom were brought there merely to see what would be proposed, and not with a view to take any part in the business."[31] The Federalists suspected that Smith had helped organize the abortive meeting and exulted at the discomfiture of their opponents. Federalist James Winchester jubilantly told McHenry that Smith had been in Baltimore when the protreaty petitions were circulated and that he was "conscious that his conduct opposed the sense of his constituents." Winchester also reported that the general resented the censure implied in the petitions and had tried very hard to suppress them. At one recent social gathering, Winchester related, several Federalists had gone so far as to tell Smith he could not and would not be reelected in the fall.[32]

Smith returned to Philadelphia and on April 22 delivered a long, highly emotional speech criticizing the Jay Treaty. He said there was "so little good contained in it, and so much evil to be apprehended from it," that he wished the president would never have signed it. Nevertheless, he declared his intention to vote for the appropriation bill because the treaty was not unconstitutional and failure to approve it would cause the British to renew their seizures and condemnations of American vessels. On May 1 the bill finally passed the House by a vote of fifty-one to forty-eight as Smith voted with the Federalists.[33]

The question is whether Smith's decision to vote for the appropriations represented his own judgment or was the result of the recent Federalist agitation in Baltimore. There can be no doubt that the pressure on Smith was both severe and continuous. During the last two weeks of April a committee of Federalists claiming to represent public opinion in Baltimore carefully scrutinized his actions in Con-

30. *Federal Gazette & Baltimore Daily Advertiser*, April 21 and 22, 1796.
31. Ibid., April 23, 1796.
32. James Winchester to McHenry, April 22, 1796, McHenry Papers.
33. *Annals of Congress*, 4th Cong., 1st sess., 1796, pp. 1153, 1155–1156, 1280.

gress. They wrote him letters criticizing his opinions about the treaty and insisted that he obey the instruction. Since many of the men attacking him were old friends and fellow merchants, the very group whose interests he was most concerned about, Smith must have been perplexed and hurt. He deeply resented the Federalists' committee and their insulting attitude. In one letter to the committee he pointed out that its popular mandate was dubious since only a few hundred had signed the petitions and there were over forty thousand people in the district. Furthermore, he called the committee's efforts needless because he had decided to vote for the treaty funds "before I was honored with those instructions."[34]

While Smith might have been engaging in some face-saving rhetoric, there were indications that independently of the pressure from Baltimore, perhaps in spite of it, he had indeed already made up his mind to support appropriations for the Jay Treaty. At no time had he declared any intention to vote against the legislation. His resolutions of January 15 and January 26 showed that he was anxious to correct specific evils in the treaty rather than to destroy it altogether. Even before McHenry had persuaded Oliver to circulate the instruction, Smith had apparently come around to the view that the Jay Treaty was better than no treaty at all. Federalist senator Rufus King of New York, writing two weeks before the final balloting, thought Smith definitely intended to vote for the appropriations bill but feared that "his pride will be so wounded by *this instruction* that he may vote agt. his judgement to prove his independence."[35]

Thus the attempt by the Federalists in Baltimore to force the general to vote for the appropriations seems to have been unnecessary. Rejecting Smith's protests that even without instructions from his constituents he intended to vote for the funds, the Federalists had questioned his honesty and attempted to curb his independence. They had attacked him personally and he was understandably offended. After the appropriations bill had passed Smith could not control an impulse to strike back. He angrily chided businessmen who could denounce the pressure-group tactics of the Democratic-Republican societies while at the same time using the same tactics themselves. Ironically Smith and the Baltimore Federalists had split

34. This extensive correspondence was published on April 28 and 30, 1796, in the *Federal Gazette & Baltimore Daily Advertiser;* see also Winchester to McHenry, May 1, 1796, McHenry Papers; S. Smith to Thorogood Smith et al., April 28, 1796, printed in the *Federal Gazette & Baltimore Daily Advertiser,* May 5, 1796.

35. King to Hamilton, April 20, 1796, Hamilton Papers.

over an issue they agreed upon. Such a situation had resulted from Smith's equivocal voting record and suspicion and fear on the part of the Federalists. They refused to believe that his efforts to alter some of the more obnoxious aspects of the treaty were sincere. Party strife had already reached the point in Baltimore where anything less than unqualified political loyalty was unacceptable. The antiadministration party in Baltimore was equally misinformed about Smith. Seeing his support for Livingston's resolution and the frantic efforts of the Federalists to secure his vote for appropriations, they assumed that his real desire was to oppose the treaty. Like the Federalists they had trouble understanding a man who based his actions on economic rather than party interests.[36]

The Federalists in Baltimore had thrust Samuel Smith into the hands of their enemies by their mistreatment of him. If nothing else, Federalist boasts to defeat the general's try for a third term would have forced him to seek political support from groups in his district other than the merchants, bankers, shipowners, and insurance men on whom he had formerly relied. In answer to the Mechanical Society's resolution lauding his conduct he wrote: "I am not a little gratified by the approbation of a society, at once so numerous and respectable; a society who have always been the supporters of order and good government."[37] So obvious an appeal for the allegiance of an antiadministration organization confirmed the Federalists in their earlier assumptions. "It may be politic for aught I know for him to count on numbers since he has so openly relinquished all claim to support from *orderly* and 'responsible' citizens," observed a staunch Federalist.[38] Despite their menacing rhetoric the Federalists did not seriously challenge Smith at the polls in 1796 and he again won reelection. In the presidential contest, however, the Federalists secured seven of Maryland's eleven electoral votes and thus made an important contribution to John Adams' narrow victory over Thomas Jefferson.

With the Jay Treaty crisis Smith reached an important turning point in his political career. Until 1796 he had been a very rich man who had possessed enough leisure time to gratify his wish to be a politician. As a merchant and a leading citizen of Baltimore he had encountered little difficulty acquiring the support of other rich busi-

36. *Annals of Congress,* 4th Cong., 1st sess., 1796, pp. 1156–1157; William Jessop to S. Smith, April 23, 1796, printed in the *Federal Gazette & Baltimore Daily Advertiser,* April 23, 1796.

37. S. Smith to Jessop, April 24, 1796, printed in the *Federal Gazette & Baltimore Daily Advertiser,* April 27, 1796.

38. Winchester to McHenry, May 1, 1796, McHenry Papers.

nessmen who together made up the ruling establishment of the city. The treaty issue had destroyed the relative calm of Baltimore politics by injecting into them the partisanship of political parties. No longer a gentleman's pastime, politics in Baltimore had become a deadly serious affair where only tough professionals could hope to succeed. The easy path for Smith after his unhappy experiences in April of 1796 would have been to retire gracefully and resume his station at S. Smith & Buchanan. Instead, he preferred to try to keep his position, which meant that he had to make the difficult transition from gentleman-politician to being a brass-knuckles, nuts-and-bolts politico.

His letter to the Mechanical Society was the beginning of Smith's efforts to construct a coalition in Baltimore capable of controlling the city. Within a short time he gathered other political societies around him, such as the Baltimore Republican Society, the Carpenter Society, and the Society of French Patriots. Made up of many different groups, the memberships of the societies shared a common dislike for the merchant oligarchy of Baltimore and the Federalist administration in Philadelphia that was allied with that oligarchy. The societies were drawn to Smith both because he was now an outcast from the ruling elite of the city and because he had the wealth and position to integrate the scattered groups striving for local power into an effective political force. Mutual enemies and complimentary resources had attracted Smith and the societies to each other.[39]

Smith could also depend upon the militia in the political struggles of the 1790s. The rank and file followed him not only because they respected him as their commander, but also because most of them came from the same social strata in Baltimore from which the membership of the societies were drawn. They were naturally sympathetic to anyone opposing the merchant establishment, even if he was another merchant. The officers in the Baltimore militia were as devoted to their general as were the common soldiers. For the most part the officers were well-to-do businessmen, but they were also personal friends of Smith's and owed their commissions to his nomination. As party strife in Baltimore increased after 1796, the officer corps took a more active part in politics, meshing the structure of the militia with that of the Republican party. Smith's two military aides, John Barney and Isaac McKim, soon emerged as leading figures in the Republican

39. *Baltimore Daily Intelligencer,* October 6, 1794; J. Thomas Scharf, *Chronicles of Baltimore* (Baltimore, 1874), p. 83; George Salmon to McHenry, October 7, 1798, in Bernard C. Steiner, ed., "Maryland Politics in 1798—McHenry Letters," *Publications of the Southern History Association* 10 (March 1906): 106; Diary of William Plumer, February 13, 1807, William Plumer Papers, Library of Congress.

party, and the same was true of such lower-echelon officers as James Biays, Jacob Small, and Nicholas Moore. Moore, for example, replaced Smith in the House of Representatives in 1803, when the general moved up to the Senate.[40]

The third element of Smith's political machine consisted of his political allies among the merchants and big businessmen of Baltimore. The political upheaval in Baltimore over the Jay Treaty had divided the ruling group into two unequal parts. The majority, led by James McHenry, John Eager Howard, and others remained bound to Federalism. A much smaller group followed Samuel Smith toward the Republican party. The Republican businessmen, besides the militia officers, consisted mainly of Smith's business associates and relatives. The general's most active political lieutenants in the late 1790s were his brother, Robert Smith, a prominent local attorney, and his business partner, James A. Buchanan. William Patterson and Jonathan Hollins, who were brothers-in-law of the general, and William Buchanan also diligently worked for Smith. All were merchants, while Patterson and Hollins were also involved in Baltimore banking and insurance companies. Though not numerous, these men provided Smith's organization with money, leadership, and respectability. Together with the militia and the societies they soon made the general the most powerful political figure in Baltimore.[41]

Both in Philadelphia and Baltimore Smith had by 1796 associated himself with the emergent Republican party. It remained to be seen, however, in what ways this new attachment would affect his conduct in Congress. A Republican merchant was almost a contradiction in terms as far as national politics were concerned, for the interests of each one clashed with the other. Yet in the next few years Smith managed to vote as a merchant in Congress and yet become a leader in the Republican party not only in Maryland but also nationally. The answer to the puzzle is that the marriage of Smith and the Republicans was one of convenience. The party would serve as a vehicle to fulfill the general's political ambitions, and in return he would use his substantial influence to deliver Baltimore's votes to Republican candidates for national office.

40. *Federal Gazette & Baltimore Daily Advertiser,* October 5 and August 7 and 8, 1798; *Maryland Journal and Baltimore Advertiser,* September 5, 1794; Eugene Perry Link, *Democratic-Republican Societies, 1790–1800* (New York, 1942), pp. 181, 182, 206; Renzulli, "Maryland Federalism," p. 213.

41. Winchester to McHenry, April 22, 1796, McHenry Papers; Winchester to McHenry, April 18, 1798, in Steiner, ed., *James McHenry,* pp. 305–306.

6

Politics and the
French Crisis

SAMUEL SMITH's new alliance with the Jeffersonian Republican party
was severely tested by the deepening crisis with France after 1796.
News of the Jay Treaty had convinced the French government that in
its continuing war against a coalition of European nations led by Great
Britain the United States must now be counted as an enemy even
though technically neutral. Smith and all Americans soon learned that
the price of friendship with England was the enmity of France, as
newspapers began carrying accounts of American ships and crews
being seized by the French. The situation closely resembled that of
1793 and 1794, when England had similarly struck at American commerce. Then Smith had worked frantically in Congress to pass any
and all measures that promised relief for his fellow merchants. Now
that France appeared as the chief threat to trade, the question was
whether Smith would allow the pro-French, antimilitary prejudices
of the Republican party to affect his conduct in the House of Representatives.[1]

The Marylander soon made it plain that he remained a merchant
first and a party man second. On January 5, 1797, Smith submitted a
resolution to the House asking that a special committee be appointed

1. *Federal Gazette & Baltimore Daily Advertiser,* June 18, 1796; Irving Brant,
James Madison; Father of the Constitution (New York, 1950), p. 445.

to study the current condition of the military establishment. The resolution won approval and Smith was appointed chairman of the committee. Nearly three weeks passed before the committee reported its findings, which included recommendations to increase the size of the army and alter its organization. The committee's report faced a storm of criticism from House Republicans, one of whom, John Williams of New York, made a motion to reduce the number of infantry regiments in the army from four to two. Smith objected that a decrease in strength would dangerously expose the frontier, where almost all American soldiers were stationed. Williams' motion was barely defeated, but a day later a Republican effort to cut only one regiment from the army succeeded. On both occasions Smith voted with the Federalists.[2]

Hoping to bolster the military in order to meet the French challenge, Smith instead found himself desperately trying to maintain the army at its present and very inadequate level of strength. A week after the House acted to do away with one-fourth of the nation's army, Smith introduced a bill that would have supplied appropriations for all of the regiments, including the one that had been abolished. A major debate ensued, in which Smith's chief antagonist was Albert Gallatin of Pennsylvania. Gallatin, in the process of becoming an expert on government finances, insisted that three regiments were more than sufficient for the country's needs and estimated that over $100,000 could be saved by the reduction. Smith answered that economy must be measured against the security needs of the United States and should not be made an end in itself. This clash of opinions between Smith and Gallatin was the beginning of a political and personal rivalry destined to span several decades. But on the specific issue of the army's size Smith was apparently the more persuasive of the two men, for the House did make provision for four regiments. Smith found, however, that his committee's proposals for expanding the army had no chance of being passed.[3]

The competition between those favoring military preparedness and those who felt the central government should reduce its expenditures continued over an administration bill allowing the government to

2. Thomas Jefferson to James Madison, January 8, 1797, in Paul Leicester Ford, ed., *The Writings of Thomas Jefferson*, 10 vols. (New York, 1892–1899), 7: 104; U.S., Congress, *The Debates and Proceedings in the Congress of the United States . . . 1789–1824*, 42 vols. (Washington, D.C., 1834–1856), 4th Cong., 2d sess., 1797, pp. 1818, 1944, 1952, 1963, 1969; hereafter cited as *Annals of Congress.*

3. *Annals of Congress*, 4th Cong., 2d sess., 1797, pp. 2067, 2071–2073, 2094.

complete the building of three frigates. These were the same warships that had originally been authorized by Congress in 1794. At that time war with Algiers had appeared imminent, but after a peace treaty was signed construction on the vessels had been halted. French seizures and the renewed hostility of the Barbary powers now induced the administration to seek funds with which to finish the ships. As a party, the Republicans in the House questioned the necessity of maintaining a fleet. Once again, however, Smith joined the Federalists in fighting to preserve and strengthen the navy. The general told the House that if the United States had possessed a navy when the European war had begun in 1792, it would have been possible to negotiate advantageously with either England or France. With a navy, he said, our government could have taken the position with either belligerent that "we will throw our weight into the opposite side, if you continue to insult and injure us." As he had four years earlier, the Marylander maintained that only military power impressed the great European nations. Very likely Smith looked at Gallatin while telling the House that France and England together had stolen over nine million dollars in American property. So great an amount, concluded the general, would have built a respectable navy, "which would have kept us from a situation in which we are subject to indignities and insults from every power who chooses to commit them against us."[4] Gallatin responded in the same manner as he had to the army bill: the navy was an unnecessary luxury that diverted the country from the more essential task of eliminating the national debt. A three-ship navy, Gallatin continued, could do little good under any circumstances. At some future time, however, if the nation still wanted a navy after the debt was retired, then one might be built.[5]

Gallatin's remarks prompted Smith to make one of his most significant speeches on naval and commercial policy. Since 1789, he began, revenues collected from import duties amounted to $75,000,000, of which only $700,000 had been allocated to the navy. The rest had been spent on protection for the frontier, the salaries of government officials, the public debt, and other governmental expenses. "Go where you will," Smith asserted, "and you see wealth, independence, and happiness, arising from the prosperity introduced by commerce."[6] Smith castigated representatives from western and southern states, the frontiers of which were defended because of the revenues created

4. Ibid., p. 2117.
5. Ibid., pp. 2128–2130.
6. Ibid., pp. 2134–2135.

by commercial activities, but who "rise, as in a mass, to vote against any protection being given to commerce." Those westerners and southerners remained unmoved by his eloquence and the House temporarily abandoned the plan to increase the navy.[7]

While Smith fretted, the Republicans celebrated their success in keeping America defenseless. But their joy was short-lived, for in March of 1797 reports arrived that the Directory, the ruling body of France, had refused to receive the American minister, Charles C. Pinckney, and had ordered him out of the country. The sudden deterioration in the official relations between France and the United States threw the Republican party into confusion. Thomas Jefferson voiced the desires of many when he wished that an "ocean of fire" separated America and Europe. Smith, too, was stunned and expressed disbelief that the news of Pinckney's treatment was accurate. All doubts evaporated on May 16 when President John Adams confirmed the information before a special session of Congress and called for increases in the army and navy as well as new harbor defenses to meet the crisis.[8]

The two parties in the House had difficulty agreeing to an answer to the president's address. The draft submitted by a Federalist-dominated committee bristled with bellicose anti-French sentiments that appalled the peace-minded Republicans. Smith surprised both Republicans and Federalists by also urging that the message be toned down, since, he said, it could precipitate an unwanted war. What the Marylander wanted was for Congress to arm the country and the administration to assume a tough line with France. As in the earlier dispute with England, he hoped that the mere threat of war would force France to abandon her policy of disrupting American trade. He reasoned that France was caught up in a major war, that its merchant marine had been sunk or blockaded by the British, and therefore that it would not jeopardize its only remaining link with the outside world, American neutral trade. By bolstering the armed forces and warning France that it risked not only losing American trade but also war, the United States could reasonably expect a change in French behavior. The question of actually declaring war against France was something else again. While war would hurt France it also would put the United States into the unhealthy position of tying

7. Ibid., pp. 2136, 2148–2151.

8. Jefferson to Elbridge Gerry, May 13, 1797, in Ford, ed., *Writings of Jefferson*, 7: 123; S. Smith to James McHenry, April 5, 1797, in Bernard C. Steiner, ed., *The Life and Correspondence of James McHenry* (Cleveland, 1907), p. 211; *Annals of Congress*, 5th Cong., 1st sess., 1797, pp. 57–58.

itself more closely to Great Britain. War meant the end of all trade with France and necessarily a greater dependence on British markets. More than ever American merchants would find themselves at the mercy of British laws and the good will of British merchants. It was this logic that led Smith to plead for moderation in the House of Representatives. Eventually the House approved a response to the president far more restrained in tone than the original Federalist draft and one that reflected Republican desires for new diplomatic efforts to settle grievances with France.[9]

In late May 1797 John Adams named Charles C. Pinckney, John Marshall, and Elbridge Gerry as ministers plenipotentiary to France. The appointment of a new mission encouraged optimism that a peaceful solution might be reached—which in turn reduced the pressure on Congress to enact the defense measures President Adams had asked for. Nevertheless, on June 5, Federalist William Loughton Smith of South Carolina presented a series of resolutions in the House that would have implemented all of the president's recommendations. The first resolution outlined a comprehensive national plan for port and harbor fortifications. Representing a city that he knew from experience was open to naval assault, Smith had no trouble in whole-heartedly supporting the measure. Two days later, however, he voted against a second resolution permitting merchant ships to carry cannon and defend themselves from unlawful attack. He asserted that even though the law of nations allowed neutral nations to arm their vessels in their own defense, American merchants opposed such action because it would mean war with France. Smith accused the Federalists of inconsistency, reminding them that in 1794 they had gone to great lengths to avoid war with Great Britain and instead had initiated negotiations. Now, however, they appeared willing, by arming the merchantmen, "to fight and sink the vessels of a particular nation," which would inevitably provoke the French into declaring war. Thus Smith, despite apparent vacillation, consistently followed a policy of supporting all efforts to improve the nation's defensive capacity, but opposed any aggressively hostile gestures because of a "dread of the immediate and ultimate effects of war."[10]

Throughout the fall and winter of 1797–1798 Congress and the

9. *Annals of Congress*, 5th Cong., 1st sess., 1797, pp. 214–223.

10. Jefferson to Horatio Gates, May 30, 1797, and Jefferson to Edward Rutledge, June 24, 1797, in Ford, ed., *Writings of Jefferson*, 7: 131, 152–153; *Annals of Congress*, 5th Cong., 1st sess., 1797, pp. 240, 255, 260–261, 267, 289; see the open letter from S. Smith printed in the *Federal Gazette & Baltimore Daily Advertiser*, August 3, 1798.

country waited impatiently for word from Pinckney, Marshall, and Gerry in Paris. "The mind of Congress," wrote Federalist congressman James A. Bayard of Delaware, "as well as the rest of the world seems suspended as to the measures our nation should adopt in relation to France."[11] The government, he went on, soon expected information from the ministers "which will enable us to act with decision." Vice President Jefferson joined most other Republican leaders in believing that war with France could be avoided. Finally, on March 4, 1798, dispatches from the American emissaries reached Philadelphia. Although the bulk of the papers were in code, the president did send Congress one document describing a French commercial decree ordering the arrest of all neutral ships found carrying English goods. The new decree flagrantly violated accepted interpretations of international law and made a large segment of the American merchant marine liable to capture. Jefferson voiced alarm at the development. "At length," he wrote Monroe, "the charm is broken."[12] Samuel Smith also manifested concern but continued to argue against a declaration of war. He maintained that new British orders-in-council rumored to be in existence would be "more injurious to the commerce and navigation of the United States than the *arrête* of the French Directory."[13] On March 19 Adams again sent a message to Congress, which, although not revealing the specific contents of the dispatches, announced there was no hope the French negotiations would be successful. Adams' message underlined the absolute necessity of laws that would protect American commerce. The president seemed to be warning Congress that war was likely.[14]

Jefferson called Adams' message "insane," but admitted that it had a great impact on Congress. The vice president encouraged Republicans to halt the drift into war by proposing that Congress adjourn. He also suggested that the Republican majority in the House call upon the president for the dispatches in the hope that the material would not prove as ominous as Adams had implied. Following Jefferson's lead the House voted by a large majority to ask the chief executive for the documents, and on April 4 John Adams obliged. The dis-

11. James A. Bayard to Richard Basset, December 30, 1797, in Elizabeth Donnan, ed., "Papers of James A. Bayard, 1796–1815," *Annual Report for 1913 of the American Historical Association,* 2 vols. (Washington, D.C., 1915), 2: 45.

12. Jefferson to James Monroe, December 27 and March 8, 1797, and Jefferson to Peregrine Fitzhugh, February 23, 1798, in Ford, ed., *Writings of Jefferson,* 7: 183, 209, 213; Dumas Malone, *Jefferson and the Ordeal of Liberty* (Boston, 1962), p. 370.

13. *Annals of Congress,* 5th Cong., 2d sess., 1798, p. 1258.

14. Page Smith, *John Adams,* 2 vols. (Garden City, N.Y., 1962), 2: 956–957.

patches, known as the XYZ Papers, revealed that the president had not exaggerated, but on the contrary had understated the significance of their contents. The three envoys reported that they had never been officially received by the French government. Instead they had been approached by three minor functionairies, referred to in the papers as X, Y, and Z, who had demanded that the Americans pay a bribe, or *douceur*, of £50,000 for the personal use of the Directory and its ministers before the talks would begin. The American emissaries were also told that the United States would be required to offer a substantial loan to France. When the Americans refused these terms, the Directory broke off all communications with them. The revelations of French arrogance left the Republicans in Congress "overwhelmed by confusion."[15]

Now that war seemed imminent, Samuel Smith dropped the role of temporizer and rallied behind a massive defense program introduced into the House by the Federalists.[16] One of the first defense bills provided more artillery for the army. "It must be in the view of every gentleman," Smith told his fellow Republicans in the House, "that we are to be involved in war."[17] This being the case, additional artillery would be needed to protect seaports and to equip the new regiments that must be added to the army. Smith showed little patience with the handful of Republicans who dared to criticize the bill as being too costly. When Wilson Cary Nicholas of Virginia, who also happened to be Smith's brother-in-law, raised this objection, the general hotly replied that this was "no time to talk of expense." He continued: "We must provide means of defense, this is our duty, and it is the duty of the people cheerfully to pay the expense."[18] During the next few weeks Smith also cast his vote in favor of bills to purchase ships for coastal defense and to establish a department of the navy. Backed by an angry public, the various defense measures soon cleared Congress and were signed into law by Adams.[19]

15. Jefferson to Madison, March 21, 1798, and Jefferson to Monroe, March 21, 1798, in Ford, ed., *Writings of Jefferson*, 7: 219, 221; *Annals of Congress*, 5th Cong., 2d sess., 1798, pp. 1358–1375. There are numerous accounts of the XYZ affair. See, for example, Stephen G. Kurtz, *The Presidency of John Adams; The Collapse of Federalism, 1795–1800* (New York, 1961), pp. 298–299; and Smith, *John Adams*, 2: 952–957. See also Theodore Sedgwick to Rufus King, April 9, 1798, in Charles R. King, ed., *The Life and Correspondence of Rufus King*, 6 vols. (New York, 1894–1900), 2: 312.

16. Alexander Hamilton to Timothy Pickering, March 17, 1798, in Henry Cabot Lodge, ed., *The Works of Alexander Hamilton*, Federal ed., 12 vols. (New York, 1903), 10: 277.

17. *Annals of Congress*, 5th Cong., 2d sess., 1798, p. 1404.

18. Ibid.

19. Ibid., pp. 1434–1438, 1462–1522, 1546–1554.

In early May the most important bill in the Federalists' plan for insuring American security, a direct tax on property, came before the House. The property tax was intended to provide the money with which to pay the costs of the new ships, regiments, and cannon that Congress had authorized. Smith approved of the proposed property tax for several reasons. In the first place he felt that it favored commercial interests since it lessened the government's dependence on import duties to pay its bills. Secondly, he thought the direct tax was the most efficient means of raising revenues because the government could borrow funds immediately from domestic and foreign banks by pledging future revenues from the tax as security. But the Marylander cautioned that the tax must be made permanent or "moneyed men" would not be willing to make loans. Smith's arguments were sound, but southern representatives who stood to lose a great deal from a direct levy on land and slaves managed to limit the duration of the tax to one year. The general castigated those congressmen who had voted for the military bills but "now they come to touch the expense, they flinch."[20]

After Congress rejected the permanent property tax, Smith began to take a more critical attitude toward defense bills. "Men may moralize as much as they please," he had said to the House during the tax debates, "it will avail nothing without money."[21] Now that the government had no sure source of income to pay for the military preparations already approved, the general could see little profit in voting for new programs. Such was his feeling about a bill to raise a provisional army of ten thousand men that the Federalists brought before Congress on May 10, 1798. Speaking in favor of the provisional army was Federalist Jonathan Dayton of New Jersey, who called upon those who desired to protect the United States to defend the bill "inch by inch" from attempts to defeat it. Smith quickly rose to deny that the provisional army bill was the "touchstone by which to determine whether members were willing to defend their country." He told Dayton that the question of the direct property tax should have been "the rallying point." By restricting the tax to one year Congress had denied to the people of the United States "the strongest possible defense of their liberties and independence."[22] When the House passed the provisional army bill a week later Smith absented himself from the chamber.[23] In his five years in Congress this had been the only military defense bill

20. Ibid., pp. 1596–1626, 1630.
21. Ibid., p. 1625.
22. Ibid., p. 1680.
23. Ibid., p. 1770.

he had not supported. He made it abundantly clear, however, that he did favor a provisional army if there was money to pay for it.

While the Marylander had cooperated with the Federalists in a common effort to prepare the United States for war, he took a firm stand against their program of political repression. In May, June, and July of 1798 Federalist majorities in both houses of Congress passed a series of bills known as the Alien and Sedition Acts. Publicly describing the laws as necessary war measures, the Federalists' real intentions were to eradicate their political enemies by branding them unpatriotic. In the heated and frequently irrational debates over the various bills, Smith played a small but courageous part by trying to modify or eliminate the more obnoxious provisions.[24]

The first of the alien bills to reach the House was the naturalization bill, which lengthened the residence requirement for citizenship from five to fourteen years. An extended waiting period, the Federalists hoped, would hamper the growth of the Republican party, which most immigrants joined. Smith said little about the measure, but voted against it, probably because many of his own constituents had recently arrived in the United States. In July of 1793, for example, over fifteen hundred French refugees had landed in Baltimore after fleeing the black revolutionaries of Haiti. Many of the French fugitives had remained in Baltimore and had contributed to the city's growth. The Marylander and other Republicans, however, did give their approval to the Alien Enemies Act, a measure that permitted the president in time of war to arrest, deport, or imprison aliens who were citizens of an enemy nation. Such a law, it was generally agreed, was vital to national security when a state of declared war existed. But the Alien Act, which allowed the president to expel any alien he judged dangerous regardless of whether the United States was at war, met the stout opposition of the Republicans. Smith announced to the House that he would vote against the bill because he believed it to be "in direct contradiction to the letter of the Constitution." With more candor he justified his vote on the grounds that there were many German and English immigrants in Maryland who would "illy receive" the law. Smith insisted that the act's broad provisions invited abuse and promoted injustice: immigrants who had been peaceful and useful citizens and who might have lived in the United States for some years could, under the terms of the Alien Act, be deported without a trial "on the information of any evil disposed person." Smith also styled the bill as a step toward despotism, but the Federalists were in no

24. James Morton Smith, *Freedom's Fetters* (Ithaca, N.Y., 1956), p. 21.

mood to listen. The bill passed on June 23 with only a small band of Republican congressmen indicating their disapproval.[25]

The capstone of the Federalists' scheme to silence political dissent was the sedition bill. In its original form as drafted by Senate Federalists, the sedition bill was so extreme that even Alexander Hamilton called it "highly exceptionable" and begged party members in the House of Representatives not to "establish a tyranny."[26] Even in the modified form in which it reached the House, the bill was a monument to intolerance. The most controversial section of the bill prescribed fines and jail terms as penalties for those convicted of publishing or speaking anything "false, scandalous and malicious" that brought the United States government, Congress, or the president into disrepute. Federalist John Allen of Connecticut introduced the sedition bill, claiming it essential to the nation's safety. To prove the need for the bill, Allen read excerpts from antiadministration newspapers to the House. He concluded that there was a plot to overthrow the government. "This combination against our peace is extensive," Allen informed his attentive colleagues, "it embraces characters whose stations demand a different course."[27] So that no one would misinterpret his meaning, Allen turned toward the Republican members and asked: "Is this House free from it?" For Allen and the Federalists, those who dared speak against the sedition bill could only be fools or traitors.[28]

Very few Republicans chose to openly take the position that the sedition bill should be defeated. One of those who did was Albert Gallatin, himself an immigrant from Geneva, who on July 5 delivered a brilliant speech striking at the legal justification for the bill. He charged that it violated the constitutional rights of freedom of speech and the press. He asked the Federalists if they were afraid "error could not be successfully opposed by truth." Samuel Smith also publicly opposed the sedition bill. On July 9 he moved an amendment to the bill that struck out the crucial words: "by any writing, printing, or speaking shall threaten any officer or person in public trust with any damage to his character, person, or estate." If his amendment had carried, Smith would successfully have killed the sedition bill. The Marylander defended his motion by arguing that the phrase he objected to conflicted with the First Amendment to the Constitution and

25. *Annals of Congress,* 5th Cong., 2d sess., 1798, p. 2022.

26. Hamilton to Oliver Wolcott, June 29, 1798, in Lodge, ed., *Works of Hamilton,* 10: 295.

27. *Annals of Congress,* 5th Cong., 2d sess., 1798, pp. 2093–2094.

28. Ibid., p. 2094.

that he "would never consent to vote for these words." By straight party vote the House defeated Smith's amendment and a day later gave final approval to the sedition bill. Smith's stand against the Alien and Sedition Acts had reunited him with the Republican party. In years to come 1798 would be seen as the darkest hour of the Republicans, and those who remained loyal during those troubled months would have special claims on the party after it achieved power. Smith, however, had to face the immediate consequences of opposing the administration, for it was an election year.[29]

The XYZ affair and the naval war with France that followed in the summer of 1798 made the Federalist party and its policies popular in many parts of the United States. In Baltimore the Federalist party hoped to capitalize on this support and defeat the "jacobinical" general in the fall elections. As their candidate against Smith, the Federalists selected James Winchester, a young and talented lawyer. In the ebb and flow of Baltimore politics during the 1790s Winchester had drifted from the Republican into the Federalist party. Indeed, as late as the early months of 1796 he had been a strong advocate of Thomas Jefferson's presidential candidacy and an officer in the Baltimore Republican Society. Sometime before the fall elections in 1796 Winchester had changed loyalties and helped the Federalists try to defeat Smith. Now in 1798 he had personally stepped forward to seek the fifth congressional district seat. Interest in Winchester's success was not confined to Baltimore alone, as Federalists from other parts of Maryland and even other states contributed their resources to his campaign. This widespread concern about the general's reelection testified to his growing importance as a political figure. If Smith could be defeated the Federalists would at once remove a formidable opponent from the House of Representatives and deal a blow to the Baltimore Republican party, which he headed.[30]

The campaign of 1798 was the most tumultuous contest of Samuel Smith's political career. Although Smith and Winchester did not declare their candidacies until August 10, the Federalists began their attack on the general several weeks earlier. On July 30 a Federalist newspaper reported that "a number of respectable merchants and other gentlemen" of Baltimore had arranged a dinner supposedly to honor Federalist senator John Eager Howard, one of the recognized party leaders in Maryland. In fact the dinner turned out to be nothing

29. Ibid., pp. 2109, 2133, 2171.

30. *Federal Gazette & Baltimore Daily Advertiser,* August 21, 1798, July 7, 1795, and October 3, 1796.

less than an anti-Smith convention, of which the high point was a toast: "May our next representative to congress be neither a *Jacobin*, nor a weathercock."[31] Federalists attending the dinner were quoted as saying that Smith had purposely not been invited to show "how much his conduct has been disapproved." Winchester's supporters appeared pleased with the publicity generated by the affair. One Federalist informed James McHenry that the dinner and toasts had "made a great noise" among the Republicans, who, he said, "look upon it as a great affront" to Smith.[32]

The most important issue of the campaign may have been introduced by accident. On August 1 an extract from an unsigned letter first printed in Frederick, Maryland, was republished in a Baltimore newspaper. The letter charged that General Smith had told President Adams at a dinner in Philadelphia that the American ministers to France should have paid X, Y, and Z the bribe they demanded since "it would be cheaper than war." According to the letter, Adams had rebuked Smith for being unpatriotic. The general reacted quickly to the attack, publishing the very next day an open letter to the people of Baltimore that denounced the story as one of the "pitiful artifices of electioneering" common in an election year. He called the account of the dinner conversation a "wanton, malicious untruth." Privately, Smith began writing to those who had been at the dinner and his anxiety indicated that the anonymous author's account was not entirely inaccurate. The same day his public letter appeared he hurriedly sent a note to the president explaining that he was being unfairly maligned in the press and denying that he had ever seriously suggested that the bribe should have been paid.[33] Smith also contacted James A. Bayard, a Federalist congressman from Delaware and another dinner guest. He told Bayard that the newspaper account of the verbal exchange with Adams was misleading. "You understood it (as it really was) a sort of jesting Conversation on my part," Smith reminded the Delawarean, "and the President, [although] expressing himself warmly neither then nor afterward seemed to think more of the subject."[34] Smith seemed to be priming Bayard for the coming

31. Ibid., July 30, 1798.

32. George Salmon to McHenry, July 31, 1798, James McHenry Papers, Maryland Historical Society.

33. *Federal Gazette & Baltimore Daily Advertiser*, August 1 and 2, 1798; S. Smith to John Adams, August 2, 1798, Samuel Smith Papers, Library of Congress.

34. S. Smith to Bayard, August 2, 1798, in Donnan, ed., "Papers of Bayard," 2: 69.

controversy as he alerted the Delaware Federalist that others might ask for his account of the incident and hoped that having read this letter, he would "not be surprized [for] an answer."[35]

On August 3 the general published another public letter further explaining the events at the president's dinner table. He asked the citizens of the fifth district to judge his conduct in Congress by his votes and speeches, rather than by anything that "escaped me in the levity of unguarded conversation." He then admitted that he had mentioned something to Adams about paying the bribe but it had been only a "hypothetical question." Smith claimed that his "hypothetical question" was based on certain parts of the emissaries' dispatches that did indeed show an inclination to pay the bribe if it would promote the success of the mission. In yet a third open letter printed in Baltimore's newspapers, Smith announced that the mysterious author of the extract was none other than Senator John Eager Howard, who had been acting as Winchester's campaign manager.[36]

Howard may never have intended his letter to be made part of the campaign. The recipient of his letter, a Doctor Thomas of Frederick, swore that he published the extract without Howard's knowledge or permission. Pushed unwillingly into the controversy, Howard felt compelled to defend his accusations now that they had become central to the election. On August 6 he wrote Bayard, as Smith had anticipated, requesting an affidavit detailing the conversation between the general and Adams. Howard's position was weak since he had not been at the dinner himself. He had learned of the conversation from Federalist congressman Uriah Tracy of Connecticut, who also was not present at the dinner but who had talked with one of the guests. In answer to a query from Howard, Tracy revealed that his information had come from Captain Donald Mitchell of Philadelphia, who had since died of yellow fever. Tracy volunteered to collect statements from others Mitchell had talked to about the events at the dinner. The fact remained, however, that Howard now had no witnesses to back up his story.[37]

Throughout August, Smith and Howard solicited testimony to support their positions. The senator remained unable to find anyone willing to say that Smith had expressed a wish that the bribe to France

35. Ibid.

36. *Federal Gazette & Baltimore Daily Advertiser*, August 3 and 4, 1798.

37. Affidavit of F. Thomas, August 5, 1798, and Uriah Tracy to John Eager Howard, August 14, 1798, Bayard Papers, Maryland Historical Society; Howard to Bayard, August 6, 1798, in Donnan, ed., "Papers of Bayard," 2: 70.

should have been paid. There was general agreement among the dinner guests that Smith and Adams had traded words over the *douceur,* but no one remembered precisely what had been said. Smith, on the other hand, had better luck. The Federalist Speaker of the House, Jonathan Dayton of New Jersey, who had attended the dinner, recalled Smith saying that the bribe should not have been paid. By the end of the month only Bayard's account was missing, and when his statement finally arrived, it confirmed Smith's story. Practically quoting from Smith's letter of August 3, the Delawarean said the general's comments to Adams were made in "a gay manner and not equivocally serious."[38] Bayard's testimony destroyed Howard's case. Dr. Thomas, the cause of the senator's difficulties, wrote Howard sympathetically: "You must have been a little disappointed in Bayard's letter after what you had heard and from the character of the man."[39] With his prestige committed, Howard had no choice but to continue his efforts.

In the middle of September Howard published his "proof" in the newspapers of Baltimore. It consisted of extracts from the statements he had received, but edited so as to appear damaging to Smith. Howard would have done better to keep silent, for his dishonesty was transparent. All could see that his information was contradictory and came from people who had only indirect knowledge of the conversation. The next day Smith's reply appeared. He skillfully exploited the weaknesses of Howard's evidence by reprinting the full texts of the letters that the senator had only excerpted. Having exposed Howard's duplicity, the general went on to reiterate that he had discussed the bribe with Adams "in pleasantry" and produced Bayard's letter as corroboration. Smith's refutation of Howard's charges was so complete that they were little heard of during the remainer of the campaign.[40]

While Howard vainly tried to brand Smith as unpatriotic, other Winchester supporters attacked the general's voting record in Congress. They attempted to show that as a congressman he had opposed efforts to resist "French outrages and French principles." Republicans easily parried these thrusts by stressing Smith's solid record of support for defense measures. Interestingly the Federalists hardly touched upon Smith's votes against the Alien and Sedition Acts. Like him, they

38. Jeremiah Wadsworth to Howard, August 17, 1798, Bayard Papers; Jonathan Dayton to S. Smith, August 18, 1798, Smith Papers; Bayard to Howard, August 30, 1798, Bayard Papers.

39. Thomas to Howard, August 30, 1798, Bayard Papers.

40. *Federal Gazette & Baltimore Daily Advertiser,* September 4 and 5, 1798.

realized that the laws were becoming unpopular throughout Maryland. Stymied at every turn, Winchester's campaign was faltering by the end of August and many Federalist leaders openly predicted that "Genl. Smith will be rechosen."[41]

In frustration Winchester turned to scurrility as his chief weapon. Writing under the pseudonym "Republican," he charged that in 1794 and 1795 S. Smith & Buchanan had been under contract to the French government to deliver supplies to the French West Indies. The French consul in Baltimore, Winchester continued, had issued Smith's ships documents protecting them from seizure by the French navy. Since the United States was practically at war with France, Winchester asserted that Smith's dealings with the French were *"wholly inconsistent* with his *obligations* as a representative." Smith, who must have been heartily sick of defending himself in the newspapers, answered that in 1794 and 1795 the United States and France were at peace, that he had never had a contract with the French government, and that the documents from the French consul were credentials stating that the ships were bound for French and not English ports. He appended a statement signed by merchants of both parties which said that until the XYZ affair it had been common practice for merchants to secure such credentials in order to avoid capture. Although Winchester claimed that he had proved his charges, they also disappeared from Federalist campaign literature. The contest reached a low point on September 7 when two Federalists reported publicly that three years before they had heard Smith say that as commander of the militia he would not oppose an invading French army. "Can any person conceive," Smith asked incredulously, "why I should act such a part?"[42]

The number and seriousness of the Federalist charges against Smith kept Baltimore Republicans on the defensive throughout the campaign. Whenever possible they emphasized Winchester's former connections with the Republican Society, a sensitive memory for many Baltimore Federalists.[43] The Republicans also took every opportunity to characterize Winchester's supporters as Old Tories, whose attachment to England made them "enemies of their country." Smith's most reliable support during the campaign came from the militia. On

41. Ibid., August 15 and 23, 1798; William Hindman to McHenry, August 12, 1798, McHenry Papers, Maryland Historical Society.

42. *Federal Gazette & Baltimore Daily Advertiser*, September 4, 5, 7, 8, and 13, 1798.

43. Ibid., August 28, 1798; James Nash to McHenry, August 24, 1798, James McHenry Papers, Library of Congress.

August 3 several militia companies ostentatiously marched through the streets of Baltimore to Smith's home, where they were provided with ample quantities of alcoholic beverages. The Federalists deplored the impropriety of the episode and accused Smith of buying votes. Federalist newspapers carried letters condemning militia captains who "attempt to turn their companies into political engines to suit their own private views." One Federalist wondered how the militiamen could cast their votes impartially "after drinking the general's whisky or rum."[44] Another Winchester supporter, using the pseudonym "Philo-Republican," tried to discredit Smith in the eyes of the militia by quoting portions of Smith's speech to the House in 1795, when he had argued that a more efficient militia law was needed because of the poor showing by the militia during the Whiskey Rebellion. "Philo-Republican" said Smith's remarks implied that he believed the Maryland militia had behaved in a cowardly manner.[45] If the Federalists hoped that "Philo-Republican" would succeed in separating Smith and the militia they soon realized their error. A letter signed by ten militia captains appeared in the newspapers defending the general and praising his behavior during the "western expeditions." "His deportment," the captains said, "was, in every instance, such as endeared him to the men under his command."[46]

The tensions that had been building for two months exploded into violence in late September when "general Smith's friends" broke up a Federalist meeting and beat a number of Winchester's followers. On September 27 Smith personally led a mob into a pro-Winchester rally and unsuccessfully attempted to disperse the crowd. The threat of rioting was so serious that the election judges ordered all weapons confiscated from persons in the vicinity of the polls. The voting took place in the first week of October, and the results showed Smith had won reelection by a margin of two hundred out of the thirty-five hundred votes cast. Slim as the victory was, it signaled the end of the Federalist party's effectiveness in Baltimore. The official explanation by the Federalists of their defeat was printed in the *Federal Gazette* a few days after the election. The editor stressed the importance of Republican mob violence, which he blamed for keeping many Federalists away from the polling places. He gave much of the credit for Smith's victory to the votes of the skilled laborers of Baltimore "who were very numerous, and from being united in societies, act syste-

44. *Federal Gazette & Baltimore Daily Advertiser,* August 7, 1798.
45. Ibid., August 16, 1798.
46. Ibid., August 18, 1798.

matically." But it was the militia that the *Federal Gazette* believed had given Smith the election. Many of the militia, the paper charged, were reluctant to vote against a man under whom they might some day have to fight. Smith had apparently visited every militia meeting in the city and county of Baltimore in his capacity as major general of the Third Maryland Division and campaigned for himself. According to the *Federal Gazette,* the general had unashamedly reminded the militia of his deeds during the Revolution and by "addresses to their passions" won their political support. One factor the editor neglected to mention was Smith's immense personal wealth. By one estimate the general spent over six thousand dollars of his own money during the campaign.[47]

The years 1796 and 1797 had been turbulent ones for Smith. Both in Philadelphia and Baltimore he had moved toward greater political prominence. His votes against the Alien and Sedition Acts gained the attention of the national leaders of the Republican party, but it was his victory in 1798 that made him a force to be reckoned with in national politics. In the first place Smith had proven himself an able politician by winning in an election year dominated by the Federalists. Secondly, and more importantly, Smith's success had handed the Republican party control of Baltimore and therefore given it an opportunity to win the entire state of Maryland from the Federalists. As the acknowledged leader of the Baltimore Republicans, Smith automatically obtained a position of leadership in the national party. Thomas Jefferson soon opened a friendly and confidential correspondence with the general, as both men looked ahead to the elections of 1800 and hoped that the Republican triumph in Baltimore would be the forerunner of a national victory.[48]

47. Ibid., September 28 and 29 and October 4 and 5, 1798; George Salmon to McHenry, October 7, 1798, McHenry Papers, Library of Congress.

48. Jefferson to S. Smith, August 22, 1798, in Ford, ed., *Writings of Jefferson,* 7: 275–280.

7

The Election of 1800

THE YEARS 1798 and 1799 were difficult ones for American merchants because of the undeclared war between France and the United States. As the toll of commercial ships seized by French privateers and naval vessels mounted, Samuel Smith and other Baltimore merchants found that trade with the West Indies, Europe, and the Mediterranean was becoming prohibitively hazardous. Soaring insurance rates and dwindling supplies of money and credit combined to bring on a business recession in the city. Ships lay idle in the harbor while warehouses bulged with goods that could be neither sold nor exported. In addition to the losses he sustained as a result of the war Smith also learned that most of the western lands he had purchased had been seized for nonpayment of taxes. Samuel and Robert Smith and their brother-in-law Wilson Cary Nicholas had all been partners in the original land deal but had entrusted George Nicholas, Wilson's brother and another brother-in-law of the Smiths', with the responsibility of maintaining legal title to the 150,000 acres of Kentucky property. George Nicholas, however, died in 1799 after a long illness during which he had failed to keep up tax payments on the land. Furthermore, George also left a large family that his brother and the Smiths had to support. Despite these setbacks Samuel Smith survived the war years with no irreparable damage to his fortune. Indeed he had both the confidence and the resources to begin construction on his large and expensive country home northeast of the city.[1]

1. Stuart Weems Bruchey, *Robert Oliver, Merchant of Baltimore, 1783–1819* (Baltimore, 1956), pp. 188–201; S. Smith to Wilson Cary Nicholas, September

Aside from his business interests and his duties with the militia, Smith devoted most of his attention to the approaching presidential contest in which the leader of the Republican party, Thomas Jefferson, was challenging President John Adams' effort to win reelection. The campaign was especially bitter in Maryland, where popular dissatisfaction with the war and Federalist domestic policies, particularly the Sedition Act, had made the Republicans serious contenders for state power. The changing balance of parties in Maryland prompted the Federalists, still firmly in control of the government in Annapolis, to make an attempt in 1800 to alter the method of choosing presidential electors. Under the old district system, which permitted the citizens to select their electoral representatives, the Federalists suspected that Jefferson would win three of Maryland's ten electoral votes. By eliminating the district system and allowing their majorities in both houses of the state legislature to appoint electors, the Federalists planned to give Adams and his vice-presidential running mate, Charles C. Pinckney of South Carolina, all of Maryland's electoral votes.[2] Samuel Smith identified Robert Goodloe Harper, a former South Carolinian who had recently moved his law practice to Baltimore, as the author of this scheme and alerted other Republicans to the consequences: "Mr. Harper is agitating this state & I fear will succeed in passing the [electoral-vote] legislation [;] if so we will lose all Maryland."[3]

Smith and other Republicans reasoned that only by winning control of the lower house of the Maryland legislature in the fall elections of 1800 could the Federalist strategy be frustrated. For this purpose Smith began a round of intense electioneering. Confident of his own reelection to the House of Representatives from Baltimore, the general felt free to assist the campaigns of Republican candidates to the state legislature in other parts of Maryland. In August he told Wilson Cary Nicholas that he had become a "political preacher," traveling around the state debating leading Federalists before local political gatherings. On October 12 he wrote Nicholas that he had campaigned in Anne Arundel, Frederick, and Baltimore counties and

---

5, 1799, Wilson Cary Nicholas Papers, and Cary Nicholas Fink, "Smith," Smith-Carter Papers, University of Virginia Library.

2. *Federal Gazette & Baltimore Daily Advertiser*, October 1, 1800; Alexander Hamilton to James McHenry, August 27, 1800, in Bernard C. Steiner, ed., *The Life and Correspondence of James McHenry* (Cleveland, 1907), p. 466; Libero Marx Renzulli, "Maryland Federalism, 1787–1819" (Ph.D. diss., University of Virginia, 1962), pp. 276–277.

3. S. Smith to Nicholas, June 24, 1800, Samuel Smith Papers, Library of Congress.

"confidently routed my political opponents." Smith's success as a stump-speaker prompted Baltimore's Federalists to launch a newspaper attack against him in late September and early October 1800. The public prints charged that he was "insidious," "ambitious," and suggested darkly that his opposition to the Federalists bordered on treason. They even ridiculed Smith's use of Aesop's Fables in his campaign speeches.[4]

As he had in 1798, the general used his position as commander of the militia for political ends. During the campaign Smith suddenly felt called upon to address militia meetings throughout the state, and his message to the troops was unvaryingly political and pro-Republican. His effectiveness spurred Federalist papers to new virulence against him. Federalist editors attempted to limit Smith's influence by inflaming traditional rural jealousies against Baltimore. Maryland farmers were warned that Smith was a conniving big-city politician, "publicly interfering in your actions." The *Federal Gazette* charged Smith with building a subtle conspiracy based on a low opinion of the political awareness of the people. Smith's "self-created city clubs," the paper added, were trying to dominate the selection of representatives to the legislature in all parts of Maryland.[5] Affecting indifference to such attacks, Smith refused to reply. Instead he stepped up the tempo of his campaign by denouncing John Adams as a monarchist who had once said that "America should never be happy until [it] had an hereditary chief magistrate and Senate."[6]

The crucial election of the state legislature took place in early October 1800. The outcome pleased Smith, who confided to Jefferson that the election "exceeded our most sanguine expectations." He estimated that forty-nine Republicans had been elected and "40 will be sufficient to prevent a change in our present mode of Elections."[7] The local elections had shown that many Marylanders strongly disapproved of the Federalists' machinations, and Smith now began assuring friends that five and possibly six Republican electors would be selected in Maryland's presidential balloting.[8] Federalists agreed that the attempt to abolish the district method of choosing electors had failed. James McHenry, the Federalist leader in Baltimore, con-

4. S. Smith to Nicholas, August 14, 1800, quoted in Fink, "Smith," Smith-Carter Papers; S. Smith to Nicholas, October 12, 1800, Nicholas Papers; *Federal Gazette & Baltimore Daily Advertiser*, September 24 and 29, 1800.

5. *Federal Gazette & Baltimore Daily Advertiser*, October 1, 1800.

6. Ibid., October 24, 1800.

7. S. Smith to Thomas Jefferson, October 8, 1800, Thomas Jefferson Papers, Library of Congress.

8. S. Smith to Nicholas, October 12, 1800, Nicholas Papers.

ceded that a Republican majority in the House of Delegates was a certainty and declared that "all expectations of an election of electors of President & C., by our Legislature, may be considered as completely extinct."[9]

Maryland Republicans gratefully acknowledged Smith's effectiveness in the legislative elections throughout the state. One party leader noted that Smith's "industry and zeal" greatly contributed to the victory of Republican candidates in Harford, Cecil, and Kent counties. Thomas Jefferson personally sent his congratulations to the general "on the triumph of republicanism in the city and county of Baltimore." Samuel Smith had made a significant contribution to the Republican victory. Partly because of his work Marylanders again went to the polls in November 1800 to choose their presidential electors rather than to allow a political faction in the legislature to do the job for them.[10]

The electoral vote at stake in Baltimore was virtually uncontested by the Federalists. James McHenry grudgingly admitted that Samuel Smith had built a powerful and unbeatable political machine. He believed it foolish to make exertions for the Federalist candidate, "not from any indifference to the good old cause, but from a kind of conviction that our labor would be lost."[11] The Baltimore election returns justified McHenry's pessimism and again demonstrated the general's political dominance within the city: the Republican electoral candidate defeated his rival by a margin of five to one. Outside of Baltimore the Republicans enjoyed similar success. No less than five of the ten presidential electors chosen were Republicans, one more than the party elected in 1796 and two more than the Federalists had predicted before the balloting began.[12]

Samuel Smith's concern with the presidential election of 1800 went far beyond an interest in the selection of electors in Maryland. In early 1800, long before the state elections, he and Wilson Cary Nicholas had approached President Adams' secretary of the navy, Benjamin Stoddert of Maryland, to ask whether "some means could not be adopted for a reconciliation or union . . . of parties."[13] Although they

9. McHenry to Oliver Wolcott, October 12, 1800, in George Gibbs, ed., *Memoirs of the Administrations of Washington and Adams, Edited from the Papers of Oliver Wolcott,* 2 vols. (New York, 1846), 2: 433.

10. Gabriel Christie to S. Smith, December 19, 1802, Smith Papers; Jefferson to S. Smith, October 17, 1800, Jefferson Papers.

11. McHenry to Wolcott, November 9, 1800, in Gibbs, ed., *Memoirs from Oliver Wolcott,* 2: 445.

12. Manning J. Dauer, *The Adams Federalists* (Baltimore, 1953), pp. 106, 257.

13. Timothy Pickering to McHenry, February 11, 1811, in Steiner, ed., *James McHenry,* p. 567.

talked circumspectly, Smith and Nicholas apparently hinted at a plan by which moderate Republicans would vote for Adams' reelection in 1800 if he agreed to appoint some Republicans to the Cabinet and support Jefferson as his successor in 1804. The political circumstances at the time made such a scheme plausible. Adams' decision to send a new peace mission to France in 1799, and the abrupt dismissal of some cabinet members loyal to Alexander Hamilton had seriously divided the Federalist party. Consequently Hamilton and others were conspiring to defeat the president's bid for reelection.[14]

The Republicans gleefully observed this internecine struggle, but could not be certain it would mean Jefferson's victory. The Smith-Nicholas scheme would not only have preserved the country from the excesses of the extreme Federalists, but would also have insured Jefferson's eventual accession to the presidency. In May, however, news arrived of a surprising Republican triumph in New York, where the party had captured all of the state's electoral votes. Jefferson's prospects brightened, and talk of a coalition ceased. Although Hamiltonian Federalists long insisted that Smith and Nicholas had consummated a deal with Adams, there is no proof to substantiate their claims.[15] Significantly, the correspondence of Jefferson, James Madison, and other national Republican leaders lacks any reference to a plan to coalesce with moderate Federalists, which indicates that the general and his brother-in-law acted on their own initiative. Perhaps they seriously hoped to lay the groundwork for a Jefferson-Adams alliance or, at the least, to widen the rift between Adams and Hamilton. At any rate, Smith had established contacts with moderate Federalists that would prove valuable in the future.[16]

By December 15, 1800, Smith and his fellow Republicans knew they had won the presidential election and had done so with impressive but paradoxical party unity.[17] Unexpected solidarity and discipline

14. Benjamin Stoddert to John Adams, October 27, 1811, in Charles Francis Adams, ed., *The Works of John Adams*, 10 vols. (Boston, 1850–1856), 10: 5–6; Dauer, *Adams Federalists*, p. 248.

15. The coalition plan was not fully exposed until 1811. See the following letters: Adams to Stoddert, October 15, 1811, Stoddert to Adams, November 30, 1811, S. Smith to Adams, December 1, 1811, and Adams to S. Smith, December 13, 1811, in Adams, ed., *Works of John Adams*, 10: 3–9.

16. If such was Smith's plan, it was successful. Hamiltonian Federalists were convinced that Adams had conspired with the Republicans in 1800 to secure his reelection. See Pickering to McHenry, February 11, 1811, in Steiner, ed., *James McHenry*, p. 567.

17. Aaron Kitchell to E. Elmer, December 11, 1800, Gratz Collection, Historical Society of Pennsylvania, Philadelphia; Jefferson to Aaron Burr, December 15,

among Republican electors gave Jefferson and Aaron Burr, the Republican vice-presidential candidate, an equal number of electoral votes. This was possible because each elector had two votes, and the Constitution at that time had no provision for allowing them to designate whom they preferred for president. If one Republican elector had voted for Jefferson and not Burr, the situation could have been avoided. Party leaders felt deeply chagrined. Jefferson despondently penned a note to Burr saying that "it was badly managed not to have arranged with certainty what seems to have been left to chance."[18] But chagrin gave way to consternation as Samuel Smith and other Republican leaders realized the seriousness of the political challenge now facing them. Meeting for the first time in the new national capital at Washington, D.C., the House of Representatives prepared to decide between Jefferson and Burr as required by the Constitution. The second article of that document provided that in case of a tied election the House should settle the matter by voting as state delegations. Each state was to have one vote, and a majority of the representatives of each state determined which candidate should receive that state's vote. Although there was a Federalist majority in the House, Republicans controlled eight of the sixteen state delegations—one short of the number needed to break the tie and elect Jefferson. The Federalists held majorities in six state delegations, while two states, Maryland and Vermont, were divided between the two parties and therefore had no vote. Thus the Federalists quite possibly could have withheld the presidency from Jefferson. The situation severely challenged the new American nation, since the crisis over the presidency also involved the transfer of political power from one party to another, something that had never before occurred in the United States. The electoral vote tie inevitably tempted the ousted Federalists to exploit the situation for their own benefit, even to the point of discarding constitutional process and the wishes of the people. Potentially, then, the dispute Samuel Smith and his colleagues in the House had to settle went beyond the selection of a president: it involved the very future of the country.[19]

1800, in Paul Leicester Ford, ed., *The Writings of Thomas Jefferson*, 10 vols. (New York, 1892–1899), 7: 466–467; see also Wolcott to his wife, December 11, 1800, and Hamilton to Wolcott, December 16, 1800, in Gibbs, ed., *Memoirs of Oliver Wolcott*, 2: 456–458.

18. Jefferson to Burr, December 15, 1800, in Ford, ed., *Writings of Jefferson*, 7: 466–467.

19. Morton Borden, *The Federalism of James A. Bayard* (New York, 1955), pp. 73–95.

During the winter months in Washington no one could be sure what the Federalists intended, and rumors were rife. Jefferson ominously reported that "high-flying Federalists" hoped to prevent the House from choosing a president and to let the government "devolve on a President of the Senate." Throughout the nation in both word and deed Republicans made clear their determination to resist should the Federalists try to violate the Constitution. In Pennsylvania the Republican governor drafted plans to mobilize the militia and distribute arms in case the Federalists attempted to steal the presidency. Another Pennsylvanian, John Beckley, also panicked at the vision of a Federalist usurpation and predicted civil war should it occur. Wilson Cary Nicholas hinted that his state was another one that would not accept a Federalist coup.[20] One Republican warned that the "public mind in Virginia is in a State of Ferment," and if the Federalists seized the presidency, "Virginia would instantly proclaim herself *out of the Union.*"[21]

As the time approached for the House of Representatives to vote, both political parties carefully scrutinized Aaron Burr to determine whether or not he would actively seek the office. Burr, a brilliant New York lawyer, had masterminded the Republican victory of 1800 in his state. His political adroitness was admired, but many also considered him devious and untrustworthy. A number of congressional Federalists hoped that his ambition would lead him to accept their support in electing him president; such support, they felt, would make him virtually a Federalist president. Burr at first seemed more interested in convincing fellow Republicans of his good faith than in conspiring with the Federalists. On learning that a tie electoral vote was virtually certain, Burr immediately wrote Samuel Smith, whom he had known for some years, denying all rumors that he would compete with Jefferson for the presidency. The New Yorker, in effect, asked Smith to be his political spokesman in Washington. Smith, who had never wavered in his support of Jefferson and who may have had misgivings about Burr's intentions, published the letter immediately in an effort to undercut the Federalists' efforts on Burr's behalf. On December 24, 1800, after the final election returns confirmed the tie

20. Jefferson to Burr, December 15, 1800, in Ford, ed., *Writings of Jefferson,* 7: 466–467; Governor Thomas McKean to Jefferson, January 10 and March 19, 1801, Jefferson Papers; John Beckley to Albert Gallatin, February 15, 1801, Albert Gallatin Papers, New-York Historical Society; Nicholas to John Breckinridge, January 20, 1801, Breckinridge Family Papers, Library of Congress.

21. Joseph Hopper Nicholson to Caesar Rodney, January 15, 1801, Jefferson Papers.

vote, Burr once again wrote the Marylander restating his disinterest in the presidency.[22]

Burr's protestations may have lulled Smith's suspicions, but only temporarily. On December 29, 1800, Burr dispatched a third letter to the general that seemed to imply greater interest in becoming the chief executive. He angrily related that one Republican had demanded to know if Burr would resign the presidency in favor of Jefferson should he be elected, a suggestion he found "unnecessary, unreasonable, and impertinent." The New Yorker noted that he had been made a candidate against his will and was now insulted by those who had used his name. Yet, if the House should choose him for the office, Burr concluded, he would accept the position. After this outburst Burr inexplicably invited Smith to meet with him in Philadelphia. The general arrived in that city in early January 1801, hoping to obtain a definite pledge from Burr that he would refuse the office under any circumstances. Almost certainly, Smith attended the conference with Jefferson's knowledge.[23] But the encounter with Burr only served to confirm his growing mistrust of the New Yorker. After much verbal fencing, Smith bluntly asked him "what would be done if the Federal members would not give up [their support of Burr]." Burr responded that the "House of Representatives must make a choice" and that "if they could not get Mr. Jefferson they could take him." Smith declared that solution impossible because the Republicans would never agree to abandon Jefferson.[24] The Marylander later confessed himself "mortified" at Burr's attitude. He left Philadelphia convinced that Burr coveted the presidency and would strive to obtain it.[25]

When Smith returned to Washington, he found what appeared to be more proof that Burr was aggressively seeking support for his candidacy. In a carefully worded letter to Burr the general reported on the activities of a man named David Ogden, who had circulated among the New York congressional delegation, urging its members to back their fellow New Yorker rather than Jefferson. Smith warned

22. Robert Goodloe Harper to Burr, December 24, 1800, printed in *Niles' Weekly Register*, January 20, 1823; Burr to S. Smith, December 16, 1800, Smith-Carter Papers; Burr to S. Smith, December 24, 1800, McGregor Folder, University of Virginia Library.

23. Burr to S. Smith, December 29, 1800, Smith-Carter Papers; Christie to S. Smith, December 19, 1802, Smith Papers; Philadelphia *Aurora*, January 6, 1801; Borden, *Federalism of Bayard*, pp. 82–83.

24. Christie to S. Smith, December 19, 1802, Smith Papers.

25. Deposition of Samuel Smith in the New York court case of *Aaron Burr v. James Cheetham*, March 1806, Smith Papers.

Burr to discount Ogden's belief that there was a chance he could be elected, since the eight Republican delegations in the House would persevere in their loyalty to Jefferson. *"Be assured,"* Smith wrote, *"Believe me,"* he insisted, "those Eight States are unmovable." Moreover, after analyzing the situation in the House of Representatives, Smith concluded that Jefferson would easily obtain the one vote that he needed to become president.[26]

Despite Smith's suspicions, he had misconstrued Burr's intentions. While Burr was probably honest in saying that he would serve as president if elected, there is no evidence that he wished to deny Jefferson the post or that he encouraged the Federalists in the House to support him. Many well-placed individuals testified to these facts, including Governor George Clinton of New York and other leading Republicans. Burr himself wrote his son-in-law on January 17, two weeks after meeting Smith in Philadelphia, that he believed "all will be well," and that Jefferson would be elected. Those Federalists who were actually involved in the attempt to replace Jefferson with Burr also agreed that Burr in no way tried to secure his own election. Indeed, James A. Bayard accused the New Yorker of acting a "miserable and paultry part" during the election in the House of Representatives. The Delawarean complained that Burr had actually tried to discourage the Federalists. Without knowledge of this correspondence, Smith continued to believe that Burr was conspiring with the Federalists. This fundamental misunderstanding helps to explain the Marylander's subsequent actions.[27]

In the months preceding the actual vote in the House of Representatives, Samuel Smith had established himself as a center for negotiations. Enjoying the friendship of both Jefferson and Burr and with a reputation as a political moderate, it seemed only natural that the Marylander would continue in this capacity during the crucial period when the House made its final decision. His position was not an enviable one. Operating in a crisis atmosphere and under great pressure, Smith and his colleagues engaged in activities that they would later regret and deny. Nevertheless, the general's role as a conduit of

26. S. Smith to Burr, January 11, 1801, Smith Papers.

27. George Clinton to DeWitt Clinton, January 13, 1801, DeWitt Clinton Papers, Columbia University, New York City; Burr to Joseph Alston, January 15, 1801, and William Cooper to Thomas Morris, February 13, 1801, in Matthew L. Davis, ed., *The Memoirs of Aaron Burr*, 2 vols. (New York, 1836–1837), 2: 144, 113; James A. Bayard to Andrew Bayard, February 16, 1801, James A. Bayard Papers, Library of Congress; S. Smith to Burr, January 11, 1801, Smith Papers; Nicholas to S. Smith, December 19, 1806, Smith-Carter Papers.

information between the opposing groups in the House gave him a unique opportunity to shape the final settlement.

The House of Representatives began seven days of balloting on February 11, 1801. Until February 17 the votes remained eight states for Jefferson, six for Burr, and the two states of Vermont and Maryland evenly divided. On the evening of the first day Smith was approached by Bayard, who told him that "there was nothing in the way of an appointment" that the general could not command if he switched his vote to Burr. By doing so Smith would have broken the tie in the state's delegation and given Maryland to Burr. Smith asked if Burr had authorized the offer; Bayard replied affirmatively. Since Bayard later said that Burr refused to cooperate with the Federalists in the House, he apparently lied to Smith. To the Marylander this conversation undoubtedly appeared as one more proof of a sinister conspiracy between Burr and the Federalists.[28]

Bayard was but one of several Federalists who sought out Smith to propose deals or to ask for information. The same day that he received Bayard's proposition, the general was also contacted by Federalist Josiah Parker of Virginia, who claimed to represent a number of Federalist congressmen interested in abandoning Burr and "putting an end to the election." They wished to know what Jefferson's attitude would be, if elected, toward the public debt, the navy, and commerce. Smith answered that he had recently spoken with Jefferson, who lived in the same boarding house, about these very points. He told Parker that he understood Jefferson, as president, would hesitate to touch the debt, reduce the navy, or act in an unfriendly manner toward commerce. To be sure of his facts the Marylander again talked with Jefferson that evening without mentioning Parker's conversation. The next day Jonathan Dayton, a Federalist senator from New Jersey, approached Smith with the same questions and received the same replies. Frrom these conversations Smith learned that moderate Federalists seemed more interested in future governmental policies than in keeping Jefferson from the presidency. Furthermore, the fact that Parker and Dayton approached Smith rather than the acknowledged leader of the House Republicans, Albert Gallatin of Pennsylvania, showed that Smith had clearly emerged as Jefferson's spokesman. Federalists considered the general their most reliable contact among those close to the Virginian.[29]

On Friday, February 13, Bayard, who had now decided that the

28. Anas, February 12, 1801, in Ford, ed., *Writings of Jefferson*, 1: 291.

29. Deposition of Samuel Smith in the New York Court case of *Gillespie v. Smith*, April 15, 1806, Smith Papers.

Federalists could not elect Burr, again sought a meeting with Smith. This time the talk avoided the subject of political bribery to win support for Burr. The representative from Delaware declared that he could end the tie, but, like Parker and Dayton, he also wished to know Jefferson's attitude toward commerce, the navy, and the public debt. As the only representative from Delaware, Bayard constituted the entire state delegation, and by switching his vote to Jefferson he could have broken the deadlock in the House of Representatives. Having recently talked with Jefferson, Smith easily satisfied Bayard's curiosity on the three points of policy. But the man from Delaware was not above using his unique position to seek personal favors. Bayard also asked, as Smith recalled, what Jefferson would do about Federalists holding government jobs. He made specific reference to two port collectors who were close friends and political allies. Clearly Bayard had made his vote for Jefferson contingent upon an assurance that these two men would not be dismissed. When Smith pleaded ignorance of Jefferson's intended policy on patronage, Bayard insisted that he speak with Jefferson on the subject and bring his answer back the next day.

On Smith's report depended the outcome of the election. Should he tell Bayard that Jefferson had rejected the implied deal, the struggle in the House of Representatives would have continued and extremist elements among the Federalists might well have tried to impose some unconstitutional settlement. The confidence of the American people in their new political institutions could have been seriously shaken and civil war could possibly have resulted. Much rested on Smith's actions at this meeting. Written several years after the event, the accounts of that critical second meeting between Smith and Bayard are contradictory. According to Smith, he told Bayard that as far as the treatment of incumbent Federalist officeholders was concerned, Jefferson did not think that such men "ought to be dismissed on political grounds only." Smith also remembered telling Bayard again that he might rest assured that Jefferson would act on the other three points as Smith said he would on the day before. The Marylander recalled that Bayard then promised that Jefferson would be elected.[30]

Bayard's own account of the meetings with Smith, also written several years later, indicates his conviction that he had, through Smith, struck a bargain with Jefferson. He claimed that he told the general at their first meeting on Friday, "I should not be satisfied nor

30. Ibid.

agree to yield, till I had the assurance from Mr. Jefferson himself,"[31]
that as president he would act as the Federalists desired on appointments, the navy, the debt, and commercial policy. According to
Bayard, Smith returned the next day and said that he had conferred
with Jefferson on the points Bayard had raised and was *"authorized
by Jefferson to say, that they corresponded with his views and intentions, and that we might confide in him accordingly."*[32] On the word
authorized rests the principle difference between the two stories. Was
Smith in truth commissioned by Jefferson to complete the bargain
with Bayard? Was Smith merely speaking his own thoughts? Did
Bayard simply misinterpret what Smith told him?

The evidence indicates that Jefferson did not make a political
bargain with Bayard to secure his own election. Smith later denied
that Jefferson authorized any deals with the Federalists or was aware
of Bayard's overtures. The Marylander claimed that he had learned
of Jefferson's attitudes on the various points in general conversation,
"without [Jefferson] having the remotest idea of my object." It was
this information that Smith said he relayed to Bayard in their two
meetings. Smith asserted he never told Bayard "that I had any
authority from Mr. Jefferson to communicate anything to him or to
any other person."[33] Jefferson also said that he never empowered
Smith to strike a bargain with Bayard.[34]

The truth of the matter can never be precisely known; it appears,
however, that Smith used his role as intermediary to mislead Bayard
purposely in order to bring a quick end to the election. Although
aware that some Federalists wanted to conclude the contest, he still
believed Burr was seeking the presidency and there was no way of
knowing whether or not the New Yorker could still win. Furthermore,
the possibility remained that the Federalists would prevent any choice
at all or make one that was unconstitutional. Republicans had made it
clear that such a move would lead to a breakup of the union and
perhaps civil war. When the two men met that Saturday morning,
the temptation Smith felt to tamper with the truth must have been
great. By merely allowing Bayard to believe that Jefferson's casual
references to future policy constituted a capitulation to Federalist
terms, Smith could have and probably did make a significant contri-

31. Deposition of James A. Bayard in the New York court case of *Gillespie v.
Smith*, April 1806, Bayard Papers.

32. Ibid.; italics are mine.

33. S. Smith to Richard H. Bayard and James A. Bayard, Jr., April 13, 1830,
Smith Papers.

34. Anas, April 15, 1806, in Ford, ed., *Writings of Jefferson*, 1: 313–314.

bution to ending the "aweful crisis." Many years later Albert Gallatin admitted that he believed this to be the case. Gallatin asserted that Smith misled Bayard because the Marylander erroneously feared a defection to Burr by some Republican congressmen.[35]

The Saturday meeting proved to be decisive. After leaving Smith, Bayard wasted no time in initiating procedures to end the election. He called a caucus of Federalist House members and announced that he would vote for Jefferson, a move assuring Jefferson the ninth vote he needed for election. The Delawarean successfully won the acquiescence of many in his own party. Some Federalists later said they were willing to drop Burr after Bayard claimed that he had received "assurances" from Jefferson that "certain points of Federal policy . . . would be observed in case Mr. Jefferson was elected."[36] On February 17, 1801, several Federalist representatives from Maryland and Vermont cast blank ballots, thus placing those states in the Republican column and giving Jefferson the necessary margin of victory. Ironically, Bayard himself had managed to avoid the embarrassment of casting his ballot for the Virginian.[37]

The election of 1800 marked a major turning point in Smith's political career. Prior to 1800 the general had been known as an important political figure in Baltimore and a respected if relatively obscure member of the House of Representatives. His contributions to Jefferson's successful candidacy, from the time he and Nicholas first talked with Stoddert to the meeting at which he deceived Bayard, now entitled him to some of the fruits of victory. When the new administration assumed power no one could doubt that Smith would be an important influence. Yet it remained to be seen whether Smith could adjust himself to party discipline if it contradicted his loyalties to American commercial interests.

35. Margaret Bayard Smith's notebook, found in Gaillard Hunt, ed., *The First Forty Years of Washington Society* (New York, 1906), pp. 1–25; Gallatin to Henry Muhlenberg, May 8, 1848, in Henry Adams, ed., *The Writings of Albert Gallatin*, 2 vols. (Philadelphia, 1879), 1: 250.

36. George Baer to Richard H. Bayard, April 19, 1830, Bayard Papers.

37. James A. Bayard to Richard Basset, February 17, 1801, in Elizabeth Donnan, ed., "Papers of James A. Bayard, 1796–1815," *Annual Report for 1913 of the American Historical Association*, 2 vols. (Washington, D.C., 1915), 2: 127.

8

···

A Jeffersonian Leader

THE FIRST four years of Republican rule were an era of almost un-
mixed blessings for Samuel Smith. At no other period would he enjoy
such material success and political influence. In Baltimore his political
control remained unchallenged while his wealth rapidly grew. Fifty
years old, with a martial bearing and quiet dignity, Smith was proud
of his accomplishments. By his own estimate he owned over $400,000
in land and stock. This did not take into account, however, his half-
share of S. Smith & Buchanan, which made an annual profit of at
least $200,000. Nor did it include his fashionable house in the center
of Baltimore, let alone his lavish country estate a few miles north and
east of the city. Named Montebello after a minor French victory at
that place in Italy in the late eighteenth century, Smith's country
home was designed by himself and completed in 1800. With its
marble-paved, columned porch, its huge central bay, and its furnish-
ings collected from all corners of the world, Montebello was a testa-
ment to its owner's affluence and taste. The dark-paneled study held
other clues to the general's personality. Behind busts of Benjamin
Franklin and Thomas Jefferson stood shelf upon shelf of the world's
great literature. Perhaps reflecting his early training, Smith's collection
was heavily weighted with Greek and Roman authors as well as more
recent French novels. But English works were certainly not neglected.
In addition to the ubiquitous Locke could be found volumes by
Fielding and Pope. The library indicated Smith's wide-ranging intel-

lectual interests and showed that despite his brief formal education, he never lost the taste for learning.[1]

Smith could also take satisfaction in the general condition of his family. Five of his sisters and a brother had survived to adulthood and all had done well for themselves. Robert Smith, already a well-known lawyer and politician in Baltimore, was about to begin a career in national government, and the sisters had married respectable men in Baltimore and Virginia. In his immediate family, however, Smith suffered some sorrows. In 1797 Margaret bore the last of twelve children, Anne, who died five years later. Indeed, only six of the twelve reached maturity and of these, Louis, the oldest and his father's favorite, died in 1805 of tuberculosis while visiting Europe. The other son, John Spear Smith, was a most promising young man destined for a long and honorable life. Like their aunts, Smith's daughters married well: Mary's husband was a prominent English jurist, Lord Mansfield; Sidney married into the wealthy Patterson family of Baltimore; Margaret chose her spouse from the Nicholas clan of Virginia; and Laura wed a young Baltimore attorney of good family. Much to Smith's joy Montebello was often filled with his many grandchildren. A loyal family man, the general aided his son, brothers-in-law, and sons-in-law in every possible way. For some he obtained government appointments and for others he handled their financial affairs. All, at least for the time, repaid him with affection and political support.[2]

In March of 1801 Smith, along with nearly a thousand other people, crowded into the Senate chamber of the yet unfinished Capitol building to witness Thomas Jefferson's inauguration, the first to be held in Washington. After long years of often arduous opposition the Republican party had finally achieved national power. As Smith and other Republican stalwarts watched their leader take the oath of office and then strained to hear his nearly inaudible inaugural address, they could take pride in their accomplishment. They could also count themselves lucky that Jefferson's administration was beginning under such favorable circumstances. Domestically, the economy was booming and every section of the country was experiencing growing prosperity. Moreover, the Republicans could rely on being free of a crippling political opposition, at least temporarily, since the recent elections had left the Federalists disorganized and fragmented. A large majority

1. List of property of Samuel Smith, 1800, Samuel Smith Papers, Library of Congress; Cary Nicholas Fink, "Smith," Smith-Carter Papers, University of Virginia Library; Lawrence Hall Fowler, "Montebello, Maryland," *Architectural Review* (November 1909), pp. 146–149.

2. Smith Family Geneaology, Smith-Carter Papers.

in the House of Representatives and a slim one in the Senate assured the president's party of a relatively free hand in constructing national policies. In foreign affairs Jefferson began his term with the United States at peace in a peaceful world. President Adams' diplomatic initiative of 1799 had led to the signing of a convention with France in 1800 that both ended the undeclared war and extricated America from the entangling alliance of 1778 that had caused so much embarrassment. More important, Great Britain and France signed the Peace of Amiens, which momentarily halted the war in Europe and ended the insults and injuries the belligerents had subjected the United States to as a neutral. At the start at least the Republicans would not be confronted with the agonizing dilemmas that had torn the Federalist party apart.

Peace in Europe removed the major obstacle that in the past had prevented completely cordial relations between Smith and the Republican party. Although he had in actuality been a Republican since 1796, the general had never hesitated to vote against the party when issues affecting commerce or defense were involved. Now that the end of hostilities had nearly eliminated the attacks on American trade, he could and did enthusiastically support Jefferson's administration and most of its programs. But despite his irregular voting record Smith had been counted among the ranks of the Republican party ever since that party can be said to have existed. He was a veteran of the struggles over the Alien and Sedition Acts and the election of 1800, not to mention his contributions to the party in Baltimore. Few were surprised, therefore, when the president offered Smith a high position in the government.

Less than a week after the inauguration Smith received word that Jefferson hoped he would enter the Cabinet as secretary of the navy. "If you can be added to the administration I am forming," the president wrote Smith, "it will constitute a magistracy entirely possessed of the public confidence."[3] Jefferson bluntly told the Marylander there were two reasons why he would be a valuable addition to the government. The first was political: the general was to be the representative of commercial interests in the administration. Furthermore, Jefferson wished Smith to act as an intermediary between merchants, most of whom were Federalists, and the president, with the goal of winning their "acquiescence" to Republican rule. The second reason Jefferson wanted Smith for the post was that he was one of only a small number

3. Thomas Jefferson to S. Smith, March 9, 1801, in Paul Leicester Ford, ed., *The Writings of Thomas Jefferson*, 10 vols. (New York, 1892–1899), 8: 13.

of Republicans qualified to administer the department. The Virginian reminded Smith that the "knowledge of naval matters" in America was largely monopolized by the Federalists, whom it was politically impossible to appoint to office. Therefore, it was the Marylander's "moral duty" to accept the office.[4]

Although flattered, Smith refused with some reluctance. "The conflict with myself has been very great," he answered the president, explaining that the condition of his private affairs and the "disapprobation" of his constituents forced him to reject the offer. Later, however, after learning that Jefferson had been unable to find anyone willing to take the job, Smith agreed to run the navy department temporarily, but without pay and without giving up his seat in Congress. The president gratefully approved the arrangement. At the suggestion of Vice President Burr, the secretary of war was also appointed secretary of the navy, with the understanding that Smith would actually be in charge.[5]

The general took over the navy department at a time when tension was once again building between the United States and the pirate states of North Africa. In recent months the Barbary Powers, with whom there had been an uneasy peace for several years, had resumed their depredations on American commerce. With war threatening in the Mediterranean, it became Smith's task to organize the United States navy for the coming conflict. Congress, he found, had complicated his task by passing a law in the previous session ordering seven of the thirteen American frigates built for the quasiwar with France taken out of service. Acting on his own authority, the Marylander divided the remaining vessels into two fleets. One he immediately ordered to the Mediterranean, while the second was kept in port with instructions to relieve the other in eight months. Thus, when the Pasha of Tripoli declared war against the United States in May of 1801 for refusing to meet his demands for more tribute, a small but powerful American squadron was already on its way to the area.[6]

In his brief stint as acting head of the navy department Smith also

4. Ibid.
5. S. Smith to Jefferson, March 17 and 20, 1801, Thomas Jefferson Papers, Library of Congress; Jefferson to S. Smith, March 24, 1801, in Ford, ed., *Writings of Jefferson*, 8: 28; Aaron Burr to S. Smith, March 24, 1801, Smith-Carter Papers.
6. S. Smith to Jefferson, May 4, 1801, Jefferson Papers. Jefferson had little to do with the navy department and gave Smith a free hand in running its affairs. "It is the department I understand the least," he wrote the general, "and therefore need a person whose complete competence will justify the most entire confidence and resignation" (Jefferson to S. Smith, April 17, 1801, Smith-Carter Papers).

took steps to promote the careers of promising young officers, to see that adequate naval yards were built, and to improve the Potomac River ship channel. Smith informed the president in early July that he was resigning the position.[7] Jefferson was obviously sorry to lose Smith but graciously thanked him for his services: "you have done for us gratis, what the emoluments of office have not been sufficient to induce others to undertake," the president's commendation to Smith read, "and it is with equal truth and pleasure I testify that you have deserved well with your country."[8] Jefferson complimented the general even more by appointing his brother, Robert Smith, to be the permanent secretary of the navy. Although Robert was a lawyer with limited experience in naval affairs, Jefferson undoubtedly hoped that he would be guided by his brother. Moreover, the appointment of Robert Smith was probably dictated by a desire on Jefferson's part to maintain good relations between the administration and the Maryland Republicans, of whom Samuel Smith was the principal leader.[9]

Samuel Smith had not been entirely candid with Jefferson in detailing his excuses for refusing to become secretary of the navy. It was not true, for instance, that his business was in need of his constant attention. S. Smith & Buchanan was if anything more profitable than ever. As for supervising the business, Smith had long since given over most of the responsibility to his partner, James A. Buchanan. The general's real reason for turning down the navy department post appears to have been related to his personal political ambitions. For one thing, Smith preferred his position in the House of Representatives, believing, perhaps with justification, that he could exercise more influence there than in the newest and least significant of the Cabinet positions. For another, the general had already decided that, as a reward for his services on behalf of the party, he wanted a major diplomatic appointment.[10]

As early as November 1801 Smith directly solicited the president for a ministerial post. "Our relations with foreign nations being chiefly of a commercial nature," Smith told Jefferson on one occasion, "has

7. S. Smith to John Rutledge, May 12, 1801, John Rutledge Papers, Southern Historical Collection, University of North Carolina, Durham; Burr to S. Smith, May 2, 1801, Smith-Carter Papers; S. Smith to Jefferson, April 6, 1801, Jefferson Papers; Jefferson to S. Smith, July 9, 1801, Smith-Carter Papers.

8. Jefferson to S. Smith, July 9, 1801, Smith-Carter Papers.

9. Jefferson to Robert Smith, July 9, 1801, Jefferson Papers; Dumas Malone, *Jefferson the President: First Term, 1801–1805* (Boston, 1970).

10. Jefferson to Gouverneur Morris, May 8, 1801, in Ford, ed., *Writings of Jefferson*, 8: 49; John Randolph to Joseph Hopper Nicholson, October 1, 1801, John Randolph Papers, Virginia State Library, Richmond.

induced me to suppose that my information and knowledge of the commercial Interest of our country may be useful to our nation in making arrangements abroad."[11] The Marylander went on to stress his genuine interest in becoming a diplomat and pledged retirement from his business activities if offered such a position. Jefferson did not reply favorably to this inquiry but Smith persisted in his efforts. In October 1802, when rumors reached Washington that the American ministers in England and France intended to resign, Smith tried to enlist the influence of his brother-in-law, Wilson Cary Nicholas, in persuading Jefferson to name him to one of the openings. He pointed out to Nicholas that his wealth and commercial knowledge made him "equal to the appointment." Nicholas, who was a business associate of Smith's as well as an in-law, replied tactfully that more was required of an envoy than money; diplomacy demanded men "trained to the artifices of legal and political disposition," which Smith was not. He enclosed a letter of recommendation to Jefferson that Smith could read and then send "if you think proper." The letter said only that Smith was available for either post. Nicholas' reaction apparently discouraged the general, for he did not pursue the matter any further.[12]

The general's ambitions for a career in the foreign service were no secret in Washington and on one occasion inadvertantly involved him in an embarrassing diplomatic tiff between France and the United States. In the summer of 1803 Jerome Bonaparte, youngest brother of the French Emperor, visited Baltimore on his way home from Santo Domingo, where a French army had failed to reconquer the black republic. Jerome naturally excited a good deal of interest within Baltimore society, and his stay was marked by a steady round of parties. At one such affair, held at the home of Judge Samuel Chase, Jerome met the strikingly beautiful Betsy Patterson, daughter of William Patterson and Samuel Smith's niece. After a brief but frenzied romance the two were married on Christmas Eve over the vehement objections of the French chargé d'affaires, Louis Andre Pichon.[13]

Pichon, correctly anticipating that Napoleon would not be pleased with the match, had done everything in his power to prevent the ceremony. Having failed, the Frenchman cast about for an excuse

11. S. Smith to Jefferson, November 25, 1801, Jefferson Papers.

12. S. Smith to Wilson Cary Nicholas, October 12, 1802, Wilson Cary Nicholas Papers, University of Virginia Library; Nicholas to Smith, January 1803, Smith-Carter Papers.

13. Irving Brant, *James Madison; Secretary of State, 1800–1809* (New York, 1953), pp. 166–167; J. Thomas Scharf, *Chronicles of Baltimore* (Baltimore, 1874), p. 294.

and thought he had found one in Samuel Smith's desire to be named to an important diplomatic post. Writing to Talleyrand, the French foreign minister, Pichon claimed that Smith had engineered the marriage in order to improve his chances for an appointment as the next American minister to France. "He has long aimed at the diplomatic career for which he is little qualified," Pichon asserted, "and this motive and the near return of Mr. [Robert] Livingston have decided his taste."[14] Pichon's charges were echoed by several of Smith's enemies in Congress, although they had nothing but suspicions to support their accusations. Not only would such a Byzantine intrigue have been out of character for the general, but also it should be noted that Jerome's and Betsy's obvious ardor for each other needed no outside encouragement from anyone.[15]

Even if Smith was not entirely successful in promoting his own career, he often helped others obtain offices. "Let me again press your appointment of my friends," he once unabashedly wrote Secretary of State James Madison; "be assured you will be satisfied."[16] Most of Smith's patronage requests involved his family or those personally close to him. In 1801, for example, he was instrumental in having a relative of his business partner appointed a consul in the French West Indies. Later he succeeded in securing a minor judicial post for one of his brothers-in-law. Federal offices in Maryland also drew his attention, since they could materially increase his power in state politics. He dispatched numerous letters to Jefferson and Madison filled with the names of "good Republicans" that he deemed worthy of preferment. Smith's greatest influence was exercised in the selection of consuls and port collectors. These jobs necessarily had to be filled with individuals experienced in commercial affairs and trusted by the merchants with whom they must deal. Since Smith was both a Republican and a successful merchant, his recommendations naturally carried great weight with the administration and the Republican majority in Congress.[17] On at least one occasion in 1803, the Senate refused to approve a consular nomination after Smith, who was then a member

14. Henry Adams, *History of the United States of America during the Administrations of Thomas Jefferson and James Madison,* 9 vols. (New York, 1889–1891), 2: 377.

15. Ibid.

16. S. Smith to James Madison, April 5, 1803, James Madison Papers, Library of Congress.

17. S. Smith to Jefferson, June 22 and March 20, 1801, Jefferson Papers; S. Smith to Madison, July 9 and 12, 1801, and May 4, 1804, Madison Papers; Jefferson to Albert Gallatin, November 16, 1801, Albert Gallatin Papers, New-York Historical Society.

of the Senate, described the man as incompetent. Senator John Quincy Adams of Massachusetts called the rejection the first he had witnessed, "and it was done on General Smith's declaring that he knew the man and that he was in every way unfit for the office."[18]

During these early years of Jefferson's presidency Smith frequently used his position as a party leader to transmit the views of merchants and other businessmen to the administration. In the summer of 1802, for example, the Marylander vigorously objected to a new tax regulation promulgated by Secretary of the Treasury Albert Gallatin that cancelled the practice of refunding import duties American merchants paid on foreign sugar. Smith, who never had gotten along with Gallatin, plainly told the secretary that the change in policy was "impolitic" because it adversely affected the rum industry in America. As the owner of a distillery himself, the general was qualified to evaluate the effect of increased taxes on sugar; they would make American rum less competitive in world markets. Without avail Smith warned Gallatin that unless the regulation was repealed it would harm the Republican cause in areas where distilling was a major enterprise, such as New England. On another occasion and with a similar lack of success, the Marylander urged the administration not to carry out a plan to reduce the size of the American fleet in the Mediterranean because the loss of protection to American ships would drastically increase the cost of insurance to merchants. Although rarely effective in getting the administration to tailor its policies to commercial interests, Smith did provide a link between merchants and the president that would not otherwise have existed. Jefferson and the business community may not have liked each other, but through Samuel Smith they could at least communicate.[19]

Besides his efforts to wield influence in the administration, Smith also labored to make himself President Jefferson's principal spokesman in the House of Representatives. Before the election of 1800 House Republicans had been led by Madison and later by Gallatin. Now both men held cabinet positions. If the Republican majority in the House was to cooperate with the president in governing the nation, then a new legislative leader had to be found, one able to command the confidence of Jefferson and the Republican representatives. In compe-

18. Diary of John Quincy Adams, January 19, 1803, Adams Family Papers, Massachusetts Historical Society. See also William Plumer, "Notes of Proceedings in the United States Congress," January 29, 1805, William Plumer Papers, Library of Congress.

19. S. Smith to Gallatin, August 13, 1802, Gallatin Papers; S. Smith to Madison, April 1, 1803, Madison Papers.

tition with three other men, William Branch Giles and John Randolph, both of Virginia, and Joseph Hopper Nicholson, a fellow Marylander, Smith aspired to become the majority leader in the House. Apparently none of these men possessed in sufficient measure the requisite abilities, for by Christmas of 1801 Jefferson still had made no choice, and the leadership in the House remained in confusion. Perceptive Federalists began commenting on the "rivalry and jealousy among the leaders" that kept the Republicans disorganized. In the early months of 1802 Giles seemed to have triumphed, but illness soon forced his retirement and reopened the scramble for power.[20] "Who will, in the absence of Mr. Giles, be the leader of the House is uncertain," commented a Federalist senator, "John Randolph, Samuel Smith and Joseph Hopper Nicholson, have each laid in their claims."[21] From Jefferson's point of view the dispute did not end satisfactorily; Nicholson faded into obscurity and Smith transferred to the Senate in 1803. By a process of attrition the talented but violently erratic Randolph emerged as Jefferson's lieutenant in the House.[22]

While he maneuvered to win the position of floor leader, Smith actively promoted administration measures in the House. During the first years of Jefferson's term the Republicans concentrated on redressing grievances against the previous Federalist administrations. The president and his supporters first moved against the Judiciary Act of 1801. Passed by a lame-duck Federalist majority in Congress shortly before Jefferson took the oath of office, the law created a host of new offices for marshals, attorneys, and clerks, as well as sixteen circuit court judgeships. President Adams had promptly named Federalists to these posts, signing many of the commissions only hours before he left office. To Smith and other Republicans the Judiciary Act and the "midnight judges" symbolized the arrogance and reckless partisanship of the Federalist party; and so, in January 1802 the Republicans acted to repeal the legislation.[23]

The repeal bill provided the first test of the cohesiveness of the Republican majority in the House as the Federalists used every device at their command to win over enough votes to defeat the

20. Roger Griswold to Rutledge, December 14, 1801, Rutledge Papers; Malone, *Jefferson the President: First Term,* p. 446; Dice Robins Anderson, *William Branch Giles* (Glouster, Mass., 1965), pp. 85–90.

21. Plumer to Oliver Peabody, December 22, 1802, Plumer Papers.

22. Noble E. Cunningham, *The Jeffersonian Republicans in Power; Party Operations, 1801–1809* (Chapel Hill, 1963), pp. 73–75.

23. Morton Borden, *The Federalism of James A. Bayard* (New York, 1955), pp. 106–125; Anderson, *Giles,* pp. 83–85.

measure. The Senate had already passed the repeal bill by one vote when the House debate began in February. Led by Smith's old friend James A. Bayard, the Federalists took the position that it was unconstitutional for Congress to abolish the judicial positions. They reminded the Republicans that the Constitution specifically stated that judges shall hold their offices during good behavior and their salaries shall not be reduced while they are in office. The only legitimate method for removing the judges appointed under the Judiciary Act, insisted the Federalists, was by impeachment. The major burden of defending the repeal bill against charges of unconstitutionality was borne by William Branch Giles, but on February 27 Smith assisted his colleague with a long and careful analysis of the constitutional question. The general informed the House that he had not only studied the relevant portions of the Constitution himself, but also had conferred with leading lawyers to determine the validity of the Federalists' arguments. On the basis of his research Smith had predictably deduced "that Congress had the Constitutional power to pass the [repeal] bill on your table." As evidence for his contention Smith noted it was the practice in England and in many of the American states to remove judges from the bench by a joint address of the legislature. This precedent alone, he commented, justified Congress in dispensing with judicial offices it had created. Smith also accused the Federalists of having passed the Judiciary Act of 1801 solely for political purposes. Smith's speech, although overly long and not one of his better efforts, did help to rally those Republican representatives who were wavering and, if Bayard can be believed, had "openly cursed" the repeal bill. On March 3 the measure passed by a vote of fifty-nine to thirty-two, with only one Republican deserting the party.[24]

The general also supported the president by voting for a bill to end all internal taxes and for a constitutional amendment changing the presidential elector system in order to avoid any repetition of the situation that had occurred in the election of 1800. Henceforth electors would cast one vote for president and one for vice president. Nearly all Republicans could agree upon these issues. Since they were largely of symbolic significance and certainly had little or no impact on

24. U.S., Congress, *The Debates and Proceedings in the Congress of the United States . . . 1789–1824,* 42 vols. (Washington, D.C., 1834–1856), 7th Cong., 1st sess., 1802, pp. 846–854, 982; hereafter cited as *Annals of Congress.* See also James A. Bayard to Richard Bassett, February 12 and March 2, 1802, in Elizabeth Donnan, ed., "Papers of James A. Bayard, 1796–1815," *Annual Report for 1913 of the American Historical Association,* 2 vols. (Washington, D.C., 1915), 2: 148.

commerce, Smith could and did back them without reservation. But behind the scenes, away from the publicity generated by the Republican attack on the Federalist system, the Marylander ceaselessly labored in the House to promote policies beneficial to American trade.[25]

Smith's efforts on behalf of the mercantile community were facilitated by the fact that he was chairman of the Committee on Commerce and Manufactures, one of the five standing committees in the House of Representatives. In 1801 and 1802 the seven-man committee consisted of five Republicans and two Federalists. Although Smith was the only merchant on the committee, five other members represented districts or states with important commercial interests. Under Smith's leadership the Committee on Commerce and Manufactures became a powerful advocate for legislation favoring the protection and expansion of American trade. In contrast, the Committee of Ways and Means and its chairman, John Randolph, mirrored rural and agrarian interests. With control over appropriations, that committee was in a position to block many of Smith's proposals. As a result the two committees sniped at each other in a continuing battle over their respective prerogatives.

One clash between the committees took place in December 1801, when Smith rose and made a motion that would have instructed the Committee on Commerce and Manufactures to investigate the whole subject of import duties. The implication was that the committee had reason to believe changes were needed in American taxing policies as they affected trade. Instantly a member of the Ways and Means Committee was on his feet loudly complaining that Smith's motion would intrude in an area properly belonging to his committee. The general answered that "it was necessary for the subject to be discussed by commercial men," since they were better acquainted with the topic. In this instance the House agreed with Smith and approved his motion. A year later the Marylander made a frontal assault on the Ways and Means Committee by suggesting that its membership should be increased. He very likely was trying to pack the committee with men less amenable to Randolph's domination and thus dilute the Virginian's control. Randolph, however, managed to avoid the blow by persuading the House not to act on the plan.[26]

When he was not skirmishing with Randolph, the chairman of the

25. *Annals of Congress,* 7th Cong., 1st sess., 1802, pp. 1058–1062, 2d sess., 1802, p. 492.

26. Ibid., 1st sess., 1801, pp. 317–319, 2d sess., 1802, pp. 275–278.

Committee on Commerce and Manufactures somehow found time to initiate a flood of constructive legislation. A great deal of it concerned such routine matters as the building of lighthouses or action on petitions for special privileges submitted to Congress by groups of merchants. Smith's most important project was to persuade the administration to secure agreements with European nations that would reciprocally lower import duties. Fewer taxes on trade would, he thought, inevitably lead to greater commercial intercourse and prosperity. Smith had submitted this plan before, in 1796, but then he had been a member of the opposition. Now as an influential leader in the ruling party he reintroduced the measure in December 1801. Arming himself with his usual array of statistics, Smith gave a lengthy explanation and defense of his scheme before the House. Six years earlier he had correctly predicted that discriminatory duties would cause other nations to retaliate by enacting heavy "countervailing" duties against American trade. The outcome of this war of tax regulations was that international trade had been impeded. It was true, he admitted, that the American duties had helped the domestic shipping industry by giving it a competitive edge in importing goods into the United States. On the other hand, Smith added, both France and Great Britain had imposed discriminatory duties of their own, thereby excluding American merchant vessels from trade routes they had formerly used without restriction. Smith contended that the discriminatory duty system had ultimately been detrimental to the nation's commercial interests, since the valuable tobacco and cotton exports from the southern states were being carried to Europe in French or British ships rather than American ones.[27]

Having demonstrated the shortcomings of the present tax laws, Smith tried to convince the House that only by negotiating mutual reductions in duties could the larger interests of American trade be protected. The Marylander, anticipating his critics, testified as to the capacity of American merchants to survive in a free-trade situation. "No man that knows the character of an American merchant," he declaimed, "will doubt his ability to sustain such a competition."[28] Smith's proposal, despite his closely reasoned arguments, did not favorably impress either the Federalists or other merchants. William Plumer, a Federalist senator from New Hampshire, considered the plan objectionable on several counts. Not only would it violate the most-favored-nation provision of the Jay Treaty, but also it would

27. *Ibid.*, 2d sess., 1802, pp. 283–284, 523, 1st sess., 1801, p. 325.
28. *Ibid.*, 1st sess., 1801, p. 330.

"injure the commerce of the eastern states [and] lessen the number of our seamen."[29] Plumer's view was shared by many Federalists in the House and, with Republicans apathetic about the matter, they had little difficulty in tabling the general's bill.

At the next session of Congress Smith tried a new approach. On January 10, 1803, he again presented his scheme to the House, but this time in the form of a lengthy report on discriminatory duties prepared by the Committee on Commerce and Manufactures. The report offered proof that Great Britain, acting under the terms of the Jay Treaty, had severely restricted the American carrying trade to England by levying countervailing duties. It also showed that France, Denmark, and Sweden had similarly raised their import duties on goods brought in on American vessels. At the end of the report Smith inserted a resolution embodying the principle of reciprocal reductions in duties. It differed from his earlier bill in that the president was to be given authority to lower American duties without approval from Congress.[30]

Because of the documentation and the greater publicity it received, Smith's plan drew more attention than it had previously. The passage of a year, however, had not changed the adverse opinion held by most merchants. The Philadelphia Chamber of Commerce even went so far as to send Congress a resolution expressing its disapproval.[31] Robert Waln, a Philadelphia merchant, explained to a friend in Congress that it was generally believed repeal of the discriminatory duties would harm rather than help the mercantile community. Waln observed that New England, which relied heavily on the carrying trade and on the ship-building industry for its prosperity, would be badly hurt if it lost the protection of the duties: "Experience has demonstrated the benefits of the present system," the Philadelphian concluded, "it secures to American vessels the whole import trade."[32] The majority of American merchants obviously did not share Smith's confidence in the enterprise and efficiency of the American business-man. They were willing to sacrifice the possibility of expanding the American portion of the carrying trade to Europe for the security of monopolizing the import trade.

Against such conservative intransigence Smith was helpless. Swamped by letters and petitions pleading that the system of dis-

---

29. Plumer to [?] Livermore, December 21, 1802, Plumer Papers.
30. *Annals of Congress*, 7th Cong., 2d sess., 1803, pp. 347–351.
31. Robert Waln to Plumer, January 17, 1803, Plumer Papers.
32. Ibid.

criminating duties be maintained, the House delayed and delayed again the consideration of Smith's resolution. Finally, on February 12, Samuel Latham Mitchill of New York, a Republican member of the Committee on Commerce and Manufactures and one of Smith's most consistent supporters, moved to end all consideration of the resolution, since there was "no possibility of adopting it, even if it should be argued." Mitchill praised Smith's plan as "intriguing" and said he hoped it could be adopted at some future time. "However speculative men might think on the point," the New Yorker told his colleagues, "the great body of practical men bore strong testimony against it."[33] The general did not again propose his idea until 1815, when events forced his fellow merchants to recognize its wisdom.

The reciprocity plan was Samuel Smith's last major effort in the House of Representatives. In the fall of 1802 the Republicans had gained control of the Maryland legislature and, as one of their first actions, elected Smith to a full term in the United States Senate. Undoubtedly flattered by this further evidence of his importance, he must at the same time have felt some regret at leaving the House, where he had served with distinction for over a decade. In retrospect his decision to enter the Senate appears strange. It was not that he endangered his political hold on Baltimore, for he was able to dictate who would succeed to his seat in the House. What is perplexing is why he would surrender the power he had accumulated as a party leader in the House and as chairman of the Committee on Commerce and Manufactures. Possibly Smith felt discouraged by his inability to achieve undisputed possession of the floor leader's job. If so, he may well have seen the Senate as a place where his ambitions would have a better chance of fulfillment. As a new member of the Senate, however, Smith certainly did not have the same influence he had commanded in the House.

During his first years in the upper chamber the Marylander conducted himself much as he had in the House. On important party issues such as the Louisiana Purchase, the Twelfth Amendment, and the Louisiana government bill, Smith stood firmly with the administration.[34] But without fanfare he continued to champion commercial interests just as he always had done. In December 1803 the general led

33. *Annals of Congress,* 7th Cong., 2d sess., 1803, p. 517.

34. Ibid., 8th Cong., 1st sess., 1803–1804, pp. 9–256 passim; Plumer, "Proceedings in Congress," December 13, 1803, Plumer Papers; Cunningham, *Jeffersonian Republicans in Power,* pp. 92–93; Samuel Flagg Bemis, *John Quincy Adams and the Foundations of American Foreign Policy* (New York, 1965), pp. 126–127.

the resistance in the Senate to a bill repealing the national bankruptcy act that had been originally passed in 1800. The law had been shown to be unjust and frequently ineffective. Farmers especially felt that under the bankruptcy act they were discriminated against in favor of commerce. Smith admitted that the law had shortcomings but insisted that it was better to modify than to destroy it. If Congress repealed the act, he warned that state governments would pass legislation unpalatable to businessmen. "Gentlemen from commercial cities who are most acquainted with the subject are in favor of the law," he told the Senate, "they know that it is in favor of creditors."[35] Despite his plea, the Senate voted to approve the repeal bill by a vote of nineteen to twelve.[36]

In the fall of 1803 American commerce was once again imperiled as the Napoleonic wars resumed and the belligerents began to reinstate restrictions on neutral carriers. The renewal of the European war placed an immediate strain on the relations between Smith and the administration. Anxious as always to shield American commerce from attack, the Marylander found himself advocating policies not in agreement with those of the president and his advisors. One such clash of opinion took place in the winter of 1803–1804, when President Jefferson informed Congress that Moroccan cruisers had captured American merchant ships in the Mediterranean. The House responded by passing a bill authorizing the president to employ the navy to protect commerce and to issue commissions to privateers allowing them to seize Moroccan vessels. When the bill reached the Senate it was referred to a committee chaired by Smith. Pleased by the tough line adopted by the House, he wasted little time in issuing a report favorable to the bill. Before the Senate could take final action, however, a special message from Jefferson arrived announcing that an agreement had been signed with Morocco. The president's message implied that the legislation before the Senate was no longer necessary, and it was sent back as a matter of procedure to Smith's committee.[37]

Normally nothing more would have been heard of the bill, but Smith had decided it was far too valuable to be lost. Within a few days, as chairman of the committee, Smith reported out an amended version of the bill that would have permitted the navy to protect American commerce from anyone, not merely the Moroccan pirates. In the context of worsening relations with England, the Federalists correctly interpreted the bill to mean that the United States would

35. Plumer, "Proceedings in Congress," December 13, 1803, Plumer Papers.
36. *Annals of Congress*, 8th Cong., 1st sess., 1803, p. 215.
37. Plumer, "Proceedings in Congress," January 18, 1804, Plumer Papers.

resist English interference with its trade and prevent the impressment of sailors on American ships. Great Britain, the Federalists believed, would never retreat from her declared right to keep contraband from the enemy and to reclaim British citizens from neutral ships. War, therefore, would be inevitable.[38] "The provision is in general terms," William Plumer said of Smith's bill, "but it is designed and can operate only, against the British nation."[39] The Federalists were not alone in feeling that the bill was too obviously directed at the British. On February 4, 1804, Wilson Cary Nicholas, also a newcomer to the Senate, told that body that he was "authorized" to say the bill would harm the officially friendly relations between the United States and Great Britain. Furthermore, there were delicate negotiations in progress that would be destroyed if the bill passed. Nicholas then moved to indefinitely postpone consideration of his brother-in-law's bill. Although he had never mentioned the president's name, no one could doubt who had "authorized" Nicholas to speak. Interestingly, Smith did not yield to Jefferson's wishes and vigorously fought the postponement motion. The combined weight of the president and the Federalists finally succeeded in killing the general's bill, but even on the final vote he and nine other Republican senators obstinately refused to give up their support for the measure.[40]

A much more serious difference between Smith and Jefferson occurred in January and February 1805, when the administration moved to curtail American trade with the rebellious French colony of Haiti in the West Indies. American merchants had taken advantage of the protracted Negro revolution on that bloody island to establish trade relations ordinarily prohibited by France. The French had been no more able to suppress this intercourse than to put down the revolt itself. On occasion armed American merchantmen had even fired upon French vessels trying to arrest them for violating the law. Under French diplomatic pressure Jefferson asked Congress to put a stop to the trade, and a bill entitled "an act to regulate the clearance of armed vessels" was soon sent from the House of Representatives to the Senate. The measure prohibited all armed American ships from sailing to the West Indies unless their owners deposited funds with the government equal to twice the value of the ship and cargo as a guarantee that their arms would not be used for illegal purposes. Republican senators who were merchants themselves or closely con-

---

38. Plumer, "Proceedings in Congress," February 28, 1804, Plumer Papers.
39. Plumer, "Proceedings in Congress," February 29, 1804, Plumer Papers.
40. *Annals of Congress*, 8th Cong., 1st sess., 1804, p. 264.

nected with mercantile interests in their states joined the Federalists in deploring the legislation.[41]

The armed-vessels bill was sent to a special Senate committee headed by Samuel Smith. On January 21 he returned the measure to the Senate with an amendment striking out every part of the bill save the enacting clause. For a few days Smith verged on the brink of a complete and irreconcilable break with the administration. Many wondered how Smith could remain in the Republican party after such an open disavowal of a presidentially sponsored bill. Following a heated debate the Smith amendment was defeated by three votes. Besides the general, four other Republicans and eight Federalists comprised the minority.[42] Smith did not take the outcome of the vote with good grace. "It appeared," the Marylander was overheard to say by one Federalist senator, "that our Executive were more anxious to restrain our commerce, lest our merchants should by some means injure the French government, than they were to demand from France the millions they had wantonly robbed from our merchants."[43] Opponents of the armed-vessels bill vainly tried for the next two weeks to soften some of its more stringent provisions, but on February 22 the Senate approved the measure without amendment. The president had made the bill a test of party loyalty, and the Republican dissidents, despite their reservations, finally fell into line and voted for the law.[44]

On March 4, 1805, Jefferson took the oath of office for the second time. He and his party could look back on four years of dazzling success. The country was more populous, more wealthy, and more united than it had been four years earlier. The physical size of the nation had been doubled by the Louisiana Purchase. Party strife had been more subdued than at any time since 1791, and Republican majorities in Congress had grown to the point that only a corporal's guard of Federalists remained. For the most part Samuel Smith had been in the mainstream of developments. As a representative and a senator he had been in the front rank of the Republican party's leadership. For four years he had participated in the exercise of power; but Jefferson's first term would turn out to be only an interlude in a political career characterized by vigorous independence. The re-

41. Plumer, "Proceedings in Congress," January 10, 1805, Plumer Papers; *Annals of Congress*, 8th Cong., 2d sess., 1805, pp. 34–39.

42. *Annals of Congress*, 8th Cong., 2d sess., 1805, p. 49.

43. Plumer, "Proceedings in Congress," February 5, 1805, Plumer Papers.

44. Plumer, "Proceedings in Congress," February 22, 1805, Plumer Papers; *Annals of Congress*, 8th Cong., 2d sess., 1805, pp. 50–63.

sumption of hostilities in Europe signaled an end to the generally happy relationship between the Marylander and the national Republican party. As the figures for American ships seized by the belligerents mounted, Smith's dissatisfaction with the administration's handling of the crisis grew. For four years he had reconciled the dilemma of being both a merchant and a Republican. It was an open question as to how much longer he would be able to bridge the ever-widening chasm between the two.[45]

45. See Samuel Flagg Bemis, *A Diplomatic History of the United States* (New York, 1936), p. 140.

9

Critic of the President

THE TRANSFER of the national capital to Washington in 1800 had both advantages and disadvantages for Samuel Smith. While he could now travel from his home to Congress in less than a day, he found living conditions in Washington primitive compared to those in Philadelphia. During his first years in the new capital, Smith, like most congressmen, resided in one of the boarding houses clustered about Capitol Hill. In 1801 he stayed at Conrad's, located to the south of the Capitol overlooking the Potomac River. Among his fellow boarders was Thomas Jefferson, who remained until he moved into the president's mansion. For one year, 1802, the general roomed in Mrs. Williams' boarding house along with several other prominent Republicans, including Vice President Aaron Burr, John Randolph of Virginia, De Witt Clinton of New York, Robert Wright of Maryland, and Wilson Cary Nicholas. Sometime in 1803 Smith built a house in the vicinity of Capitol Hill, which permitted Margaret to stay with him during the four or five months a year the congressional session usually lasted.[1]

Washington as Samuel Smith knew it in the first decade of the nineteenth century was not an impressive community save for its natural scenic beauty. In 1804 its population, even counting nearby Georgetown, was less than seven thousand. The British chargé

1. John Randolph's Diary, September 3, 1802, Virginia State Library, Richmond; Gaillard Hunt, ed., *The First Forty Years of Washington Society* (New York, 1906), pp. 9–10.

d'affaires, Augustus Foster, reported that the city had no streets. He described Washington as being mostly wilderness, adding that he had found the snipe-hunting good around Capitol Hill. The absence of passable roads made movement around Washington difficult and, as contemporary records show, hazardous. Carriage accidents with serious injuries to the passengers were not unusual; Margaret Smith had nearly died in one such accident while visiting her husband in 1802. In sharp contrast to the general crudeness of Washington were the magnificent chambers in which the two houses of Congress met. Smith and his senatorial colleagues held their sessions in a room that one member pictured as "large, elegant, and well furnished." In the chamber each senator sat in a mahogany chair behind a writing table piled high with reference books and printed copies of pending bills. The desks were arranged in a semicircle around a canopied platform from which the president of the Senate presided. As a senator, Smith was entitled to writing paper, free use of the mails, and subscriptions to eighteen weekly newspapers of his choice.[2]

When not engaged in the nation's business Smith participated in Washington's sometimes glittering social life. His position in government as well as in the Republican party made him a much-sought-after guest. He dined frequently with the president and attended parties given by Cabinet officers and diplomatic representatives. Apparently the general enjoyed these social interludes, for at least one prominent lady recalled that his "pleasantry & wit" had enlivened a recent party. The Smiths themselves entertained on a grand scale at tremendous cost. The general estimated that between June 1803 and July 1804 his expenses in Washington had been $10,000, of which a large portion had gone for dinners and parties.[3]

If Samuel and Margaret tired of Washington, and the general's work permitted, they could easily make the journey back to Baltimore. With over thirty-five thousand inhabitants in 1805, Baltimore had much more to offer in the way of theaters and shops than did Washington. Proximity to Baltimore also meant that Smith could keep up with his responsibilities in the militia and at S. Smith & Buchanan. Under his partner, James Buchanan, the firm had continued to prosper.

2. Augustus Foster, Notes on the U. S. of A. [1804], pp. 11, 22–23, Augustus Foster Papers, James A. Bayard to Andrew Bayard, February 26, 1802, James A. Bayard Papers, and William Plumer's Autobiography, December 1803, William Plumer Papers, Library of Congress.

3. Margaret Bayard Smith to unknown recipient, February 8, 1801, Mrs. Samuel H. Smith Papers, Library of Congress; S. Smith to Wilson Cary Nicholas, July 21, 1804, Wilson Cary Nicholas Papers, University of Virginia Library.

Although the war in Europe was beginning to affect American trade, the company was still making sizable profits, especially by reexporting to England coffee originally purchased in the West Indies for Maryland wheat. However pleasant, the trips to Baltimore were still luxuries for the general, and there were times when his duties as a legislator kept him close to his desk in the Senate chamber. Certainly one of those times was in the winter of 1805–1806, when the United States once again had to face the problem of remaining at peace in a world at war.[4]

The convening of the first session of the Ninth Congress in December 1805 was of more than usual interest to Smith. Not only was he concerned about growing French and British interference with American commerce, but also he was worried about his relations with the administration, which had become strained during the past year. With some relief he discovered that his position in the Republican party was still secure. Indeed, the Republican majority in the Senate felt no qualms in choosing Smith president pro tem, an honor that surprised and embarrassed him. Of more practical importance, Jefferson and the administration continued to respect his requests for patronage. Soon, however, developments in America's foreign relations created new issues over which Smith and the president disagreed and which threatened to drive the Marylander out of the party.[5]

The first foreign crisis faced by the new Congress involved not English and French attacks on American commerce but rather a dispute with Spain over the location of the Florida border. The terms of the Louisiana Purchase had been aggravatingly vague about the southern boundary of the territory, giving rise to conflicting claims on the part of Spain and the United States. By the end of 1805 both sides were near the point of using armed force to seize and hold the disputed areas. Jefferson, in his annual address to Congress in late December, had announced that American army units had been put on alert along the Florida border and warned that clashes with Spanish troops were possible. Republicans cheered the president's "energetic

4. S. Smith to W. C. Nicholas, August 22, 1804, Nicholas Papers, University of Virginia Library; *Federal Gazette & Baltimore Daily Advertiser*, September 29, 1803.

5. Diary of Plumer, December 2, 1805, Plumer Papers; S. Smith to unknown recipient, Smith Letterbook, Library of Congress; U.S., Congress, *The Debates and Proceedings in the Congress of the United States . . . 1789–1824*, 42 vols. (Washington, D.C., 1834–1856), 9th Cong., 1st sess., 1805, p. 10, hereafter cited as *Annals of Congress*; S. Smith to Thomas Jefferson, January 22 and December 28, 1806, Samuel Smith Papers, Library of Congress.

and warlike" attitude, but excitement turned to dismay a few days later when Jefferson sent Congress a secret message on the Florida question. In this second communication the president urged a different course of action, asserting that war with Spain was neither necessary nor probable. Instead of asking for funds to increase the size of the army, he suggested that through the good offices of France, Spain might be persuaded to sell Florida. Many Republicans were stunned by the apparent duplicity of Jefferson's strategy and objected to the way the public was being misled. In the House of Representatives an administration bill appropriating two million dollars, intended as bribes for French officials to facilitate the proposed sale, passed over the stiffest resistance, as John Randolph led a small group of Republicans into permanent opposition to the administration.[6]

In January 1806 the appropriations bill reached the Senate, where Smith and several other Republican senators expressed criticism. Republican Stephen Bradley of Vermont challenged the president's preoccupation with obtaining Florida by offering an amendment to the bill which specified that the money could also be used to purchase Canada. Smith supported the Bradley proposal, reasoning that the port of Halifax, home of the British fleet harassing American shipping and impressing American seamen, was worth far more to the United States than Florida. The Marylander also made plain his dislike for the plan to spend two million dollars on bribing French ministers. The scheme, Smith contended, required absolute secrecy, yet every diplomat in Washington knew of the two million bill and its purpose; it would now be better and probably cheaper to openly approach Spain with an offer. Besides, he argued, the country could ill-afford to squander so much money on such a risky venture when funds were badly needed for the defense establishment. The two million bill confronted Smith with the same dilemma as the president's efforts to close the Haitian trade a year before. He either had to support a measure he disapproved of or break with Jefferson. Finally, after strongly condemning the appropriations bill on the floor of the Senate, he simply walked out of the chamber refusing to vote for or against the measure. Several Republican senators found the strain on their loyalty too great; six of them voted for the Bradley amendment, six

6. *Annals of Congress,* 9th Cong., 1st sess., 1805, p. 12; Diary of Plumer, December 3, 1805, Plumer Papers; *Annals of Congress,* 9th Cong., 1st sess., 1805, pp. 18–19; Norman K. Risjord, *The Old Republicans* (New York, 1965), pp. 46–50.

to reduce the amount of the appropriation, and three against final passage of the bill.[7]

Even after the two million bill had been signed into law, Smith continued to denounce it. He told one senator that the act had "thrown an immense responsibility on the President," who, he prophesied, "will endanger his popularity."[8] Two months later he was still proclaiming to his correspondents that the matter of the Florida purchase had been badly handled by the administration. In one letter he said: "There has been much folly in the business, much imbecility."[9] In May the general wrote Wilson Cary Nicholas that Jefferson's plot to buy Florida was "Machiavellian." Smith was not made any happier when the president reopened the question of trade with the Negro revolutionaries of Haiti.[10]

Just before Christmas of 1805 Republican George Logan, at the request of Jefferson, asked the Senate's permission to bring in a bill prohibiting all trade with the black republic in the West Indies. Logan justified this new legislation as a necessary supplement to the armed-ships legislation of the previous year. That law, he said, had not halted the illegal traffic between the United States and Haiti. Samuel Smith combined forces with Senator John Quincy Adams of Massachusetts in trying to keep the bill from even being considered by the Senate. Observing that Logan had not brought forward any evidence proving the new law was necessary, the Marylander reminded the Senate that since the armed-ships law went into effect France had made no further formal complaints about the trade. Smith refused to accept Logan's contention that the American trade with Haiti violated the law of nations. Since Haiti was in fact free of French domination, trade with the island was legitimate. Furthermore, he noted, the Haitian trade annually brought $200,000 in revenue to the United States treasury. To end commercial relations would thus be costly as well as a dishonorable concession to French power. Once again, however, Smith said a great deal and did nothing. The Senate voted to consider the bill and then passed it on February 20, 1806. On both occasions the general voted with his party.[11] It was not party loyalty,

7. Diary of Plumer, January 30 and February 3 and 7, 1806, Plumer Papers; *Annals of Congress,* 9th Cong., 1st sess., 1806, pp. 80–81, 86–87.

8. Diary of Plumer, February 8, 1806, Plumer Papers.

9. S. Smith to unknown recipient, April 29, 1806, Smith Letterbook.

10. S. Smith to W. C. Nicholas, May 16, 1806, Smith-Carter Papers, University of Virginia Library.

11. *Annals of Congress,* 9th Cong., 1st sess., 1805–1806, pp. 26–31, 41, 52.

however, but worsening relations with England that explained his strange behavior. He was unwilling to antagonize the French at a time when the full energies of the nation would be needed to confront the British. "Pressed as we are by other nations," he argued, "it may be good policy for us to make Friends."[12]

The Maryland senator's preoccupation with the British was understandable. In the summer of 1805 the English courts had handed down the famous *Essex* decision that reversed previous rulings. Henceforth American shippers must prove that when they imported enemy goods into the United States it was done in good faith and not as a device to avoid compliance with English laws prohibiting neutrals from carrying cargoes from one enemy port to another. Part of a plan to drive United States merchantmen from the oceans, the *Essex* decision was potentially a devastating blow at the huge American reexport trade. If rigorously enforced, the ruling would prevent United States vessels from any longer picking up cargoes in the Spanish and French colonies and, after paying nominal import duties in the United States, transshipping them to European ports past the British blockade. Even more offensive to the Americans was the high-handed manner in which the new interpretation was implemented. Long before the *Essex* decision was known in the United States, the Royal Navy began arresting scores of American ships in the West Indies for violating a law they did not know existed.[13]

News of the mass seizures soon reached American ports, and indignant merchants began sending petitions to Congress complaining of "ruinous interference" with their trade by the British.[14] Sympathetic to the plight of the merchants, Smith was initially pessimistic that Congress would take any action. "It is indeed a mortifying thing," Smith lamented, "that we cannot in an effectual manner resent the Insults and Injuries of G.B." He told friends that nothing would be done because of the "agriculturalists" who controlled the government and who "have no idea of honor, dignity, or use of National Character."[15] The Marylander was temporarily buoyed, however, by the hard language of the president and Secretary of State Madison in regard to the recent aggressions. In January of 1806 Madison distributed a report to Congress carefully refuting the British justifications

---

12. S. Smith to unknown recipient, January 30, 1806, Smith Letterbook.

13. Bradford Perkins, *Prologue to War; England and the United States, 1805–1812* (Berkeley, 1963), pp. 80–83.

14. See, for example, *Annals of Congress*, 9th Cong., 1st sess., 1806, pp. 45, 51–52.

15. S. Smith to unknown recipient, December 16, 1805, Smith Letterbook.

for infringing on the rights of neutral commerce and impressing American seamen. A month earlier in his annual address, Jefferson had also mentioned the renewed crisis with Britain. He had asked Congress for an increase in the naval establishment and a reorganization of the militia system to make it more efficient.[16]

Although Smith wanted much more in the way of military preparations, he welcomed the president's recommendations, especially the one concerning the militia system. Having for many years been a proponent of militia reform, he was able to present a plan to the Senate almost immediately. His elaborate scheme, one he had been pushing since 1796, would have created a number of categories within the structure of the militia to which men were to be assigned on the basis of age. The single most important innovation of the plan was a provision permitting the president to call up for duty some part of the militia on his own authority. Smith also insisted that all militia had to be better armed and disciplined. If adopted, the Smith plan of militia reform would eventually have provided the United States with a military force adequate to its needs and therefore would have reduced the need for a larger standing army. The administration, however, did not throw its weight behind the general's proposal, backing away from the clearly understood policy stated in Jefferson's annual address. Without the president's approval, Smith's militia bill was doomed. Other defense bills submitted in response to Jefferson's call for military preparedness shared a similar fate. The Marylander voted with the minority in favor of measures to build more harbor fortifications, to construct naval ships-of-the-line, and to add three hundred thousand men to the regular army. It was understandable why Smith once again concluded that the "agriculturalists" cared very little for American commerce.[17]

If the president would not act with dispatch to protect American commerce as well as to end the illegal impressment of American seamen by the British, Smith and other congressmen decided that the legislature must take on the burden. Assuming the lead in the Senate, the general reintroduced on February 12 a resolution he had first proposed a decade earlier during the Jay Treaty debates. It provided for a ban on foreign ships landing any goods in the United States that were not of the growth or manufacture of the country to which the ships belonged. Vessels of nations that did not discriminate against the American reexport trade were to be exempt. Once more the

16. *Annals of Congress*, 9th Cong., 1st sess., 1805–1806, pp. 12–13, 69.

17. Ibid., pp. 17, 21–22, 25, 27–31, 36; Diary of John Quincy Adams, February 25, 1806, Adams Family Papers, Massachusetts Historical Society.

only country that could possibly be affected by such a law was England. Smith wished to force England to stop its attacks on the American reexport trade by threatening to curtail the profitable arrangement by which British ships brought cargoes from all parts of the globe to American ports. Many in the Senate thought the law a desirable one, but the president did not give it his support and the bill died in committee.[18]

With his usual energy, Smith shifted his attention to a new and even more promising project: a nonimportation law directed against Great Britain. The idea was not new, of course, but it had been used effectively in the past and both Jefferson and Madison were much attracted to economic coercion as an alternative to war. Smith could hopefully anticipate a favorable reception from the administration for a nonimportation bill. The House of Representatives already had before it a resolution calling for an end to the importing of British goods. The author of the resolution was Andrew Gregg of Pennsylvania who, like Smith, was trying to fill the vacuum in leadership left by Jefferson and Madison. Smith's own plan for nonimportation, submitted to the Senate in February of 1806, differed from Gregg's in that it was selective. Rather than keeping out all British goods, the Smith bill singled out important manufactured items such as linen, shoes, hats, nails, and windows. Smith contended that total nonimportation of British goods would deprive the United States of essential revenues, but selective discrimination against British products that might be purchased elsewhere would cost less and hurt England as much.[19]

Convinced of the merits of his nonimportation bill, the Marylander personally contacted Secretary of the Treasury Gallatin and Secretary of State Madison in a futile effort to win the administration's endorsement. Smith, now aware that he would get no assistance from the executive branch, insisted on presenting his nonimportation scheme to the Senate in the form of a resolution. The upper house responded favorably on February 12 and a month later the general brought in his plan as a bill. With unusual eloquence Smith defended nonimportation as a means to preserve the American reexport trade, a trade he considered essential to the nation's economic well-being. The United States historically had an unfavorable balance of trade with

18. *Annals of Congress,* 9th Cong., 1st sess., 1806, p. 90; Diary of Adams, Adams Papers.

19. *Annals of Congress,* 9th Cong., 1st sess., 1806, p. 413; S. Smith to James Madison, February 1806, James Madison Papers, Library of Congress; S. Smith to unknown recipient, December 16, 1805, Smith Letterbook.

England, and only the reexport trade allowed the country to over-come this imbalance and pay its debts. Smith's bill would very likely have passed the Senate if the administration had not bestirred itself to active opposition. Apparently fearing that the Gregg and Smith bills were too strong, the president and his advisors sought to defeat them by initiating a nonimportation proposal of their own, and both houses of Congress quickly accepted the substitution. Although Senator Smith voted for the administration's nonimportation measure, he recognized that it had little more than symbolic value. In its final version the law prohibited the importation of English silk, tin, leather, and a few other products that altogether constituted a small per-centage of the goods normally bought from Britain. The law was not even to take effect for nine months and then was delayed again until December 1808. Smith could emphatically agree with John Randolph, who styled the measure as a "milk and water bill," and with William Plumer, who believed the law had not "sufficient energy" to affect British policy but might bring retaliation.[20]

Up to this point Samuel Smith had reacted to the second British crisis as he had to the first a dozen years before. Then, too, he had forcefully backed measures for increasing the nation's military capacity and to pressure England by economic coercion. By proving to England that the United States was prepared to fight in defense of its interests, the Marylander had hoped John Jay could obtain concessions in peaceful negotiations. Jay's Treaty (with all its weaknesses) had avoided war and freed American commerce from British assaults for the better part of a decade. Now, in 1806, Smith, along with many others in Congress, fervently hoped that the earlier pattern could be reproduced. Yet they were stymied by the lack of decisive leader-ship from the executive. Whereas Washington and Hamilton had generated ideas and then worked with their supporters in the legis-lature to gain Congressional approval, Jefferson and Madison seemed paralyzed. Whether true or not, a substantial number of congressmen, including Samuel Smith, appeared to feel there had been an abdi-cation of responsibility by the president and that if the country was to be saved they must be the ones to do it. It thus became the object of many, if not a majority, of the legislators to force Jefferson to follow in George Washington's footsteps and combine anti-British legislation with diplomatic initiatives to end the confrontation between the two

20. S. Smith to Madison, February 1806, Madison Papers; *Annals of Congress,* 9th Cong., 1st sess., 1806, pp. 90–91, 161–164, 232, 451, 557; Diary of Adams, March 10, 1806, Adams Papers; Perkins, *Prologue to War,* pp. 108, 112; Plumer to John Goddard, April 14, 1806, Plumer Papers.

nations. This attitude was most clearly expressed in the three resolutions drafted by a Senate committee chaired by Smith. The first
resolution condemned as illegal the Rule of 1756, that piece of
unilateral British legislation which prohibited any trade in wartime
not also permitted in peacetime. It was under this law that so many
American ships in the French and Spanish West Indies had been
seized. The second resolution requested the president to enter into
negotiations with Great Britain and demand restitution for American
losses. The third resolution had been Smith's nonimportation plan,
and was meant to give the president something to bargain with.
Drafted by Smith and John Quincy Adams, the three resolutions comprised a coherent policy almost identical with that followed by
Washington and the Federalists in 1794 and 1795—save that now
Congress and not the president had assumed the lead.[21]

With the exception of the third resolution, which Jefferson managed
to block, the Smith-Adams coalition was remarkably successful. The
first resolution, which did little more than repeat the main points of
Madison's report on neutral trade, passed easily. The second resolution,
calling on Jefferson to send a new diplomatic mission to London, was
far more controversial. Many Republican senators felt it would be
improper for the Senate to dictate to the president that he should
send ministers and conduct negotiations. They pointed out that
Jefferson had already stated publicly that negotiations with England
would be fruitless and therefore the resolution might compel him to
take actions he deemed not in the national interest. As the debate
raged, Smith remained silent, leaving the defense of the resolution to
others. The most important vote took place on February 13, 1806,
when a motion was made to strike out the essential provisions of the
resolution. Party lines blurred as thirteen Republicans and one
Federalist voted for the motion while nine Republicans and seven
Federalists voted against it. The next day by a vote of twenty-three to
seven the resolution received Senate approval. Only six of the nineteen
Republican senators opposed the measure, an indication of how much
influence Jefferson had lost among his own party.[22]

It is difficult to see the passage of the second resolution as anything
but a vote of no-confidence in the president. During the debates one

21. *Annals of Congress,* 9th Cong., 1st sess., 1806, pp. 101, 190–191; Diary
of Adams, January 31 and February 1 and 5, 1806, Adams Papers. In his recent
book, *The Democratic Republic, 1801–1815* (New York, 1968), pp. 151–156,
Marshall Smelser takes a much less pessimistic view of Jefferson's leadership in
this period.
22. *Annals of Congress,* 9th Cong., 1st sess., 1806, pp. 90–112.

SAMUEL SMITH,
C. 1788–1793.

*By Charles Willson
Peale. Independence
National Historical
Park Collection,
Philadelphia.*

MONTEBELLO.

By W. Birch. Copy from original owned by Maryland Historical Society, Baltimore.

GENERAL AND MRS. SAMUEL SMITH, C. 1800.

*By William Edward West after Gilbert Stuart. Collection of Maryland
Historical Society, Baltimore.*

ASSEMBLY OF THE TROOPS, HAMPSTEAD HILL, SEPTEMBER 1814.

By Thomas Ruckle. Copy from original owned by Maryland Historical Society, Baltimore.

SAMUEL SMITH, AGE EIGHTY-FOUR.

By unknown American artist. Collection of Maryland Historical Society, Baltimore.

Republican had gone so far as to refer to the measure as censuring Jefferson's conduct. Smith, among others, was not deterred by charges of deserting the party in a time of need. The Marylander had come to view the president not as a party leader nor even chief executive, but as a barrier to vitally necessary steps to protect American property and honor. To one fellow senator Smith confided that Jefferson had to be pushed into negotiations for he was too "timid" to begin them himself.[23] Republican senator George Logan, recently one of Jefferson's closest aides in the upper chamber, shared the Marylander's misgivings. "I have no confidence in the President," he was overheard to say, "he will not negotiate unless we resolve it is necessary—He has shamefully neglected the interests of this nation by not making a treaty with Great Britain years ago."[24] The open avowal of such sentiment underlined the loss of rapport between Jefferson and the Senate Republicans.

Having passed the second resolution, the Senate elected a committee to convey it to the president. Those receiving the most ballots were Samuel Smith and Samuel Latham Mitchill of New York. The two men met with Jefferson in the president's house for a conference none of the participants could have relished. Smith and Jefferson both agreed that the meeting was unpleasant. The president remembered that the committee had not only given him the resolution but emphasized the strong feeling behind it in the Senate. Under the pressures of the moment Jefferson admitted losing his temper and angrily rejecting the Senate's request. Smith reported to Wilson Cary Nicholas that the chief executive had received the committee "cooly" and had given Smith and Mitchill reason to believe "he would not take the advice."[25] In practice the president could not so easily dismiss the Senate's resolution, especially because most Republican senators had voted for it. When the House of Representatives seconded the Senate's call for a mission to Britain, Jefferson could do nothing but comply. "I found it necessary, at length," he wrote the current American minister in London, James Monroe, "to yield up my own opinion to the general sense of the national council."[26] Although worse was yet to come, the fortunes

23. Ibid., p. 95; Diary of Plumer, February 13, 1806, Plumer Papers.

24. George Logan to Jefferson, March 12, 1806, George Logan Papers, Historical Society of Pennsylvania, Philadelphia.

25. *Annals of Congress,* 9th Cong., 1st sess., 1806, p. 138; Jefferson to James Monroe, March 10, 1808, in Paul Leicester Ford, ed., *The Writings of Thomas Jefferson,* 10 vols. (New York, 1892–1899), 9: 179; S. Smith to W. C. Nicholas, March 11, 1806, Smith-Carter Papers.

26. Jefferson to Monroe, March 10, 1808, in Ford, ed., *Writings of Jefferson,* 9: 179.

of Thomas Jefferson and the Republican party had clearly plummeted to their lowest point since the Alien and Sedition Acts. While the executive and legislative branches fought each other instead of the British, the national government was becoming thoroughly disorganized, and the Republican party itself was in shambles, the congressional wing of the party standing in open rebellion to the policies of the president.

The arrival of warm spring weather in Washington found Samuel Smith in the midst of a personal crisis. More than ever he wanted the government to do something about the British fleets that had virtually blockaded every American port, seizing American ships and sailors at will within sight of land. The reluctance of Jefferson to assist American trade had driven the Marylander farther and farther from the president. During the winter months of 1805 and 1806 he had disagreed with every facet of the administration's foreign policy and had been a leader among those in Congress who had tried to circumscribe the president's freedom of action. Nevertheless, he had avoided public attacks on Jefferson and therefore had stayed within the Republican party, if such a structure can be said to have been present in 1806. In March and April his tenuous connection with the administration was strained even more by what he considered to be personal slights by the president.

Following congressional approval of the Two Million Act, Jefferson had nominated John Armstrong, the American minister to France, and the veteran diplomat James Bowdoin to be ministers plenipotentiary to Spain; their assignment was to induce Spain to sell Florida to the United States. Rumors circulated through Congress, however, that Jefferson would soon appoint a third member to the mission and that Samuel Smith was his choice. When the Senate took up the Spanish nominations, it promptly approved the uncontroversial Bowdoin, but John Armstrong was a different matter. His performance as minister to France had been faulted by many who felt that he had not been aggressive enough in prosecuting American claims for damages arising from the quasiwar. Samuel Smith was known to be disgruntled with Armstrong's handling of the *New Jersey* case. Owned by a Baltimore firm, the *New Jersey* had been seized by the French, and Armstrong had failed to negotiate a satisfactory settlement to cover the loss. Smith told one fellow senator that he suspected Armstrong had not pressed the *New Jersey* issue because he and his in-laws, the powerful Livingston clan of New York, stood to benefit financially if other claims were given precedence. The Senate, as a sign to the president of its displeasure with Armstrong, delayed acting on the appointment and named a special committee to inquire into the New Yorker's fitness. The committee, of which Smith was a member, returned with a report unfavorable to Armstrong. When the Senate again took up the nomination, the Marylander led the fight to defeat it. On March 15, 1806, the Senate finally balloted, and by the deciding vote of Vice President George Clinton, also a New Yorker, consented to the nomination. Besides Smith, over one-third of the Republican members had defected from the president; and, if John Quincy Adams can be believed, there were many others who would have liked to vote nay. Vice President Clinton told Jefferson that the antipathy toward Armstrong in the Senate was so great that "any treaty made by him would be in danger."[27]

Because of his opposition to Armstrong's nomination, as well as his loudly expressed dislike of the Two Million Act, Smith probably would not have accepted a place on the Spanish mission. What injured his pride was that after all the rumors of an impending appointment none had been offered. Jefferson tried to soothe the general's feelings by letting it be known that only his attacks on Armstrong had prevented his designation as one of the ministers. But Smith learned from his brother Robert, who as secretary of the navy had attended all the Cabinet sessions, that his name had not even been mentioned for the post.[28] Jefferson's gesture had done far more harm than good. Smith was not only disappointed, but also convinced the president had perjured himself. "There are such things as the lie downright, the fib, and the white lie," he angrily told Wilson Cary Nicholas, "which of these were the case you will decide for yourself, when the P. said I had been thought of."[29]

Smith had also entertained hopes that the president would appoint him to the diplomatic mission soon destined to start negotiations in London. In view of the Marylander's role in pressuring the president to open the talks, his expectations of a reward from Jefferson were unrealistic. Nevertheless, reports that a merchant would be sent along as part of the mission and that Samuel Smith had been selected came from several sources in and out of Congress. Robert told him that in

27. *Journal of the Executive Proceedings of the Senate . . . 1789–1948*, 90 vols. (Washington, D.C., 1828–1948), 2: 25, 26, 29; hereafter cited as *Senate Journal;* Diary of Plumer, March 17 and 18, 1806, Plumer Papers; Irving Brant, *James Madison; Secretary of State, 1800–1809* (New York, 1953), p. 361; Diary of Adams, March 12, 13, and 17, 1806, Adams Papers; S. Smith to W. C. Nicholas, March 21, 1806, Smith-Carter Papers.

28. S. Smith to W. C. Nicholas, May 16, 1806, Smith-Carter Papers; Jefferson to W. C. Nicholas, April 13, 1806, in Ford, ed., *Writings of Jefferson*, 8: 435.

29. S. Smith to W. C. Nicholas, May 16, 1806, Smith-Carter Papers.

one Cabinet meeting the president had asserted a "practical merchant of talent" must be named to the mission. But when the nominations reached the Senate, Smith's name was not among them. In letter after letter to his brother-in-law, Wilson Cary Nicholas, he poured out his feelings of anger and mortification at being passed over. "Everybody expected such an offer to me," one note to Nicholas read, "the question was, will he accept?"[30] Three weeks later Smith returned to the same theme: "I could but ask myself what have I not done to serve these men?"[31] If given an opportunity to answer this last question, the president might have had a great deal to say.

To Smith's further humiliation Jefferson chose William Pinkney, a Maryland Federalist, to join James Monroe in London to conduct the forthcoming negotiations. Seemingly the president had gone out of his way to reprimand Smith for his recent antiadministration activities. Not only had he refused to name the general to the London mission, but also he had picked instead a man from the opposite party who was a local political enemy of Smith's. The Marylander protested Pinkney's appointment as a blow to the morale of the Republican party. He charged the president with saying in effect that he "could not find a man fit for a minister to London in all his party." With more reason he claimed the Pinkney nomination had visibly strengthened the Federalist party in Maryland. By April of 1806 the long-standing friendship between Jefferson and Smith had ended. Driven apart by policy differences and political ambition, the two men no longer communicated with each other directly, preferring to use Wilson Cary Nicholas as an intermediary.[32]

During the next year, while Pinkney and Monroe talked with the British government, Smith maintained a sullen silence, at least in public. Congress could do little until the envoys had agreed upon a treaty, and one, it was hoped, that would remove the British cruisers operating at the entrances of every American port. On most issues that came before the Senate in this period Smith supported the Republican position but almost without comment. Nothing but habit, the absence of new issues, and the hope that Monroe and Pinkney would be successful kept the Marylander from severing his ties with the party.[33]

In private letters written during these long months of political iso-

30. Ibid.
31. S. Smith to W. C. Nicholas, April 8, 1806, Smith-Carter Papers.
32. Ibid.; S. Smith to W. C. Nicholas, May 24, 1806, Edgehill-Randolph Papers, University of Virginia Library.
33. S. Smith to W. C. Nicholas, April 7, 1806, Nicholas Papers, University of Virginia Library; Risjord, *The Old Republicans,* pp. 40–71.

lation, Smith continued to speak harshly of Jefferson and the manner in which he had been treated. He referred admiringly to John Randolph of Roanoke, who also had been alienated by Jefferson and who, with several other congressmen, had left the Republican party. Blessed with great ability and a gift for oratory, the former majority leader had caused the administration infinite embarrassment. Conceivably, Smith might have seen in Randolph an example of what course he should pursue in the Senate; it must have been a temptation to join the eccentric Virginian in heaping public sarcasm on Jefferson and Madison. But Smith, unlike Randolph, was no ideologue so committed to his principles that he could not bend or compromise. Smith too had principles, but he had learned to be flexible in the tactics he used to fulfill them. While it was not out of the question that he might become a schismatic, things were not yet so bad as to justify the sacrifice of the perquisites he enjoyed as a powerful figure in the ruling party. To become a schismatic meant an end to patronage, the opportunity to influence policy, and the chance that at some future time the president might appoint him to a diplomatic position. So while he privately applauded Randolph's "manly language" in criticizing the president, the general carefully avoided making the same error that had left the Virginian a loud but quite powerless figure.[34]

In February of 1807 news reached Smith that the treaty with England upon which he and many others placed such great hopes was nearly completed. He learned from Robert, who habitually reported Cabinet secrets to his brother, that even though the president had not seen the full text, he had already decided not to accept it since the issue of impressment had not been resolved. Jefferson confirmed Robert's information on March 3, 1807, when he advised a Senate committee that the treaty was so exceptionable he would not even send it to the upper chamber.[35] The president's decision upset Smith, since the negotiation had been held at least in part because of his labors, and he had placed great faith in a treaty as a means to free American commerce from British attack. Although he had not read the treaty, Smith's first reaction to Jefferson's announcement was to suspect the president of suppressing it for personal reasons. "It is well known that he was coerced by the Senate to the measure," the Mary-

34. S. Smith to W. C. Nicholas, March 11, 1806, Smith-Carter Papers; S. Smith to unknown recipient, March 5, 1806, Smith Letterbook.

35. Henry Clay to William Prentiss, February 13, 1807, in James F. Hopkins, ed., *The Papers of Henry Clay*, 2 vols. (Lexington, Ky., 1959), 1: 280; Robert Smith to S. Smith, February 9, 1807, Smith Papers; Diary of Adams, March 3, 1807, Adams Papers; Diary of Plumer, March 4, 1807, Plumer Papers.

lander wrote Nicholas, "and he refuses to submit it to their approbation—what a responsibility he takes!!"[36] Smith warned Nicholas that Jefferson ran grave political risks. If because of his rejection of the treaty the British continued or increased their depredations on American trade, then "what will be the outcry?"[37]

On March 14 Smith wrote Secretary of State Madison, repeating in more muted language what he had told his brother-in-law. Madison responded by sending the Marylander a copy of the treaty and asked for his opinion. Smith, who had known only generally what the treaty contained, was amazed at the severity of the commercial provisions. He judged they would have been more injurious to American trade than the Jay Treaty had been. Presumably the Marylander felt at least mildly chagrined that he had thought and said so much about the administration before he had had the facts. He frankly admitted to Madison that he would never have voted for the treaty, but insisted that the president should have allowed the Senate to make its own judgment. The effort to end the crisis with Britain by peaceful negotiation had collapsed, and in its aftermath there was a tentative reconciliation between the president and some of his Republican critics —including Samuel Smith. Because the British refused to make substantive concessions to the Americans, the long-simmering controversy had escalated into an immediate emergency. Relations had deteriorated to the point where war could begin at any time. In these new circumstances the Republicans began to rally around Jefferson, temporarily burying their differences in order to face the challenge to the nation's safety.[38]

Smith's alienation from the Republican party leadership ended suddenly and dramatically in the final days of June 1807. Newspapers in every state carried stories describing a naval encounter between the newly commissioned United States frigate *Chesapeake* and the British warship *Leopard*. On June 22 the *Leopard* met the *Chesapeake* in international waters, and the British captain demanded that the commander of the American vessel surrender several deserters from the Royal Navy. Although his ship's guns were unmounted, the American officer refused. The *Leopard* responded with a broadside that severely damaged the *Chesapeake* and killed several sailors; a boarding party then removed several seamen alleged to be deserters.

36. S. Smith to W. C. Nicholas, March 4, 1807, Thomas Jefferson Papers, Coolidge Collection, Massachusetts Historical Society.
37. Ibid.
38. S. Smith to Madison, March 14, April 3, and April 18, 1807, Smith Letterbook.

Throughout the United States citizens congregated to protest the atrocity. In cities from Boston to Charleston mass meetings drew up petitions to the president urging him to retaliate promptly.[39] For Smith there was no question as to what his role should be. A week after the attack he penned two letters to James Madison. The first reported on a large public meeting in Baltimore called to condemn the British action; the general had been its chairman. "I deemed it prudent," he told the secretary of state, "to take the lead to which the voice [of the crowd] unanimously called me."[40] Smith related that the assembly had agreed on two resolutions, which were being sent to the president. He assured Madison that most people in Baltimore would support any firm policies the government chose to pursue, including war, but, he added, something had to be done immediately. "If we tamper too much with the natural ardor of the People," he told the secretary, "we shall moderate it down until we become a pusillanimous race."[41]

In his second letter to Madison, Smith listed specific steps the government should take in the crisis. He suggested that the United States prevent British ships from purchasing supplies along the coast. At the same time the president should demand "satisfaction" from England for the outrage and Congress should be called into early session in October. "These measures," he predicted, "would show that we meant something serious." The Marylander also proposed that as soon as Congress met it should be presented with legislation laying an embargo on American shipping for a period of possibly three months. During that time American vessels would sail into port, where in case of war they would be safe. The three months could also be used to build up American military power. Again and again Smith stressed the need for an effective answer to the British aggression. Either England must be made to pay reparations, he said, or "We must go to War."[42]

Throughout the next few months the administration continued to seek and receive Smith's advice. Secretary of the Treasury Albert Gallatin frequently contacted him on ways and means of financing a war should it come. Smith recommended to Gallatin that the Bank of the United States could be forced to lend the government sufficient funds by threatening not to renew its soon-to-expire charter. On

39. See Brant, *James Madison; Secretary of State*, pp. 380–391.
40. S. Smith to Madison, June 30, 1807, Thomas Jefferson Papers, Library of Congress (all subsequent references to the Jefferson Papers are to this group of papers found in the Library of Congress).
41. Ibid.
42. S. Smith to Madison, June 30, 1807, Jefferson Papers.

another occasion he informed the secretary that the Spanish government might be willing to sell the United States $15,000,000 in gold that it had been unable to ship from South America because of the British blockade. The irrepressible general indicated his availability for an appointment as a special agent to negotiate the bargain.[43]

Gallatin also inquired of Smith as a military man what defense measures the government should take and what plan was best for an invasion of Canada. The general answered that he believed a war with England would not involve land battles inside the borders of the United States. He predicted that the war "must necessarily be principally maritime." The war at sea, he said, should be carried on by privateers, since the small American navy would certainly be eliminated early in the contest. The country, he told Gallatin, must expect a blockade of its ports and harbors, but he was optimistic that "swift schooners" would easily avoid the British ships. As for Canada, Smith felt that the American army would have no trouble in conquering it. He asserted that he had given especial attention to the British naval base at Halifax and had dispatched one of his own vessels to spy out the best method of capturing the city. At the end of August, Jefferson, for the first time in over a year, personally wrote Smith thanking him for his assistance and promising that many of his proposals would be acted upon. The *Chesapeake* and *Leopard* affair had been a great insult to the United States, a symbol of America's impotence in a hostile world, but it had cleared away for a brief moment the complexities of politics in America and restored a lost unity to the Republican party.[44]

Summoned by the president, Congress gathered in October, with Samuel Smith reassuming the role of presidential spokesman in the Senate. Almost daily the general traveled in his carriage to the president's house, where he joined other Republican leaders in hammering out policies. In the course of these discussions it became clear that despite much sentiment for war both in Congress and the Cabinet, Jefferson had already decided to seek a peaceful solution. Following the suggestion of Smith and others as well as his own prejudices, the president resolved to meet the British depredations on American vessels as well as the less-publicized French attacks with a total embargo on American shipping. Smith was assigned the task of guiding

43. See, for example, Albert Gallatin to S. Smith, July 17, 1807, and S. Smith to Gallatin, July 10, 1807, Smith-Carter Papers; S. Smith to Gallatin, July 13, 1807, Jefferson Papers.

44. Gallatin to S. Smith, July 17, 1807, Smith-Carter Papers; S. Smith to Gallatin, July 26, 1807, and Jefferson to S. Smith, July 30, 1807, Jefferson Papers.

the embargo bill through the Senate, which he did with impressive speed. On his motion the rules of the Senate were suspended and the bill given three readings. On the same day it was introduced, the Senate passed the embargo bill by a vote of twenty-two to six and sent it along to the House of Representatives. Not in many years had the Republican majority in the upper chamber displayed such discipline.[45]

As finally approved, the embargo law was far different from the plan Smith had sent to Madison a few months before. Then he had seen an embargo as a prudent measure necessary to protect American property. It was, in other words, to be a prelude to some other action, such as a declaration of war. Jefferson's embargo scheme was intended to be a substitute for war. He was proposing to keep American ships and goods at home until France and England would be so badly hurt economically that they would change their policies, at least as they affected American trade. That Samuel Smith, the traditional champion of mercantile interests, would support a law virtually ending all American commerce for an indefinite length of time seems paradoxical. Yet there were persuasive reasons behind his action. The general was patriotic and sincerely deplored the attack on the *Chesapeake* as a blow to American honor. He had been willing to declare war against Britain, a far more radical response than an embargo. Furthermore, he was very much aware that his constituents in Maryland wanted England punished and were willing to accept an embargo instead of war. The general had personal as well as political reasons for approving the plan. S. Smith & Buchanan was losing ships at an alarming rate to the Royal Navy and the French privateers, who between them were rapidly extinguishing all neutral commerce. The Embargo at least held out the promise of ending this gloomy situation. Privately, Smith told his fellow senators that the Embargo should bring quick results because the French and British sugar islands in the West Indies were dependent on American food. England and France would soon have to accept the American demands or face the possibility of starvation in their colonies.[46]

45. See, for example, Jefferson to S. Smith, November 5, 1807, Jefferson Papers; Diary of Adams, October 30 and December 14 and 18, 1807, Adams Papers; *Annals of Congress,* 10th Cong., 1st sess., 1807, pp. 19, 50–52; Jefferson to Joel Barlow, December 10, 1807, in Ford, ed., *Writings of Jefferson,* 9: 168–169.

46. William Buchanan to S. Smith, January 31, 1808, Madison Papers; M. C. Nicholas to W. C. Nicholas, November 24, 1807, William Hollins to W. C. Nicholas, April 5, 1808, and William Patterson to W. C. Nicholas, May 11, 1808, Nicholas Papers, Library of Congress; S. Smith to W. C. Nicholas, August 14,

In its operation the Embargo law proved badly defective. There were many loopholes in the legislation that unscrupulous businessmen used to get their ships out of port. In addition, there was large-scale smuggling not only from every port, but also by land across the canadian and Florida frontiers. More and more of Smith's time had to be spent sponsoring supplementary enforcement bills and defending them before the Senate. By the summer of 1808 the Embargo had not visibly affected either England or France, and the near-rebellious opposition to the law in New England and among some elements in the Republican party made its repeal only a matter of time.[47] Even the president came to believe that it would be impossible to maintain the system much longer. "Should neither peace nor a revocation of the decrees and orders in Europe take place," he wrote, "the day cannot be distant when that [Embargo] will cease to be preferable to open hostility."[48] Jefferson was not yet ready, however, to subject the United States to the horrors of war. He determined to keep the Embargo as long as he could.[49]

When the second session of the Tenth Congress met in November 1808, the high spirits and chest-thumping nationalism of the year before had dissipated. In the fall of 1807 the country had been united and ready for even the most extreme measures; a year later sectionalism and factionalism were rampant. Congress was made no happier by the president's annual address, which strongly recommended the Embargo be continued and further strengthened. In the Senate a committee of which Samuel Smith was a member was chosen to decide what, if any, new enforcement legislation was needed. Before the committee had time to present its report, James Hillhouse, a Federalist from Connecticut, introduced a resolution calling for total repeal of the Embargo. Hillhouse sensibly pointed out that the measure had harmed no one but Americans and therefore ought to be abolished. As

1807, Nicholas Papers, University of Virginia Library; S. Smith to Madison, August 20, 1807, Madison Papers; S. Smith to W. C. Nicholas, August 24, 1807, Smith-Carter Papers; S. Smith to Jefferson, August 24, 1807, Jefferson Papers; Diary of Adams, December 18, 1807, Adams Papers.

47. *Annals of Congress,* 10th Cong., 1st sess., 1808, pp. 64–79, 104–105, 153–157, 361–363; Diary of Adams, January 5 and February 13, 19, and 21, 1808, Adams Papers; Samuel Taggart to Rev. John Taylor, January 27, 1808, in George H. Haynes, ed., "Letters of Samuel Taggart," American Antiquarian Society, *Proceedings* n.s., 33 (1923): 301–302; Samuel Harrison to Jefferson, May 28, 1807, Jefferson Papers; Patterson to W. C. Nicholas, June 3, 1808, Nicholas Papers, Library of Congress.

48. Jefferson to James Bowdoin, May 28, 1808, Jefferson Papers.

49. Jefferson to Robert Smith, August 9, 1808, Jefferson Papers.

to what should replace the Embargo, the Connecticut senator said very little, other than that war was not necessarily the only alternative. The Hillhouse resolution was deceptively attractive, and the Republican leadership in the Senate had to move quickly to keep their wavering followers in line. Smith made two major speeches urging defeat of the resolution. Time and again he returned to two themes: that repeal of the Embargo would not free American commerce from the attacks by the French and English, and that repeal without a simultaneous declaration of war would be a disgraceful submission to the illegal decrees of the European belligerents. He assured the Senate that no one was suffering more from the Embargo than he, and that he would "join heart and hand" to repeal it when the United States was assured of a "safe and honorable trade." Republicans in and out of Congress were favorably impressed with the Marylander's presentation, especially his statistics supposedly showing that France and England were both feeling an economic pinch because of the Embargo. On December 2 the Hillhouse resolution was defeated as every Republican voted against it. Smith's arguments had helped maintain the party's solidarity, but behind the scenes Republican senators were badly split over the Embargo itself and the best course to pursue in the future.[50]

A week after the Hillhouse resolution had been lost, the committee assigned to study the president's request for new enforcement legislation brought in its report. It proposed a new law that struck at smuggling by permitting federal revenue agents to seize all goods they suspected would be shipped in violation of the Embargo. The agents were to be exempt from any lawsuits should they make a mistake. Smith loyally supported the bill, but many Republicans would have no part of it. After extensive debate the new enforcement legislation passed, though it proved a Pyrrhic victory for the administration.[51] By the end of December it was clear that the Republican party in Congress would no longer listen to the president. "What I had foreseen has taken place," Gallatin commented to a friend, "a majority will not adhere to the embargo much longer."[52] On February 3, after the House

50. *Annals of Congress*, 10th Cong., 2d sess., 1808, pp. 11–12, 16–17, 120–136, 138–161, 230–231; Taggart to Taylor, November 17, 1808, in Haynes, ed., "Letters of Taggart," pp. 318–319; Joseph C. Cabell to W. C. Nicholas, December 18, 1808, and Nicholas to unknown recipient, December 3, 1808, Nicholas Papers, University of Virginia Library; see also Nathaniel Macon to Joseph Hopper Nicholson, Joseph Hopper Nicholson Papers, Library of Congress.

51. *Annals of Congress*, 10th Cong., 2d sess., 1808, pp. 241, 298.

52. Gallatin to Nicholson, December 29, 1808, Albert Gallatin Papers, New-York Historical Society.

of Representatives had already voted to repeal the Embargo, a caucus of Republicans from both houses of Congress met to decide the party's stance on present and future foreign policy. Northern Republicans, led by Representative Ezekiel Bacon of Massachusetts, were uncompromising in their view that the Embargo must be abandoned. Smith, William Branch Giles, and other southern Republicans replied that repeal should be tied to a declaration of war against England or at least to a larger and more accelerated program of defense preparations. The majority of the caucus would not agree to either alternative; they did not want war or the new taxes more troops and ships would require. Rebuffed by their party at every turn, Giles and Smith finally asked the caucus to delay the proposed date for repealing the Embargo from March 4, 1809, until June 1. The two men were trying to spare Jefferson the embarrassment of having to sign the repeal bill on his last day in office. The northern Republicans would not even permit this small courtesy, adamantly insisting that if the Embargo was continued even a short while longer, it would cause a civil war in New England.[53]

On February 8 Giles reluctantly bowed to the will of the caucus and presented a motion in the Senate that provided for the repeal of the Embargo and the substitution of a nonintercourse act prohibiting Americans from trading with France, England, or their colonies. Samuel Smith sat silently in the Senate chamber during the repeal debates, but he undoubtedly agreed with Giles, who disowned his own measure. "The resolution before you . . . is not the one of my choice," the Virginian informed his colleagues, "nor the one by which I could wish my responsibility tested. It is the offspring of conciliation and great concession on my part."[54] The repeal bill easily passed on February 14 as both Giles and Smith voted with the majority. The nonintercourse bill, however, ran into immediate trouble. Weak and unenforceable, it was a sad attempt to preserve some shred of the national honor and to conceal as much as possible the fact that the United States had unconditionally surrendered to the decrees of France and England. In its original form the bill contained provisions allowing the president to commission privateers and American merchantmen to carry arms for their defense. Even these were abandoned when the House of Representatives would not approve them.[55]

Jefferson's presidency thus ended in great disorder and confusion.

53. Ezekiel Bacon to Joseph Story, February 5, 1808, Joseph Story Papers, Library of Congress.

54. *Annals of Congress*, 10th Cong., 2d sess., 1809, p. 353.

55. Ibid., pp. 409, 451–452.

Ironically, repeal of the Embargo settled nothing. As Smith had predicted, the British and French decrees continued to exist and under them American trade was crippled. Once more American ships were being seized and American sailors impressed. The nonintercourse law was honored mainly in the breach. At home the Embargo had left the Republican party more seriously divided than ever before. In New England the Federalist party had been brought back from the brink of the grave and restored to power. In Congress the Embargo issue had shattered the Republicans—as shown by the fact that they could not agree upon a candidate for the presidency. The election of 1808 found no less than three Republicans on the ballot. As bad as the Embargo had been, Samuel Smith continued to view it as the only feasible policy besides war. For him the end of the Embargo restored conditions to those in the spring of 1807, when he had verged on a break with the administration because of its inability to defend American commerce. A new president, however, was entering office, and the general could only hope that the next administration would be able to achieve what the old one had not.

IO

*An Independent
Republican*

No ONE could doubt that Thomas Jefferson welcomed the end of his presidency and the journey back to Monticello. His last years in office had not been happy ones. His Embargo scheme was generally regarded as a costly failure that had deeply wounded the nation and the Republican party. Yet the author of the Declaration of Independence left Washington still retaining the sincere affection of countless Americans. Samuel Smith certainly was among those who regretted Jefferson's departure. Since the *Chesapeake* affair he had grown very close to the president politically and personally. He still believed with Jefferson that the Embargo was the best policy for the nation to have followed and war the only honorable alternative. In his role as a loyal Jeffersonian, Smith had not only defended the Embargo at every opportunity, but also had actively campaigned for Jefferson's handpicked successor to the presidency, Secretary of State James Madison. At the Republican party nominating caucus held in January 1808 Smith had cast his vote for Madison, and in succeeding months he had used his influence with Republicans throughout the United States to benefit the secretary's candidacy. His greatest service was performed in Maryland, where he managed to keep the wavering Republican governor, Robert Wright, from openly declaring himself in favor of New York governor George Clinton's bid for the highest office. Smith's campaigning helped to win nine of Maryland's eleven electoral

votes for Madison, who, when the results from other states were tabu-
lated, was declared an easy victor over his two Republican challengers,
Clinton and James Monroe, and the Federalist candidate, Charles
Cotesworth Pinckney of South Carolina.[1]

Smith and Madison had never been friends, but they had enjoyed a
long political association dating back to the 1790s. Now that Smith
had worked hard for Madison's election it seemed likely that the two
men would at least begin the tenure of the new administration har-
moniously. Madison's future policy, of course, would determine how
long the spirit of amity would continue. But even before Madison's
inauguration an unforeseen incident took place that poisoned relations
between the president-elect and Smith. The dispute centered on
Madison's selections of new Cabinet officers, especially his choice for
the post of secretary of state. For his successor to this most important
position, Madison wanted his long-time friend and colleague Albert
Gallatin, then serving as secretary of the treasury. Gallatin's promotion
to the state department was obvious and logical. For eight years, as
Jefferson's fiscal advisor, the Pennsylvanian had ably administered
his department and supervised the reduction of the national debt. His
work had made him familiar with the diplomatic scene and with men
and procedures in Congress. As the president's right-hand man he
would supply financial expertise, diplomatic acumen, friendship, and
continuity with Jefferson's administration. Many in Congress, however, were displeased with Gallatin's policies in the treasury department, feeling that his commitment to economy had left the country
inadequately protected militarily. Others opposed the Pennsylvanian
on the less honorable grounds that he had been born in a foreign
country. For these reasons Gallatin's legislative enemies were numerous, and the rumor that Madison had picked him for secretary of state
elicited from them an unfavorable reaction. William Branch Giles
had no sooner heard reports of the intended appointment than he
rushed to Madison's house to protest. Giles had been one of Madison's
campaign managers and had expected as a reward to be named to

1. S. Smith to William Eustis, April 23 and June 7, 1808, William Eustis
Papers, and Jonathan Russell to S. Smith, September 13, 1808, Samuel Smith
Papers, Library of Congress; Moses Younglove to S. Smith, October 11, 1808,
Smith-Carter Papers, University of Virginia Library; Governor Robert Wright to
S. Smith, June 24, 1808, Portfolio 13, Maryland Historical Society; Libero Marx
Renzulli, "Maryland Federalism, 1787–1819" (Ph.D. diss., University of Virginia,
1962), p. 324; U.S., Congress, *The Debates and Proceedings in the Congress of
the United States . . . 1789–1824*, 42 vols. (Washington, D.C., 1834–1856),
10th Cong., 2d sess., 1809, p. 344; hereafter cited as *Annals of Congress.*

the state department himself. When Gallatin was chosen, the Virginia senator was angered and set out to discredit him. In his private talk with Madison, Giles listed nine reasons why Gallatin would be a poor choice as secretary of state. His most significant contention was that the Pennsylvanian was so unpopular in Congress that even if the Senate approved the nomination, there would be a strong tendency in both houses to oppose his programs.[2]

Madison was so disturbed by the interview with Giles that he asked Wilson Cary Nicholas to canvass the Senate quietly in an effort to determine Gallatin's chances for approval. Nicholas reported that nearly half the members of the Senate would vote against the nomination, but there was a slim possibility of a one-vote majority. What Nicholas had found in his inquiry was that Giles and Samuel Smith, the two most powerful Republicans in the Senate, were unalterably determined to defeat Gallatin's appointment. Nicholas spent long hours patiently trying to persuade his two friends not to dispute the president-elect's wishes. Smith and Giles finally convinced Nicholas that, in his words, "nothing on earth could prevent an opposition to Mr. Gallatin."[3] Giles' motives were well known, but Smith's inflexibility was surprising. Why should he antagonize Madison, whom he had helped elect? Why sacrifice the goodwill of the administration even before it took office? The only apparent answer seems to be that the general allowed his dislike for Gallatin to overcome his better judgment. For fifteen years the two men had constantly feuded with each other over issues of finance and defense. Smith saw Gallatin as the architect of national weakness, and the prospect of having him in the state department during a period of foreign turmoil may have caused the Marylander to overstep the bounds of prudence.

Madison was not pleased with Nicholas' assessment of senatorial opinion, but there was no profit in provoking a divisive intraparty struggle so early in his administration. After considering several possibilities, he decided to keep Gallatin in the treasury department and elevate Robert Smith from the navy to the state department. News of

2. James Madison to Joel Barlow, February 7, 1809, James Madison Papers, Library of Congress; Raymond Walters, *Albert Gallatin: Jeffersonian Financier and Diplomat* (New York, 1957), p. 210; Irving Brant, *James Madison; The President, 1809–1812* (New York, 1956), p. 24; Augustus Foster, Journal of the U. S. of A., November 23, 1811, Augustus Foster Papers, Library of Congress; William Branch Giles to Creed Taylor, March 27, 1808, Creed Taylor Papers, University of Virginia Library; John Randolph to James Monroe, January 1, 1809, James Monroe Papers, and Giles to Madison, February 27, 1809, William Cabell Rives Papers, Library of Congress.

3. Wilson Cary Nicholas to Madison, March 1809, Rives Papers.

the nomination shook the political society of Washington. Rumors of deals, conspiracies, and sell-outs became the staple conversation in the boarding houses where the politicians lived. It was hinted darkly that Smith and Giles had forced the appointment on Madison as the price of their future support. There is nothing, however, in the scattered records to prove that the naming of Robert Smith was anything but Madison's own determination. He may, indeed, have hoped that the gesture would purchase Samuel Smith's loyalty, but more likely he was anxious to keep as many ties as he could to the still popular Jefferson. Moreover, there was the added bonus that Robert Smith was less talented and more pliable than Gallatin, thus permitting Madison to dominate American foreign policy just as he had done for the last eight years. Whatever his expectations, Madison had blundered. Gallatin was angry that he had not received the state department job and positively livid that Robert Smith, an advocate of military preparedness whatever the cost, should have been the one to supersede him. The rancor between the Smiths and Gallatin was now open and avowedly bitter. Unwittingly Madison had created a situation in which the Republican party would inevitably suffer from an internal competition for power and status.[4]

In the fall of 1809 Gallatin and his supporters had an opportunity to even the score with the Smiths. The general's term in the Senate expired at the end of the second session of the Tenth Congress, and it would be left to the Maryland legislature to determine if he should be reappointed. The party composition of the legislature was consequently of extreme importance to Samuel Smith's political career. Unfortunately for Smith, the unpopularity of the Embargo in the state had led to a resurgence of Federalist sentiment. In the 1808 elections that party had recaptured a majority in the House of Delegates, while the Republicans kept control of the state senate and the governor's office.[5] When Smith's name was brought up for a new term in the

4. John Quincy Adams to Louisa Adams, March 5, 1809, in Worthington Chauncey Ford, ed., *Writings of John Quincy Adams,* 7 vols. (New York, 1913–1917), 3: 290; Nicholas, draft of a speech probably written in July 1811, Wilson Cary Nicholas Papers, Library of Congress; Brant, *James Madison; The President,* p. 25; Henry Adams, *The Life of Albert Gallatin* (New York, 1879), p. 389; Diary of John Randolph, June 22, 1809, Randolph Papers, Virginia State Library, Richmond.

5. Because of the Embargo, exports from Baltimore had fallen off more than 80 percent, while the price of a barrel of flour had dropped from forty dollars in 1806 to twelve dollars in 1808. By 1809 Baltimore was a center of smuggling operations aimed at evading the Embargo. See the *Federal Gazette & Baltimore Daily Advertiser,* August 13 and September 13, 1808.

spring of 1809, a deadlock ensued; the House of Delegates would not consent to the nomination and the Senate would not consider anyone else for the post. The Republican governor temporarily settled the dispute by appointing Smith to serve as an interim United States senator until the next legislature was elected and made a final decision. In the campaign leading to the selection of state representatives, the question of returning Smith to the Senate was the central issue. For their part, the Federalists unearthed the old charges that during the 1790s the general had conducted trade under French protections and opposed defense measures aimed at France. These shopworn allegations had little impact, but more serious accusations of corruption made by members of his own party almost cost the general his political life and his reputation.[6]

The man responsible for Smith's difficulties was Joseph Hopper Nicholson, an ancient political enemy. Nicholson had long been a resident of Baltimore, had served in the House of Representatives, and was a close friend of Albert Gallatin as well as a leading member of John Randolph's Republican schismatics. Sometime during the spring of 1809 Nicholson received a letter from Gallatin telling him of an unusual and suspicious business transaction. The secretary of the treasury asserted that Robert Smith, as secretary of the navy, had cashed bills of exchange drawn by S. Smith & Buchanan on the firm that acted as agents to supply the American naval squadron in the Mediterranean, Degen & Purviance of Leghorn, Italy. Degen & Purviance had failed to pay these bills of exchange because, so Gallatin thought, Samuel Smith's firm had not shipped sufficient quantities of bullion to the agents. In effect, Gallatin charged Smith with illegally holding government funds and using them for private investment rather than transshipping them promptly to Italy. The situation had become more complicated when Degen, one of the partners in the Italian commercial house, absconded with all of the assets of the business, most of which belonged to the United States government.[7]

Coming just as the campaign in Maryland to elect a new legislature began, Gallatin's indictment was obviously intended to harm Smith's

6. Abraham Shriver to S. Smith, May 9, 1809, Vertical File, Maryland Historical Society; S. Smith to George Clinton, May 29, 1809, Smith Papers; Randolph to James Mercer Garnett, October 3, 1809, Randolph-Garnett Letterbook, Library of Congress.

7. Albert Gallatin to Joseph Hopper Nicholson, May 11, 1809, Joseph Hopper Nicholson Papers, Library of Congress; Gallatin to John Armstrong, May 1, 1809, Smith Papers; Nicholson to Gallatin, May 14, 1809, Albert Gallatin Papers, New-York Historical Society.

chances for another term in the Senate. Nicholson was ecstatic over the revelation, regretting only that it had not been brought out sooner. He warned Gallatin that time was short and the information would have no impact on the state elections "unless the thing can be moved immediately by some Republicans in the House of Representatives, and exposed in its true colors."[8] Only by publicizing the story at the national level, Nicholson claimed, could Smith's election be prevented, because in Maryland the "Democratic Papers will publish nothing against a man who professes to support the administration and our Democrats will believe nothing published in the Federal Prints."[9] Acting on his own advice, Nicholson contacted Congressman Nathaniel Macon, the former Speaker of the House and another friend of Gallatin and Randolph. Within hours of receiving Nicholson's letter repeating Gallatin's charges, Macon met with John Randolph, who instantly saw that if the purported scandal was made public, Samuel Smith would probably not be back in the Senate. Going directly to the House of Representatives, Randolph revealed Gallatin's story of the Degen & Purviance affair and successfully moved the appointment of a committee of investigation. By June 2, 1809, the committee, chaired by Randolph and thoroughly controlled by men hostile to Smith, began collecting evidence. Less than three weeks later, however, Macon confessed that the investigation was faltering because of "unsatisfactory" information from the accountants of the army and navy departments.[10] Nicholson, despondent over the lack of results, urged that the committee rush its work and submit a report to the House before Congress adjourned. "If it is not, the Senate will be cursed with S[amuel] S[mith] for another six years," he told Gallatin, "and what is of more importance to me, I shall be called a liar, for I have mentioned the subject, and am so relied on as the authority."[11]

While Gallatin and his friends plotted, the Smith brothers remained silent. Not until after Gallatin had released his accusations to the newspapers did they react. On June 26 Samuel penned a note to the treasury secretary denying that his business conduct was unethical. He asked Gallatin to confirm or deny whether the newspapers had quoted him correctly. A few days later Robert Smith also wrote the secretary and after dismissing the charges as false, accused Gal-

8. Nicholson to Gallatin, May 14, 1809, Gallatin Papers.

9. Ibid.

10. Nathaniel Macon to Nicholson, May 24, May 25, and June 2, 1809, University of Virginia Library; Macon to Nicholson, June 20, 1809, Nicholson Papers, Library of Congress.

11. Nicholson to Gallatin, June 21, 1809, Gallatin Papers.

latin of attempting to tarnish his reputation. Robert also criticized the House investigating committee for holding its meetings so near the end of the congressional session, thus preventing him from fully rebutting the allegations. Finally, he objected that the committee had not first looked at the pertinent records of the navy department that would have explained the transaction.[12]

Gallatin did not retreat. In his reply to Samuel Smith the treasury head restated the charges, implying that they were proven beyond doubt. "The transaction such as it appears there [in the records]," he responded to the senator, "is under all its aspects, the most extraordinary which has fallen within my knowledge since I have been in this Department."[13] He added that the affair had "certainly left very unfavorable impressions on my mind." The secretary went so far as to threaten the senator with legal action to recover the money stolen by Degen, which he claimed was Smith's responsibility.[14] Gallatin's extravagance aroused Samuel Smith's well-known temper. On July 2 he again wrote the secretary of the treasury; his letter was composed with such passion that its legibility and coherence suffered. The Marylander ridiculed the secretary's ignorance of even the most usual commercial practices. Gallatin's interpretation of the dealings between S. Smith & Buchanan and Degen & Purviance he characterized as wildly inaccurate.[15]

By late July the Randolph investigation had not produced any evidence of wrongdoing by either Robert or Samuel Smith. Randolph, however, was determined to return to the full House with a report that made the Smiths at least look guilty. Although the comptroller of the navy under Robert Smith, Gabriel Duvall, had testified that the Degen & Purviance business was perfectly legitimate, Randolph decided to ignore everything save Gallatin's official report to the committee. Fortunately for the Smiths, a friendly committee member told Robert what Randolph intended to do. Alerted to their danger, the two brothers exposed Randolph's duplicity and forced changes in the report. Samuel Smith, in relating the episode to Thomas Jefferson, predicted that even though the accusation had been proven false in

12. *Baltimore Federal Republican,* June 19, 20, 21, 22, and 26, 1809; S. Smith to Gallatin, June 26, 1809, Smith Papers; Robert Smith to Gallatin, June 28, 1809, Gallatin Papers.

13. Gallatin to S. Smith, June 29, 1809, Smith Papers; see also the rough draft of the same letter in the Gallatin Papers.

14. Ibid.

15. S. Smith to Gallatin, July 2, 1809, Smith Papers.

Congress, "it has had an influence in Maryland that may lose us the October Elections."[16]

The general was not exaggerating the possible consequences of Gallatin's mischief. His opponents in Maryland, both Federalist and Republican, advertised the corruption charge throughout the state, always being careful to omit the fact that the Smiths had been exonerated by the government. As he had before, Samuel Smith demonstrated his skill and resilience as a political campaigner. In Baltimore, where the general's political strength centered, his Republican enemies limited their efforts to a malicious and fact-twisting broadside probably written by Joseph Hopper Nicholson. Smith's supporters promptly published a broadside of their own refuting their antagonists. But, unlike his congressional campaigns, Smith's fight to stay in the Senate could not be restricted to Baltimore. Since his election depended upon winning a Republican majority in the House of Delegates, he necessarily had to carry his campaign into all parts of Maryland.[17] "The Hero of Mud Fort," one Federalist commented, "is working night and day to secure his election and he has the little mission to ride about the Country, in order to solicit votes."[18] John Randolph, who closely watched the campaign, professed himself to be appalled at the spectacle of the "gallant General" galloping around the state "exhorting the people 'to vote only for such as will vote for me.' "[19] As in previous campaigns Smith spoke mainly before militia assemblies, but on occasion he sponsored barbecues to which the public was invited. Hugh M. Brackenridge, a young Pennsylvanian visiting Baltimore, attended one such gathering held in Baltimore County and carefully noted what he saw. The barbecue was held some two miles east of Baltimore, and the center of attraction was an ox that was roasted whole. Nearby there were mounds of bread, while in the shade stood stacks of barrels containing whiskey and beer. "The swilling of the liquor, and the pulling and tearing of the half-raw beef," Brecken-

16. S. Smith to Thomas Jefferson, July 23, 1809, Thomas Jefferson Papers, Library of Congress; see also S. Smith to Robert Smith, March 12, 1811, Smith Papers.

17. *Baltimore Federal Republican*, June 20, 23, and 29, 1809; see the two broadsides, "General Smith's Bill of Exchange Exposed" and "To the Freemen of Maryland," both published in July 1809, Gallatin Papers; James Boyle to S. Smith, July 21, 1809, and Moses Tabbs to S. Smith, September 8, 1809, Smith Papers.

18. James Boyd to James McHenry, August 19, 1809, James McHenry Papers, Library of Congress.

19. Randolph to Garnett, October 22, 1809, University of Virginia Library.

ridge commented, "would have done honor to the feast of the Abyssinians."[20] Well-plied with food and drink, the crowd was addressed by its host, General Smith, whom Brackenridge described as a "tall, fine-looking man with a strong clear voice well suited to field oratory." The Pennsylvanian observed that Smith was an adept and popular stump-speaker, who was "frequently interrupted by shouts of applause."[21]

Despite the best efforts of Smith's enemies, the returns in the fall elections showed that the House of Delegates was once more in the hands of the Republicans and that a majority favored Samuel Smith for another term in the Senate. A few anti-Smith Republicans tried to persuade Nicholson to announce his own candidacy for the Senate in a desperate effort to prevent the general's selection. Nicholson, however, declined, confessing to Gallatin that "the play is not worth the Candle."[22] When he learned that the state legislature had elected him to another full term in the United States Senate, the general must have experienced feelings both of exhilaration and outrage. His re-election resulted entirely from his own efforts and had been accomplished in the face of President Madison's passive hostility and Secretary Gallatin's open opposition. The national administration, made up of members of the same party to which Smith belonged, had tried to bring about his defeat. He owed nothing to these men. They had risked a great deal in attacking the Marylander and now they would have to endure the consequences.[23]

Smith was not the only Republican who was rejected by Madison's administration. There were others who, like him, had occupied positions of power and influence during Jefferson's presidency, but who found Madison unwilling to accept their advice or honor their requests for patronage.[24] William Branch Giles, for example, had been a trusted

20. Raphael Semmes, *Baltimore as Seen by Visitors, 1783–1860* (Baltimore, 1953), p. 43.

21. Ibid.

22. Nicholson to Gallatin, October 16, 1809, Gallatin Papers.

23. *Annals of Congress*, 11th Cong., 2d sess., 1809, p. 479. Smith was furious over Gallatin's interference in the Maryland election and told Wilson Cary Nicholas: ". . . no federal party can do more injury than G[allatin] did to me and the [Republican] Party in Maryland . . . however, it is past and I have triumphed in spite of him. His invidious conduct on that occasion would shock you . . ." (Smith to Nicholas, January 13, 1810, Smith-Carter Papers).

24. Smith occasionally wrote to President Madison about foreign affairs, but never received a reply. His earliest letter began: "I have been in the habit of conferring with Mr. Jefferson during his administration . . ." (Smith to Madison, March 20, 1809, Madison Papers).

lieutenant of Jefferson in Congress and an organizer of Madison's presidential campaign. But once in office, Madison had turned on Giles, refusing him suitable reward for his services. William Duane, the talented editor of the Philadelphia *Aurora,* who had stood by Jefferson in the dark days of 1798, wrote the former president that he was "little known" to Madison. Each man for individual reasons found it increasingly difficult to remain in the Republican party as long as it was directed by Madison and Gallatin. As for Samuel Smith, both friend and foe assumed that he would return from his triumph in Maryland as an adversary of the secretary of the treasury, and, indeed, of the entire administration.[25]

Even had Smith and the administration been on the best of terms, disputes over the conduct of foreign affairs would probably have caused a rupture in their relations. As it happened, personal enmity reinforced fundamental differences over policy. By the spring of 1810 the American government found itself in yet another crisis precipitated by the continuing Anglo-French war in Europe. Shortly after Madison had taken the oath of office he managed to negotiate an agreement with the British Minister, David M. Erskine, that pledged the British government to repeal the orders-in-council, at least as they applied to American commerce. Madison, acting on this agreement, had exempted England from the provisions of the Nonintercourse Act, and it appeared that the two countries were moving closer together. Erskine, however, had no authority to conclude any such arrangement with the United States, and he was disowned by his government. As a result the bright hopes of reconciliation were smashed and there was no relaxation in the enforcement of the orders-in-council. American commerce was again reduced to the humiliating position of operating when and where the British fleet dictated. It was apparent to both Congress and the president that if the United States was to escape this neocolonial subservience and reestablish the honor of the nation, then new and bolder policies could not be delayed. The need for haste was under-

25. See, for example, Randolph to Nicholson, June 6, 1810, Randolph Papers; Nicholas to Giles, December 25, 1810, Edgehill-Randolph Papers, University of Virginia Library; William Duane to Jefferson, February 4, 1809, and Jefferson to William Wirt, May 3, 1811, Jefferson Papers; Jefferson to Duane, January 25, 1811, in Worthington C. Ford, ed., "Letters of William Duane," Massachusetts Historical Society, *Proceedings* 2d ser., 20 (1907): 344–345; Duane to Henry Dearborn, July 3, 1810, Personal Papers Miscellaneous, Library of Congress; Duane to Jefferson, January 25, 1811, Jefferson Papers; Peter Carr to S. Smith, July 17, 1809, Smith Papers; Randolph to Garnett, October 22, 1809, University of Virginia Library.

lined by the fact that the foolish and ineffective Nonintercourse Act would expire in June 1810.[26]

In January 1810 a measure known as the first Macon's bill was introduced into the House of Representatives. The plan, devised by Gallatin and approved by Madison, was intended as a replacement for the Nonintercourse Act. As passed by the House, the bill continued the prohibition against armed French or British naval vessels entering American harbors, prevented the importation of goods from France, Great Britain, or their colonies except in American ships, and allowed the president to exempt either nation from its provisions should they repeal their commercial decrees. American merchant ships would be allowed for the first time since 1807 to trade legally with both France and Great Britain. Madison hoped that such a law would enable him to bargain advantageously with both belligerents. By reopening trade with France and Great Britain, the bill also promised to increase receipts for the badly depleted American treasury. But many in Congress and all over the United States, having been schooled by Jefferson to believe that war was the only alternative to the Embargo, saw Macon's bill as a cowardly capitulation to the French and British decrees; they were determined to put the country in a more aggressive posture.[27]

On January 31 Macon's bill reached the Senate and was sent to a committee of which Samuel Smith was the chairman. From the beginning it was obvious that the measure would meet stiff opposition. One "highly toned" Republican senator, Obadiah German of New York, was not untypical when he expressed a wish that it might be "laid up in dry dock." Within the five-man committee considering the bill, Smith outspokenly condemned the plan and offered a substitute bill that would have permitted merchant ships to carry cannon and capture vessels that attacked them. His proposal would also have instructed the president to use the navy to protect convoys of American merchant ships. Smith had put forward these suggestions on other occasions and they now fared no better than before; the other mem-

26. Marshall Smelser, *The Democratic Republic, 1801–1815* (New York, 1968), pp. 193–194.

27. S. Smith to Nicholas, January 13, 1810, Smith-Carter Papers; *Annals of Congress*, 11th Cong., 2d sess., 1810, pp. 575, 754–755, 1160–1161, 1175–1178; Samuel Taggart to Rev. John Taylor, February 15, 1810, in George H. Haynes, ed., "Letters of Samuel Taggart," American Antiquarian Society, *Proceedings*, n.s., 33 (1923): 343–344; Jared Ingersoll to Madison, January 28, 1810, Madison Papers; George Washington Campbell to James Holland, April 4, 1810, George W. Campbell Papers, Library of Congress.

bers of the committee felt they were too strong and refused to accept them. The Marylander, however, was able to convince the committee to adopt an amendment striking out every provision of Macon's bill except the ban on armed ships. By emasculating the bill, which he felt was too weak anyway, Smith anticipated that the door would remain open for the introduction of more meaningful legislation. By a vote of sixteen to eleven the full Senate accepted the committee's report. The distribution of the vote revealed a breakdown of Republican party discipline in the Senate as serious as that of 1806. Eleven Republicans, including most of the traditional party leaders, joined five Federalists in passing the amended bill, while eleven Republicans voted against it. Thus, on a measure understood to be the president's own, the intended keystone of his foreign policy, the administration could not muster the support of a majority of its own party in the Senate.[28]

On February 22 the Senate version of Macon's bill was returned to the House, which refused to accept the alterations, and a joint committee of the two chambers met to thrash out the differences. As one of the Senate's conferees, Smith once more submitted his convoy plan as a substitute for the bill. The committee members from the House rejected the proposal and insisted that the Senate accept the original bill. Led by Smith, the Senate conferees declined, and in the resulting impasse the committee adjourned. Upon hearing the results of the conference, Senator Joseph Anderson, a Tennessee Republican, moved that the Senate adhere to its amended version of Macon's bill. In effect this step would have killed the measure since the House had already indicated that it would not recede from the original bill.[29] On March 19 Smith rose and delivered one of his relatively infrequent prepared speeches, urging approval of Anderson's motion. He began by recounting the history of America's foreign policy since the *Chesapeake* affair and the imposition of the French and British commercial decrees. The attack on the *Chesapeake*, he said, was an "insult offered to the honor of the nation," while the decrees had driven "our com-

28. *Annals of Congress,* 11th Cong., 2d sess., 1810, pp. 549–550, 610, 577; Taggart to Taylor, February 5, 1810, in Haynes, ed., "Letters of Taggart," pp. 343–344; James A. Bayard to Andrew Bayard, February 7, 1810, James A. Bayard Papers, Library of Congress. At least one Republican, Henry Clay of Kentucky, voted against the amendment only because no substitute for Macon's bill had been offered. He once described the original measure as a "crazy vessel, shattered and leaky" (*Annals of Congress,* 11th Cong., 2d sess., 1810, p. 579; see also Henry Adams, *History of the United States of America during the Administrations of Thomas Jefferson and James Madison,* 9 vols. [New York, 1889–1891], 5: 185).

29. *Annals of Congress,* 11th Cong., 2d sess., 1810, pp. 582, 590, 610, 1463, 1559–1560.

merce from the oceans." The only choices the United States had in the fall of 1807, he continued, were "war or embargo" because, short of war, only a total withholding of American commerce would harm France and England enough to force them to free American trade from the decrees. Thomas Jefferson's Embargo, Smith told the Senate, was the best possible policy under the circumstances. "Had that measure been rigidly enforced," he contended, "it would not have failed to have compelled a removal of the unjust conduct of those nations, most certainly that of Great Britain."[30]

Turning his attention to the Macon bill, Smith could find nothing to recommend it: "In vain did I look for something therein that would tend to obtain satisfaction for the insult on the Chesapeake; in vain for anything that would tend to prevent the future impressment of our seamen; in vain for anything that would induce or coerce the belligerents to repeal their unjust orders and decrees against our lawful commerce."[31] He charged that under a "thin veil" the administration was seeking to repeal the Nonintercourse Act, which, in spite of its shortcomings, he considered of greater use than the president's plan. In failing to recommend a program for action that was stronger rather than weaker than nonintercourse, Madison, in Smith's opinion, had surrendered the neutral rights American trade was entitled to exercise. It was this sacrifice of American commerce that caused the Marylander to oppose Macon's bill. "I found in it, or believed I did that which would be ruinous to the commerce of the United States," he commented at one point in his speech, "and therefore felt myself bound by the duty I owe to my constituents to remove the veil, and leave the measure open to public view."[32] As evidence that the bill would be harmful, the general contended that the provision keeping out French and British merchant ships from American ports while allowing American vessels to trade with those nations invited retaliation. Both belligerents would have an incentive to seize all the American merchantmen they could find, which could amount to between three and four hundred thousand tons of shipping. "Such a step," he cautioned, "would bring down ruin on our merchants."[33]

Having attacked the administration's scheme, Smith stated his own solution: arm the merchantmen and use the navy to protect commerce. The general had spoken of this plan a great deal in preceding weeks, but he now undertook to explain its advantages in some de-

30. Ibid., p. 601.
31. Ibid.
32. Ibid., p. 602.
33. Ibid., p. 604.

tail. By issuing cannon to commercial vessels and defending their passage across the ocean, the United States government would flash an unmistakable message to Britain and France. That message would be that America had tried every pacific alternative in an effort to obtain justice for its legitimate trade, but in vain. Henceforth the United States would fight to protect its commerce and even wage war if it became necessary. The Marylander would probably have opposed Macon's bill under any circumstances, for he honestly believed it did nothing for the hard-pressed merchants and that war was preferable. But in the context of the dispute over who would be secretary of state and the effort to defeat Smith in Maryland, it was clear to everyone that the general's oration also constituted his personal declaration of war on the administration. In saying that he would cast his vote for Anderson's motion Smith admitted being "aware that my vote will be disapproved by many of my friends." Following Smith's address, a majority of the Senate, including many Republicans, voted not to withdraw its amendment to Macon's bill.[34]

Defeat of the first Macon's bill did little more than increase the antipathy between the president and his party in the Senate. The Nonintercourse Act was still set to expire in less than three months, and the government had no choice but to take some action before that deadline. Yet at this crucial moment Congress seemed paralyzed by indecision, and Madison exercised no executive leadership. As in 1806 when Jefferson also appeared to have abdicated his responsibilities, individual members of the House and Senate tried to fill the void. Smith, for example, put his convoy and armed-ships proposal into the form of a motion, but the Senate delayed considering it. Only a strong push by the administration could possibly force any measure through the drifting and dispirited legislature. Finally, in the first week of April, the administration shook off its lethargy and through representative John Taylor of South Carolina submitted a new proposal. First introduced in the House committee on foreign relations, it quickly acquired the unofficial title of Macon's bill number two.[35]

The Taylor plan was even less forceful than the first Macon's bill. It simply revoked the Nonintercourse Act and opened trade with the belligerents. If either France or Britain should exempt American commerce from their decrees, then the president was authorized to revive the Nonintercourse Act against the other. Even Macon, who intro-

34. Ibid., pp. 606–611.
35. Ibid., pp. 640, 1702–1703; Nathaniel Macon to Nicholson, April 3 and 6, 1810, Nicholson Papers, University of Virginia Library.

duced the bill officially in the House, held a low opinion of the measure, commenting to a friend that "it did not appear to be of much consequence." Macon number two represented the administration's abandonment of any hope that the United States could enforce its neutral rights. Madison was now putting American honor and friendship on the block to be sold to the highest bidder. A majority in the House could not bring themselves to accept this new Macon's bill and tried to put some teeth into it by an amendment increasing duties on French and English imports by 50 percent. The bill was then sent up to the Senate, where Samuel Smith was again elected chairman of the committee considering the measure. On April 24 he reported the bill back to the Senate with a host of amendments. Everything but the enacting clause of the original bill had been crossed out. What the committee presented was an entirely new measure, one that closely followed Smith's ideas. The general managed to insert in the bill that part of the expiring Nonintercourse Act prohibiting belligerent naval vessels from entering American ports. The ubiquitous convoy plan also made another appearance, a sign that Smith had even more influence with this committee than with the earlier one that had gutted Macon number one. The Senate, too, appeared more willing to follow the Marylander's lead. Disgruntled at the administration's behavior, it passed the Smith committee amendments by large margins.[36]

The Senate's repudiation of Macon's bill number two, coming as it did on the heels of the fiasco over Macon number one and only weeks before the Nonintercourse Act died, threw Congress into even worse confusion than had been recently customary. Samuel Taggart, a perceptive Federalist representative from Massachusetts, said of Congress that a "more completely divided, bewildered, disorganized set of men hardly exists." Taggart described the government as being virtually a leaderless mob: "No majority in one House can calculate on a majority in the other, nor do I believe the President has really any majority that he can calculate upon [in] either."[37] Perhaps because he was a Federalist, Taggart laid the blame for this chaos on Madison.[38] He was, however, seconded in his censure of the president by several Republicans. "Our affairs are very delicately balanced," Samuel Smith observed to Wilson Cary Nicholas during this period, "the Executive

36. Macon to Nicholson, April 3, 1810, Nicholson Papers, University of Virginia Library; *Annals of Congress*, 11th Cong., 2d sess., 1810, pp. 1763, 1914, 664, 666, 673.

37. Taggart to Taylor, April 27, 1810, in Haynes, ed., "Letters of Taggart," p. 347.

38. Ibid.

blames the Senate, the people blame the House, and the Senate knows where the blame justly attaches but are silent."[39] Led by a weak president, plagued by laws and decrees it was powerless to affect, and torn by personal and political jealousies, the American government had reached the nadir of its young existence.

The career of Macon's bill number two closely paralleled that of its predecessor. The amended Senate version commanded little support in the House, where a majority resented the casual way the upper chamber had mutilated its work. On April 30 the House voted not to accept any of the Senate amendments and returned the bill to its original form, including the provision for the increase in duties. Once more a conference committee gathered to consider an important administration bill and once more the Senate sent Samuel Smith as its chief delegate. In the negotiations both sides were unyielding. The House conferees would not accept the Senate's amendments and the Senate representatives denounced the plan to raise the duties on French and English goods as harmful to no one but the American merchants who would have to pay the additional cost. If the expiration date of nonintercourse had not been less than a month away, the committee would probably have reported itself irreconcilably divided. But some measure had to be agreed upon, and the conference committee devised the least desirable compromise: it decided to drop both the convoy idea and the proposed 50 percent duty. Passed on the final day of the congressional session, Macon's bill number two did nothing but repeal the Nonintercourse Act and bar armed belligerent ships from entering American harbors. The president still had the power to reinstitute nonintercourse against either belligerent should the other cease enforcing its decrees on American trade. United States' policy had come full circle, back to 1805 and 1806 when the government had no policy at all aimed at protecting its trade or compelling Britain and France to respect neutral rights.[40]

As Samuel and Margaret Smith left Washington in May 1810 to spend the months before the next session of Congress at Montebello, the senator must have ruefully contemplated the events of the last year. Once a member of the highest councils of government, he now found himself excluded entirely from contact with the executive

39. S. Smith to Nicholas, May 25, 1810, Smith-Carter Papers; see also Macon to Nicholson, April 27, 1810, University of Virginia Library.

40. *Annals of Congress*, 11th Cong., 2d sess., 1810, pp. 2026, 2049–2051; Jefferson to Jonathan Eppes, May 10, 1810, Jefferson Papers; Bradford Perkins, *Prologue to War: England and the United States, 1805–1812* (Berkeley, 1963), pp. 241–242.

branch and following a political course plainly contrary to that of the president's. This reversal of fortune had come with remarkable suddenness, but those who knew the Marylander were not surprised. His separation from the administration followed the same pattern of 1794–1795, when he left the Federalist party, and of 1806, when he nearly abandoned Jefferson. Beneath the highly visible but transient personal feud between Smith and the administration lay the Marylander's deeper and more abiding commitment to uphold the interests of the American commercial community. Not pique but principle explains why in 1810 Samuel Smith set himself against Madison and Gallatin.

II

Fall from Power

THE DEFECTION of Samuel Smith and other Republican legislators staggered Washington society and set it buzzing with rumors of schisms, conspiracies, and assorted plots. But President Madison had other problems besides uncooperative congressmen. Even as his foreign policy programs were being lacerated, the members of his Cabinet fell to quarreling among themselves. The principals in this untidy squabble were Secretary of State Robert Smith and Albert Gallatin. Ultimately, his brother's imbroglio would contribute to Samuel Smith's own political decline.

Five years younger than Samuel, Robert had not followed in the footsteps of his father or older brother. After serving in the Continental Army he attended Princeton University and then trained as a lawyer. He soon became one of the most successful attorneys in Baltimore, and, in 1789, he was selected as one of Maryland's presidential electors, evidence of his high standing. During the 1790s he served at various times in both houses of the state legislature and in the Baltimore city council. After his brother resigned as acting head of the navy department in 1801, Robert was appointed secretary; it was here that he first clashed with Secretary of the Treasury Gallatin. Robert handled the limited and not too strenuous tasks of his office creditably, but even his mild attempts to assert the interests of the navy within the councils of the government caused Gallatin to plan his destruction. Fearful of anything that might upset his timetable for abolishing the national debt, Gallatin twice asked Jefferson to remove Robert

Smith from office. On both occasions, however, the president declined to follow the advice of his brilliant but sometimes petty aide. Then, in 1809, Madison named Robert Smith to the state department instead of Gallatin. Angry and disappointed, the treasury secretary resorted once more to devious tactics in order to harm those whom he did not like. His publicizing of the Degen & Purviance allegations, for example, was calculated to discredit Robert as well as Samuel Smith.[1]

With this record of enmity it would have been a miracle if the two secretaries had been able to coexist peacefully. As it turned out, Gallatin was isolated in the Cabinet because Robert Smith and the other secretaries resented his influence with the president and his unrelenting efforts to reduce the budgets of their departments. It was no secret that on more than one occasion the secretary of the treasury had threatened to resign if Madison did not support his recommendations for cutting governmental expenditures. With his administration under fire from all sides, Madison could not afford to lose a man supported by many influential Republicans, including the patriarch of the party, Thomas Jefferson. The Pennsylvanian almost always got what he wanted. In addition to everything else, Gallatin and Robert Smith strongly differed on what response America should make to the British and French decrees. The secretary of state sympathized with his brother's position that the United States should react firmly, while Gallatin obstinately opposed any course of action that would cost money.[2]

Intra-Cabinet strife grew to alarming proportions in late 1809 and early 1810. In October 1809 Jefferson tried to smooth over the relations between his former aides, but without success. Neither Robert Smith nor Gallatin could be blamed entirely for the unhappy state of affairs

1. Charles C. Tansill, "Robert Smith," in Samuel Flagg Bemis, ed., *The American Secretaries of State and Their Diplomacy*, 10 vols. (New York, 1927–1929), 3: 151–201; William A. Burwell to Thomas Jefferson, February 16, 1810, Thomas Jefferson Papers, and Joseph Varnum to George Washington Campbell, March 19, 1810, George W. Campbell Papers, Library of Congress; Samuel Taggart to Rev. John Taylor, January 2, 1810, in George H. Haynes, ed., "Letters of Samuel Taggart," American Antiquarian Society, *Proceedings* n.s., 33 (1923): 338–339.

2. A. J. Dallas to Albert Gallatin, January 1, 1810, Albert Gallatin Papers, New-York Historical Society; Diary of Thomas Worthington, February 18, 1811, Worthington Papers, Library of Congress; Robert Smith to Wilson Cary Nicholas, Smith-Carter Papers, University of Virginia Library; Nathaniel Macon to Joseph Hopper Nicholson, June 23, 1809, Joseph Hopper Nicholson Papers, Library of Congress; Gallatin to Jefferson, November 11, 1809, and Walter Jones to Jefferson, February 19, 1810, Jefferson Papers; Taggart to Taylor, January 2, 1810, in Haynes, ed., "Letters of Taggart," pp. 338–339.

in the Cabinet. The fault lay with Madison, who knew of the historic antagonism between these two men and yet appointed them both to the highest official council. Just as his incompetence in handling the Republican party in Congress allowed his majorities to evaporate, President Madison's indecisiveness as an administrator perpetuated the unhealthy situation in his official family. Having foolishly brought the two men together, the president might at least have bestirred himself to moderate their differences. Instead he exacerbated the problem by favoring Gallatin and countenancing his effort to smear Robert Smith in the Degen & Purviance affair. Jefferson, as far away as Monticello, perceived immediately that much of the problem grew from Madison's unwillingness to establish his leadership. The ex-president reminded Madison that he and Alexander Hamilton had lived together for four years in Washington's Cabinet, although no two men possessed "more opposite principles." This was possible, Jefferson suggested, because President Washington had been the firm master of both.[3]

The fact that the two men causing Madison the most trouble were brothers did not escape the attention of contemporaries. There was a consensus among many that Robert and Samuel Smith were coordinating their endeavors to embarrass the administration. John Randolph and his Republican schismatics, however, went much further, choosing to see the Smith brothers as the center of a sizable conspiracy whose object was to overthrow Gallatin and replace his influence on the president with theirs. These so-called Quids pointed to Senators William Branch Giles of Virginia and Michael Leib of Pennsylvania, Congressman Wilson Cary Nicholas, and William Duane of the Philadelphia *Aurora* as the other partners in the plot to drive Gallatin out of the administration. That Randolph, Macon, Nicholson, and the rest of those who clung desperately to the states' rights doctrines of the Kentucky and Virginia resolutions of 1798 should dislike the Smiths was not unnatural. Before Jefferson took office their views had been in harmony with those of the Republican leadership. But in the intervening years the responsibility of governing the nation had made Jefferson and Madison less dogmatic and more flexible in their thinking. Moreover, since 1801 the Republican party itself had changed, acquiring a large segment of northerners who had little sympathy with the anti-

3. Jefferson to Jones, March 5, 1810, and Jefferson to Joel Barlow, January 24, 1810, in Paul Leicester Ford, ed., *The Writings of Thomas Jefferson*, 10 vols. (New York, 1892–1899), 9: 273, 269; John Randolph to Nicholson, May 2, 1810, Randolph Papers, Virginia State Library, Richmond; Jefferson to Gallatin, October 11, 1809, Jefferson Papers.

urban and antitrade prejudices of the old southern Republicans. These developments had left the Randolph Republicans alienated, a political fringe group of limited consequence. In all the administration they had rapport only with Secretary of the Treasury Gallatin, who believed with them in a limited and frugal central government. Understandably, Randolph and his supporters despised the Smiths, who represented the urban and commercial forces that seemed to have taken control of the party.[4]

Interestingly, no one in Washington besides the Randolph faction betrayed any knowledge of a conspiracy against the secretary of the treasury. Unsubstantiated, their accusations had little significance until resurrected by several generations of historians beginning with the redoubtable Henry Adams. The evidence, however, suggests that both the adherents of John Randolph and their historian-allies were mistaken in thinking that there was ever any group in or out of government that could be called a Smith faction or cabal. A survey of voting records in the Senate in 1809, 1810, and 1811 reveals that the three senators who were supposed to be members of the anti-Gallatin plot, Smith, Giles, and Leib, rarely voted together on major issues. On the two Macon's bills, for example, Giles refused to cast a vote on the final roll calls, but on preliminary procedural votes he stood on the opposite side of the question from Smith and Leib. The correspondence of the alleged plotters also rebuts the notion of conspiracy. While there are no letters proving collusion, a few exist indicating the reverse was true. William Duane once mentioned that he had never met or corresponded with the Smiths and did not particularly like either one of them. Robert Smith revealed in a letter to Wilson Cary Nicholas in June 1810 that he disapproved of his brother's attack on the Macon's bills and had tried to persuade him not to challenge the president. Other similar communications confirm the impression that the Smith faction had no reality anywhere but in the fevered imaginations of John Randolph and his friends.[5]

4. Macon to Nicholson, May 23 and June 23, 1809, and January 7, 1810, Nicholson Papers; James Mercer Garnett to Randolph, December 19, 1809, and January 23 and July 31, 1810, Randolph-Garnett Letterbook, Library of Congress; William Nisbet Chambers, *Political Parties in a New Nation; The American Experience, 1776–1809* (New York, 1963), pp. 183–185; William Cabell Bruce, *John Randolph of Roanoke, 1773–1833* (New York, 1922), p. 219.

5. Henry Adams, ed., *The Writings of Albert Gallatin*, 2 vols. (Philadelphia, 1879), 1: 388–431; Henry Adams, *History of the United States of America during the Administrations of Thomas Jefferson and James Madison*, 9 vols. (New York, 1889–1891), 4: 428–431, 5: 179–193, 327–335, 363–364; John S. Pancake, "The Invisibles; A Chapter in the Opposition to President Madison," *Journal of South-*

The concept of the Smith faction as a potent combination aiming at domination of the American government and capable of paralyzing the operations of that government at will is certainly flattering to Samuel Smith. Unfortunately for his historical position, it is also inaccurate. Worse, the deep-rooted belief, still present, that the Smith faction was a reality has obscured the far more significant and complex forces contributing to the decline of the Republican party during James Madison's first administration. Not conspiracy but an absence of domestic political opposition, the stress of an insoluble international crisis, and the mismanagement on the part of the president were the major causes of the Republican party's descent into chaos. By 1810 there was no real party structure in the national government, only shifting patterns of factional coalitions. Clintonians, Madisonians, northern Republicans, Old Republicans, admirers of Samuel Smith, the Federalists, and other splinter groups formed together in various combinations on different issues.[6] "We are all at odd and evens," the general once lamented to Wilson Cary Nicholas, "and never can get together again."[7]

The growing tension in Congress and the Cabinet reached a climax in the winter and spring of 1811 over the question of whether or not the Bank of the United States should be granted a new charter. A result of one of Secretary of the Treasury Alexander Hamilton's famous reports to Congress, the bank had been originally chartered for a period of twenty years. The institution symbolized all that orthodox Republicans considered evil in Federalism: centralization and a loose construction of the Constitution. Albert Gallatin, however, had discovered that the bank was useful, perhaps indispensable to the orderly conduct of business in the treasury department. By 1811 he had managed to bring the president around to his point of view, although twenty years earlier as a congressman Madison had led the fight

ern History 21 (February 1955): 17–37; U.S., Congress, *The Debates and Proceedings in the Congress of the United States . . . 1789–1824,* 42 vols. (Washington, D.C., 1834–1856), 11th Cong., 2d sess., 1811, pp. 575–577, 582, 611, 673–674, 12th Cong., 1st sess., 1812, pp. 189, 191–192, 192–193, 203, 211, 267, 270–271, 286, 296–297, hereafter cited as *Annals of Congress;* William Duane to Henry Dearborn, March 3, 1810, in Worthington C. Ford, ed., "Letters of William Duane," Massachusetts Historical Society, *Proceedings* 2d ser., 20: 334–338; Robert Smith to Nicholas, June 11, 1810, Smith-Carter Papers; Nicholas to unknown recipient, undated but probably written in early 1811, and Nicholas to S. Smith, October 22, 1812, Wilson Cary Nicholas Papers, Library of Congress.

6. Taggart to Taylor, April 27, 1810, in Haynes, ed., "Letters of Taggart," p. 347; Chambers, *Political Parties,* p. 191.

7. S. Smith to Nicholas, March 17, 1810, Smith-Carter Papers.

against Hamilton's plan. But the administration was not in tune with congressional Republicans, who still saw the institution as a monster, and Madison did or said little that would convince them otherwise.[8]

Samuel Smith probably did not share, at least entirely, the doctrinaire opinions about the bank held by many of his fellow Republicans. As a merchant he knew that banks were essential to the economically sophisticated American business community. But as to the Bank of the United States specifically, he had some very strong views. Smith's connections with several local state-chartered banks in Baltimore in part explain his attitude. In 1811 he was on the board of directors of the Bank of Baltimore and the Bank of Maryland and owned stock in several other banks in the city. Personal interest dictated that he be jealous of the Bank of the United States and its branch office in Baltimore, which competed with the institutions he was associated with. While some of the general's enemies felt that these arrangements with local banks determined his vote against recharter, others presumed that the Marylander was really carrying on his vendetta against the secretary of the treasury. The truth, however, was far different.[9]

Although the question of recharter was finally settled in 1811, Congress had first considered it a year earlier. At that time the Senate had named a committee to consider a recharter bill after receiving a favorable report on the bank from the secretary of the treasury. An expert on banking matters, Smith found himself on the committee and deeply involved in drafting a new charter. He made it clear during the committee debates that it was not a national bank that he disliked but the organization and operations of this particular national bank.

8. *Annals of Congress,* 10th Cong., 2d sess., 1809, pp. 456–460; James Madison to Gallatin, August 29, 1810, James Madison Papers, and Timothy Pickering to Samuel Chase, January 11, 1811, Timothy Pickering Papers, Library of Congress.

9. Irving Brant, *James Madison; The President, 1809–1812* (New York, 1956), pp. 266–269; Norman K. Risjord, *The Old Republicans; Southern Conservatism in the Age of Jefferson* (New York, 1965), p. 111; Bray Hammond, *Banks and Politics in America from the Revolution to the Civil War* (Princeton, 1957), pp. 46–212; Dice Robins Anderson, *William Branch Giles: A Study in the Politics of Virginia and the Nation from 1790 to 1830* (Menasha, Wis., 1914), p. 165; John Dos Passos, *The Shackles of Power; Three Jeffersonian Decades* (Garden City, N.Y., 1966), p. 186; Marshall Smelser, *The Democratic Republic, 1801–1815* (New York, 1968), p. 231; Raymond Walters, Jr., *Albert Gallatin: Jeffersonian Financier and Diplomat* (New York, 1957), p. 239; S. Smith to Gallatin, November 2, 1808, Gallatin Papers; S. Smith to Madison, August 8 and 10, 1810, Madison Papers; S. Smith to George Harrison, March 11, 1810, S. Smith to unknown recipient, March 20, 1810, and Harrison to S. Smith, March 10, 1810, Samuel Smith Papers, Library of Congress.

Smith complained about the Bank of the United States' misuse of power. He charged it with applying its vast economic leverage to accomplish such political goals as the strengthening of the Federalist party and the securing of its own recharter. Such activity by a publicly supported institution he found reprehensible. Sometime in the middle of March 1810 the committee presented its plan for recharter to the full Senate. The Marylander thought the proposal eliminated most of the bank's controversial features without impairing its ability to function, and at every opportunity he spoke and voted for the bill. The majority of Republican senators, however, were still uncertain as to the constitutionality of a national bank and voted to postpone any decision until the next session of Congress. On Smith's motion the Senate did agree to continue the old charter until June 30, 1812, to insure the legislature time to act.[10]

After Congress adjourned in the summer of 1810, Smith arrived back in Baltimore to find the local branch of the Bank of the United States engaged in some heavy-handed political blackmail. To force Baltimore's merchants to support recharter, the branch bank had purposely caused an economic recession by tightening credit and withdrawing funds it normally kept on deposit with state banks. Smith instantly lost his temper, flying into one of those grand rages that periodically got him into trouble. Seeking out the president of the branch bank he asserted that the institution was controlled by foreigners and loaned its money only to Federalists. Smith knew the first accusation was entirely wrong and the second nearly so. In an exchange of letters the president of the branch bank forced him to admit his errors.[11]

Smith could hardly be satisfied with this first encounter with the branch bank. Changing his method of attack, he tried to get the Republican administration in Washington to help him punish the institution. In a letter to President Madison, Smith urged that Gallatin be instructed to withdraw all federal funds from the Baltimore branch bank and deposit the monies in local banks. Only in this way, he argued, could the branch be stopped from committing further injury on the Baltimore business community. The Marylander hinted that unless his suggestion for transferring the funds was followed,

10. Henry Clay to Caesar Rodney, January 11, 1809, Rodney Family Papers, Library of Congress; *Annals of Congress,* 10th Cong., 2d sess., 1809, pp. 456–460, 11th Cong., 2d sess., 1810, pp. 598, 615–672; S. Smith to unknown recipient, March 20, 1810, Smith Papers.

11. S. Smith to Madison, August 8, 1810, and Harrison to S. Smith, March 10, 1810, Smith Papers.

there would be congressmen "who will attribute it to improper motives, and who will believe that the Sec. of the Treasury was thoroughly favoring the institution," and concluded ominously: "We certainly had better have no such institution if the consequence is that it can cave the government at its pleasure."[12] The general's letter, filled as it was with hardly concealed threats and insults, was not likely to obtain speedy compliance from the president. Then, too, Madison could not forget that the man now asking him for a favor had played a large part in embarrassing the administration during the recent Macon's bills debates. The president did not bother to answer Smith, but told Gallatin that a transfer of funds to the state banks "would not be convenient to the public."[13]

Smith was still irate over the machinations of the Baltimore branch bank and his rebuff by Madison when Congress again took up the problem of recharter. A recharter plan, far different from the Senate's scheme of 1810, was introduced into the House in January 1811. After weeks of debate, the lower chamber could not muster a majority in favor of the bill, and its consideration was indefinitely postponed, thus leaving the decision on the future of the bank in the hands of the Senate. With so much at stake, both sides poured time and money into massive efforts to sway the Senate's final vote. Gallatin worked closely with lobbyists from the bank, while the word was whispered among Senate Republicans that despite his silence the president favored recharter. The natural opposition to the bank by many Republican senators was nourished by petitions from several state legislatures protesting recharter: Virginia, Massachusetts, Pennsylvania, Kentucky, and Maryland sent instructions to their senators ordering them to vote against recharter. The binding nature of these instructions was still a matter of dispute, but since the state legislatures elected federal senators, the incumbent officeholders were wise to heed them. Smith never commented on the instructions he received from the Maryland legislature and kept so silent about his views that no one knew how he would vote even after the debates had begun. The mystery vanished when he seconded a motion made by the bank's enemies striking out that clause in the bank bill providing for the continuance of the charter for another twenty years.[14]

On February 16, 1811, the Marylander addressed the Senate on the

12. S. Smith to Madison, August 8, 1810, Smith Papers.

13. Madison to Gallatin, August 29, 1810, Madison Papers.

14. Macon to Nicholson, February 9, 1811, Nicholson Papers; Taggart to Taylor, February 4, 1811, in Haynes, ed., "Letters of Taggart," p. 353; *Annals of Congress,* 11th Cong., 3d sess., 1811, pp. 826, 122, 240.

recharter bill. Recalling that he had supported a national bank in the last session, he told the Senate that the specific plan now before the upper chamber failed to correct glaring deficiencies in the present charter. Smith rehearsed the old charges that foreigners, principally Englishmen, controlled most of the bank's stock and that the bank was partial in its loan policies to Federalists.[15] Since he had already been stung before by making these allegations and most certainly was aware that foreign stockholders could not vote for members of the board of directors, the general was obviously engaging in some conscious hyperbole. But all of this was only preparatory to his main assault, which was directed at the branch operations of the bank. The Bank of the United States, Smith declared, had at first confined its operations to Philadelphia. Soon, however, it had established branches in Boston, New York, Baltimore, and Charleston. "Wherever it extended its influence dissension commenced," the Marylander remarked, "wherever it placed its foot, it became absolutely necessary for the States to erect another bank to counter-balance its pecuniary and political influence."[16] From last summer's experience with the Baltimore branch, the general had an excellent idea of the harm the bank's "pecuniary and political influence" could do to a community.[17]

Having outlined the dangers of permitting a national bank to create branches, Smith went on to challenge the necessity of branch banks. Not only had the branch banks done incalculable injury, but also, he asserted, no one had yet demonstrated that they performed any vital function. Acknowledging that the branches aided the government by serving as depositories of revenues and by transferring federal funds to other parts of the nation, Smith recalled that state banks had conducted these operations long before the Bank of the United States was created. Anticipating another argument in favor of the bank, the Marylander emphasized the capacity and willingness of state banks to make loans to the national government. Near the end of his speech Smith indicated that although his attitude toward the bank had hardened because of the events in Baltimore, he still wanted a national bank. The plan now before the Senate, however, he found unacceptable. Any new national bank, he insisted, must be free of foreign influence and without power to establish branches.[18]

In the course of his speech opposing the bill rechartering the Bank of the United States, Smith had taken the opportunity to criticize

---

15. *Annals of Congress,* 11th Cong., 3d sess., 1811, pp. 240–242.
16. Ibid., p. 243.
17. Ibid.
18. Ibid., pp. 244–250, 259.

Albert Gallatin for using his official position to support the legislation. This remark seemed to add credibility to the view that there was something that could be called a Smith faction, and that led by Samuel Smith it was engaged in a general opposition to the administration. The general certainly disliked Gallatin, probably more than any man he had ever known. He would have been less than human had he not enjoyed the spectacle of the secretary of the treasury failing to get measures he badly wanted through Congress. But Smith was motivated less by his personal feelings about Gallatin than by his analysis of the shortcomings of the plan to recharter the bank. He considered the bank bill bad for himself, bad for Baltimore Republicanism, and bad for the country. To vote for such a measure would have been contrary to the whole pattern of his political career.[19]

Moreover, it can hardly be said that Smith bolted the Republican party when he worked against recharter. As in the case of the Macon's bills, there was no discernible orthodox party position. Even if Madison had announced his support for the bill, most Republicans would probably have continued to see the bank as the enemy of constitutional government. In the House a majority of Republicans had opposed recharter, and the same was true in the Senate. On the final vote Smith and sixteen other Republican senators voted nay. Ten Republicans together with seven Federalists voted for the bank; the tie vote was then broken by Vice President George Clinton, a Republican, who voted to kill the bank. Who then were the apostates: the majority of congressional Republicans who stood against recharter, or Madison and Gallatin, who had the support of the Federalists if not their own party? Ironically, however, the administration position eventually proved to be the right one. War was on the horizon and would begin in only eighteen months. Smith's claims that state banks could act as efficiently as branches of a national bank were, to say the least, exaggerated. Because the bank had not been rechartered in 1811, the government lost its most important financial asset on the very eve of the War of 1812. Smith helped to destroy the first Bank of the United States, but his motives were honest and his chief sin was shortsightedness. Madison, on the other hand, knew how essential the bank was to the government and yet did nothing.[20]

The death of the bank bill precipitated a crisis that had been

19. Ibid., pp. 256–259, 322–323.

20. Ibid., pp. 346–347; Macon to Nicholson, January 11, 1811, University of Virginia. This judgment on Madison's actions is disputed by Marshall Smelser and Irving Brant. See Smelser, *The Democratic Republic*, pp. 230–231; and Brant, *Madison; The President*, pp. 265–270.

building in the government for two years, ever since Robert Smith had been given the state department instead of Albert Gallatin. The secretary of the treasury, chagrined at a defeat he viewed as a personal insult delivered by Samuel Smith, and resentful of the scurrilous attacks made on him by William Duane's *Aurora*, submitted his resignation to the president. Actually the Pennsylvanian was not really sincere in saying he wished to leave the administration; his letter of resignation was carefully worded so as to leave the impression that he would stay on if certain conditions were met. Gallatin complained that he was being persecuted by "subdivisions and personal factions" within the Republican party who had delayed or defeated imperatively needed programs he had sponsored. Only a "radical and *speedy* remedy," Gallatin told the president, could reverse this situation. The secretary's insinuation was unmistakable; Madison must choose between him and the Smiths. Madison did not even reply to Gallatin's communication. Instead he immediately but indirectly opened talks with the governor of Virginia, James Monroe, to learn if he would be willing to serve as secretary of state. Monroe accepted the offer, leaving Madison with the one final problem of getting rid of the current secretary of state, Robert Smith.[21]

The president fired Robert on either March 12 or 13, 1811, citing as reasons his incompetence and his disloyalty. Neither accusation was entirely just. Robert, it is true, showed little initiative in office, but this was probably a virtue in the eyes of Madison, who preferred to handle the intricacies of high diplomacy himself. As far as the day-to-day conduct of business in the state department was concerned, Robert had performed it adequately. In calling the secretary disloyal, Madison was referring to the fact that Robert revealed Cabinet secrets to his brother and also spoke out publicly against Cabinet decisions he had not opposed when they were being discussed. If accurate, and they were, these assertions justified the dismissal. Robert, however, had been committing these indiscretions for some time, and yet the president had waited until the spring of 1811 to take action. Even more inexplicably, Madison offered this incompetent and disloyal subordinate he had just fired the position of American minister to Russia. The tendering of the Russian mission was undoubtedly aimed at easing Robert out of the state department with a minimum of

21. Randolph to Nicholson, February 14 and 17, 1811, Nicholson Papers; Diary of Thomas Worthington, February 18, 1811, Worthington Papers; Nicholson to Gallatin, March 6, 1811, Gallatin Papers; Philadelphia *Aurora*, February 13, 1811. A draft of Gallatin's resignation dated March 4, 1811, is located in the Gallatin Papers; see also Brant, *Madison; The President*, pp. 282–283.

fuss. It was a clear sign that he had no desire at the moment to open a campaign to totally eradicate Samuel Smith's influence in the government. The president could not help but realize that removing Robert would be understood as a slap at Samuel. But one of the original reasons for appointing Robert was probably to obtain his brother's support for the administration, and since that support had not been forthcoming nothing could be lost by eliminating Robert from the Cabinet.[22]

On the other hand, Madison stood to gain a great deal by bringing James Monroe into the administration. Since 1806, when the treaty he had negotiated with England had been suppressed by Jefferson, Monroe had been flirting with John Randolph and his schismatics. In 1808 he had been the Randolph faction's candidate for the presidency against James Madison. The young Virginian had shown an inclination to return to the fold in more recent years, and because of his intimate friendship with Jefferson he had been chosen governor of his state. Monroe's accession to the Cabinet meant that at one stroke Madison had weakened Randolph and his supporters and strengthened his ties to Jefferson and the Virginia Republican party, the very core of his political support. The president had also managed to end the long Cabinet dispute that had disgraced his administration. With Robert Smith gone, Gallatin now agreed to continue in the treasury department. From just about every perspective the dismissal of Robert Smith ranked as one of Madison's most adroit political acts as president.

Robert Smith, unaware of the involved considerations that lay behind his sudden exit from the Cabinet, groped about unable to decide how he should react. He was deeply resentful of his treatment by Madison, but when the president offered him the Russian post he accepted, perhaps because it might conceal from the public the full extent of his downfall. If he had stuck with this decision, much of what followed might never have happened. After a day or two of contemplation, however, the former secretary became increasingly incensed as he reviewed his final conversation with the president. He concluded that to accept the diplomatic position in Russia would give the impression that he admitted the validity of Madison's allegations. Feeling that his honor was at stake, Robert determined to defend him-

22. See Madison's memoir on the dismissal of Robert Smith, April 1811, Madison Papers; S. Smith to John Spear Smith, March 14, 1811, and Robert Smith to S. Smith, March 23 and 28, 1811, Smith Papers; Madison to Jefferson, April 1, 1811, in Gaillard Hunt, ed., *The Writings of James Madison,* 9 vols. (New York, 1900–1910), 8: 136.

self no matter what the cost. He began by turning down the Russian post and followed that by boycotting a dinner the president had arranged to honor him. It seemed that despite Madison's earnest efforts to avoid trouble, Robert Smith was bent on making some.[23]

Much more sensitive than his brother, Samuel Smith perceived instantly what had occurred. His letters indicate that he was calm but very bitter about his brother's situation during these critical days in late March 1811. His first advice to Robert was to accept the offer to become the American minister in Russia. Like Madison, he did not wish the matter blown up into a major controversy; there was no profit to be gained. The president had the right to fire a Cabinet secretary, and in this particular case he had tried to ease Robert out gently. In public, therefore, the general remained absolutely silent. In private, he used his influence with Robert to persuade him to keep his composure. At the same time, in letters to his daughter Mary Mansfield, who was living in England, he allowed his outrage full expression. The dismissal, he said, "came upon us like a thunderstroke," although for some reason the Federalists in Congress seemed to know about it in advance. The motive for the action, Smith guessed, was not to attack him but to "prepare the way for Mr. Monroe to be successor to Mr. M[adison]." Smith properly surmised that Gallatin had intrigued against Robert and was at least partially responsible for the recent events.[24]

Disregarding his brother's counsels of restraint, Robert Smith had by the end of March resolved to carry his case to the public. He informed Samuel that he intended to publish an exposé of the Madison administration. Robert predicted that his information, once known, would "lead to the injury of Mr. Madison and to my advantage." The president's overthrow was his goal, declared Robert, "and most assuredly will I effect it." Samuel Smith tried to dissuade his brother. He pointed out that while Madison was not now popular, a favorable change in the foreign situation would alter everything, and "his conduct and wisdom will be immortalized." In that case, the senator contended, everyone who had made a public assault on the president would become most unpopular. Even if the crisis with France and Great Britain persisted, Samuel believed that an attack, no matter how truthful, would have little effect since Madison's political position

23. Robert Smith to S. Smith, March 28, 1811, Smith Papers.
24. S. Smith to John Spear Smith, March 14 and 24, and May 14, 1811, Robert Smith to S. Smith, March 25, 26, and 27, 1811, and S. Smith's memorandum on the dismissal of Robert Smith, May 6, 1811, Smith Papers; S. Smith to Mrs. Mansfield, April 1, 1811, Smith-Carter Papers.

in the south and west would remain strong. Nothign, in short, could be gained by displaying the administrations's dirty linen. Prophetically, Samuel warned his brother that if he insisted on publishing his pamphlet, he would be answered by a "thousand able pens" who would "reflect on the course you take of disclosing the proceedings of the Cabinet."[25]

Robert, caught up on his own self-righteousness, was deaf to his brother's pleas, and in June he released the text of his revelations to the Baltimore newspapers. Titled grandly *Robert Smith's Address to the People of the United States,* the intemperate and lengthy document was filled with half-truths and outright lies.[26] One Republican described the pamphlet as "singular" because it was "one of the rare instances of a man's giving the finishing stroke to his own character in his eagerness to ruin his enemy."[27] More speedily than he could have imagined, Samuel Smith's predictions were fulfilled. The "thousand able pens" tore his brother's publication apart, leaving the author a pathetic and ridiculous figure.[28] The general was briefly hopeful that the pamphlet might be a success. He told his son, John Spear Smith, that it would reveal the "true ground" on which Robert had been fired. "I fancy it will surprise Madison," Samuel told his son, "and will show a littleness of mind unworthy of a great man."[29] By the first week in July, however, the mounting tide of criticism against Robert caused the senator to become more pessimistic. He was now sure that the *Address* had permanently ended Robert's political career, and he wrote his son, "indeed I consider it as the seal to the influence of the Smiths'."[30]

Robert's foolishness had now brought on the confrontation that both Madison and Samuel Smith had tried to avoid. Instead of being hurt the president had benefited from the former secretary of state's attack. Just as in 1806 John Randolph's anti-Jefferson tirades had tightened the bonds between the president and the rest of the Republican party, the same phenomenon occurred in 1811. Unwittingly Robert had done what Madison could not have done for himself: he

25. Robert Smith to S. Smith, March 26, 1811, and S. Smith to Robert Smith, March 27, 1811, Smith Papers.

26. The pamphlet was reprinted in a number of newspapers, including the Philadelphia *Aurora,* June 26, 1811; Garnett to Randolph, July 23, 1811, Randolph-Garnett Letterbook.

27. Garnett to Randolph, July 23, 1811, Randolph-Garnett Letterbook.

28. Macon to Nicholson, September 21, 1811, Nicholson Papers.

29. S. Smith to John Spear Smith, June 13, 1811, Smith Papers.

30. S. Smith to John Spear Smith, July 4, 1811, Smith Papers. See also Laura Smith to John Spear Smith, July 4, 1811, Smith-Carter Papers.

had made the president respectable to most Republicans, who had been accustomed to disregarding or ignoring him. If Republicans could not agree on how to preserve the nation's honor or commercial property, they were willing to unite against the specter of schism in the party. Many party members had said worse about the president than Robert Smith, but never publicly. He had transgressed the accepted rules of political behavior and the penalty was political oblivion. The tragedy was that although Samuel Smith had not approved of Robert's pamphlet and even had argued against its publication, he could not escape sharing his brother's ignominy. Robert was more than Samuel's brother; he was his political protegé. Two presidents had appointed the undistinguished Robert to high office partly because they wished to please Samuel. So closely was Robert identified with his brother that most thought the *Address* could only have been written with Samuel's encouragement. In any event, both brothers were branded as schismatics, and the administration took steps to curtail the general's power.

The summer and fall of 1811 were not pleasant for the general and his family. In Washington they found themselves "under a cloud" socially as Republican hostesses, including Dolley Madison, crossed them off their guest lists. In November 1811 the administration, without informing the senator, peremptorily recalled John Spear Smith as the acting United States chargé d'affaires in London. The dismissal of his son saddened Smith not only because the manner in which it was done was a further proof of his disgraced position, but also because he had long hoped John would become a career diplomat. His own downfall had made that possibility unlikely. Even back in Baltimore the general discovered that the administration was using every device at its command to wreck his political career. He learned that William Pinkney, whose nomination as minister to England he had opposed in 1806 because of his Federalism, had replaced him as the Republican party's chief agent in the city. With control over the distribution of federal patronage, Pinkney began to build a political machine rivalling Smith's. In the spring of 1812 Joseph Hopper Nicholson, Smith's old antagonist, joyfully reported with some exaggeration that the senator was almost isolated politically in Baltimore.[31]

Samuel Smith managed to survive the fiasco of 1811. By no means had his political position in Baltimore or Maryland been destroyed, as

31. S. Smith to Mrs. Mansfield, November 6, 1811, Smith-Carter Papers; John Spear Smith to Madison, April 21, 1812, Madison Papers; Nicholson to Gallatin, May 19, 1812, Gallatin Papers.

shown by the fact that he would remain in Congress for another twenty-two years, nor had his prestige within the national government been entirely erased, for he still had many friends in Congress and the administration. But in a very real sense the political odyssey he had begun twenty years before had ended. Never again would he influence presidents or sway Congress as he had in the years since Jefferson took office. Madison and Gallatin could take part of the credit, but only part, for Samuel Smith's decline. Vast demographic, economic, and social changes were leading the United States toward a new era in which the old leaders and the old issues were of less and less importance. Although fifty-nine years old the general still had many productive years before him. He belonged, however, by age and temperament to an era of America that was passing, the era of Washington and Jefferson, of the Revolution and the creation of national institutions, of an America oriented toward Europe rather than the limitless reaches of the West. That era was destined to expire not quietly but amidst the din of war.

12

<hr style="border-top: dashed;">

Prelude to Victory

THE CONFLICT between the Smiths and the administration soon faded as a topic of public interest. Attention focused instead on the un-remitting attacks by the belligerents on American commerce and the growing Indian unrest in the Northwest that many suspected the British of encouraging. Beginning in the spring of 1811, a series of events occurred that moved the United States toward war. In May the American frigate *President,* commanded by Captain John Rodgers, having been ordered to protect American commerce off the American coast, engaged the much smaller British sloop *Little Belt.* Rodgers easily overcame his adversary, and despite the unevenness of the contest his victory was considered by the American people to revenge the insult on the *Chesapeake.* The *Little Belt* affair revealed a new militancy among large groups of Americans. Meanwhile, in the western territory of Indiana, Governor William Henry Harrison began a campaign against an Indian confederacy led by the Shawnee Tecumseh and his brother, the Prophet. Ending with the indecisive Battle of Tippecanoe in November, Harrison's thrust increased tensions along the frontier. Western Americans loudly called upon their govern-ment to expel the British from Canada in order to eliminate the Indians' source of arms.[1]

As the first session of the Twelfth Congress assembled in November of 1811, the members were aware not only of the impatience of the

1. See, for example, Marshall Smelser, *The Democratic Republic, 1801–1815* (New York, 1968), pp. 208–211.

American people, but also that Macon's bill number two had failed to bring an end to the belligerents' decrees against the free flow of American neutral trade. In August 1810 Napoleon had informed the administration that he was accepting the terms of the law by exempting American vessels from the operation of the French decrees. But in the intervening months all evidence showed the emperor had lied and that American commercial ships were still being seized. Although aware of French deceit, Madison insisted that Napoleon had fulfilled the terms of Macon's bill. He told the English government that unless it suspended its orders-in-council—at least for Americans— then the United States would have no choice but to reinstate non-intercourse against Britain. Madison's gamble did not succeed, as the English navy accelerated its operations near American harbors. The painfully obvious bankruptcy of the commercial-restriction policy contributed to the rapidly developing prowar sentiment in many parts of America. Madison himself had probably decided on war even before Congress met in the late fall of 1811, but questions of timing, alliances, tactics, and financing delayed any action until June of 1812.[2]

In his annual speech to Congress in November 1811 Madison frankly confessed the defeat of his diplomatic attempts. He asked Congress to enlarge the army, reorganize the militia, and to give some attention to the state of the navy. The president's requests found strong support in both houses of Congress. In the Senate Samuel Smith, who retained much of his influence in the legislature despite his troubles with the president, voted for nearly all of the proposed defense measures. The administration seemed incapable, however, of implementing the laws it had requested Congress to pass. In March, only five months before war was declared, the administration had not recruited a single man to fill the ranks of the specially authorized twenty-five-thousand-man army.[3] One reason for the lethargy of the national government was a series of unaccountable atrocities committed by French privateers against American ships and sailors that made it difficult to justify a declaration of war against England alone. "The Devil himself," one Republican complained, "could not tell which govt. England or France is the most wicked."[4]

2. Ibid., pp. 197–199.

3. U.S., Congress, *The Debates and Proceedings in the Congress of the United States . . . 1789–1824*, 42 vols. (Washington, D.C., 1834–1856), 12th Cong., 1st sess., 1811, pp. 11–15, 33, 99, 112, 127, 163–164, hereafter cited as *Annals of Congress;* Felix Grundy to Andrew Jackson, February 12, 1812, Andrew Jackson Papers, Library of Congress.

4. Nathaniel Macon to Joseph Hopper Nicholson, March 24, 1812, Joseph Hopper Nicholson Papers, Library of Congress.

Ever since the *Chesapeake* affair the general had been among those demanding war. Earlier, he had been convinced by Jefferson that the Embargo could accomplish the same ends as war and so had temporarily moderated his original view. When the Embargo was repealed Smith had once again insisted that war was the only course open to the United States if it was to retain its honor. He had been overruled by President Madison and a majority of the Republican party, who believed war was impractical and that other forms of commercial coercion should be tried. Even his efforts to get the government to approve the arming of merchant vessels and the use of convoys had been rebuffed. In the spring of 1812 the general was as committed to war as he had been in 1809. He sensed that the administration and Congress were finally coming to agree with his point of view and he did everything in his power to encourage them. On April 3, 1812, for example, he opposed in the Senate a bill laying a ninety-day embargo on American shipping. Smith understood that an embargo was necessary before a declaration of war in order to save American ships from being trapped and caught on the ocean after hostilities commenced. He voted against the embargo bill because he felt that three months was far too long a time for such a measure. The administration, he suspected, might be making an effort to reestablish the old discredited system of peaceful coercion and thus to "sneak out of war." A short while later the Marylander also voted against a resolution sponsored by antiwar congressmen that would have adjourned the legislature immediately, before a declaration of war could be considered.[5]

For Samuel Smith it was not a question of war or peace that confronted the United States, but rather of whom the nation ought to fight and in what manner.[6] He maintained as he had to Gallatin in 1807 after the *Chesapeake* affair that a war would not be fought to any large extent on American soil. He therefore absented himself from the Senate floor during the vote on the twenty-five-thousand-man army and later criticized plans to mobilize large numbers of militia for federal service. Smith believed that the war should and would take place primarily on the ocean, perhaps on the model of the quasiwar with France. Reasoning thus, he gave his whole-hearted support to bills increasing the navy and improving coastal defenses. The general,

---

5. *Annals of Congress,* 12th Cong., 1st sess., 1812, pp. 189, 211; see also Samuel Smith's memorandum on Monroe's testimony before a House committee, March 31, 1812, Samuel Smith Papers, Library of Congress.

6. The question of strategy was debated thoroughly by congressional Republicans. See Roger H. Brown, *The Republic in Peril: 1812* (New York, 1964), pp. 108–130.

besides arguing for naval warfare, proposed that the United States declare war on both England and France rather than on England alone as the administration wished. To simultaneously challenge the two greatest nations in the world appeared as sheer lunacy to most congressmen. Smith, however, had substantial arguments behind his suggestion. In a Senate speech on May 6, 1811, the general, after enumerating the violations by France of the agreement to remove the commercial decrees as they affected American trade, told his colleagues that "national honor" required the United States to treat England and France in precisely the same way. Moreover, he might well have contended that war with both England and France was no more dangerous to American security than war with England alone. The Royal Navy had already destroyed the French fleets and so there was no chance that America would be invaded by French troops even if they could be spared from the European battlefields. It was the English fleet and the English army that the United States had to fear. Although in a war France could not hurt the United States, the United States was not powerless to inflict injury on France. War would certainly mean an almost complete halt to the shipments of American foodstuffs upon which French sugar islands in the West Indies depended. Also American privateers would soon be infesting the waters along the French coast, snapping up what little seaborne trade the British allowed to slip by their blockade. Annoyed in this way, France might sue for a quick peace with the United States, promising to genuinely exempt American shipping from its decrees in return for a possible alliance against the common and more deadly enemy, Great Britain.[7]

Smith's plan for a dual war attracted some favorable attention in Congress, but a majority of both houses obviously felt that war against one great power was more than enough for the resources of the United States. The president sent his war message to the legislature on June 1, 1812, and four days later the House of Representatives voted its approval. In the Senate the declaration ran into stiff opposition. One group of senators tried to substitute a bill that in effect would open a limited maritime war against England, and at one point the Senate even voted its approval of a motion amending the war resolution to say that letters of marque and reprisal should be issued against British public and commercial vessels. Smith spoke and voted against this plan because it did not include France. An amendment to this effect

7. *Annals of Congress*, 12th Cong., 1st sess., 1812, pp. 84, 192–193, 163, 230–231.

was defeated, and the Senate later reversed itself and threw out the limited maritime war plan. All that was left was Madison's original declaration of war. With hope of a naval war against France and England now extinct, the general swung over to complete support of the president's declaration. He may have felt that Congress had gone too far not to declare war, or that war in any form was preferable to the conditions that existed. The Senate formally gave its consent on June 18, and a day later Madison declared a state of war to be in existence. All were unaware that one of the principle causes of the hostilities, the orders-in-council, had already been repealed by the British government.[8]

With the outbreak of war Smith began spending more and more of his time in Baltimore, where, as commander of the third militia division, he bore the main burden of organizing the city's defenses. The general was perhaps the most qualified man in Maryland for the job of protecting the great port and its fifty thousand citizens. He had commanded the Baltimore militia since the Revolutionary War, and in 1778 he had directed the city's preparations against an anticipated British assault. Not only was he equipped militarily, but also he still had connections with the government in Washington and among the business elite in Baltimore that facilitated the problems of readying the city for an attack. The federal government had little in the way of resources, either in men or money, that could be committed to the defense of urban areas. In the competition for a share of those scarce resources Baltimore did very well, largely because of Samuel Smith's position as a senator. But more important was his ability to tap the reservoirs of money and men in Baltimore itself, for in the final analysis the city could not depend on any outside help. Bankers and businessmen in Baltimore listened respectfully to the general because he was one of them. They knew that his stake in the city was greater than any of theirs and so they were more willing to accept his leadership. Smith also was held in great esteem by the masses of Baltimore's less exalted citizens. In part this was due to his careful cultivation of the city's voters as a politician. Mainly, however, the people revered him as a link with the past, as a comrade of George Washington and a hero of the Revolution in his own right. This unique blending of institutional and personal authority, of official and unofficial power, of local and national influence made Samuel Smith Baltimore's most effective leader.

8. Ibid., pp. 266, 270; see also John Randolph to unknown recipient, June 24, 1812, John Randolph Papers, Library of Congress.

By the fall of 1813 Samuel Smith had created the army and built most of the fortifications that discouraged the British attack in 1814. Yet these achievements would not have been possible had not the British navy conducted raiding operations in Chesapeake Bay during the spring and summer of 1813. Before Rear Admiral Sir George Cockburn's fleet entered the Chesapeake in February, Smith had been unable to convince apathetic federal or state authorities of Baltimore's exposed position.[9] As late as the first two weeks of March, when the British squadron began moving slowly up the Chesapeake toward Baltimore, virtually nothing had been done to repair or improve the city's defenses. Finally, almost in desperation, Smith wrote Governor Levin Winder of Maryland demanding support: "The vicinity of the enemy and the facility with which he might pass a force suddenly against this City makes it necessary to be in a state of preparation to repel any attempt that may be made."[10] The general bluntly told Governor Winder that less than fifty regular army troops manned Fort McHenry and, therefore, "the defence of this important city appears to be committed to the local Militia of this State." He asserted that more muskets, cannon, tents, and every other implement of war were needed to preserve the city.[11] After personally inspecting the situation, the governor authorized Smith "to take the earliest opportunity of making the necessary arrangement of the militia for the defense of the Port of Baltimore."[12] Winder's order was vague and unsatisfactory. It did not specify that Smith had been called into active service by the governor, nor did it make clear whether he could now call up the Baltimore militia for service at the expense of the state. Smith, however, chose to interpret Winder's letter in the broadest possible way—as a full grant of power to defend the city by any means available. Significantly, Smith in his own letters always misquoted the governor's order by dropping the phrase "of the militia," thus making it appear that his commission was far broader than it was.[13]

When Smith assumed active command of Baltimore the city stood nearly defenseless. Because no fortifications existed on Patapsco Neck or on Hampstead Hill, a land invasion could not have been seriously

9. S. Smith to Gov. Robert Bowie, July 20 and September 23, 1812, and Walter Jones to S. Smith, March 12, 1813, Smith Papers.

10. S. Smith to Gov. Levin Winder, March 12, 1813, Smith Order Book, Library of Congress.

11. Ibid.

12. Gov. Winder to S. Smith, March 13, 1813, Smith Papers.

13. See, for example, S. Smith to William Jones, March 13, 1813, and S. Smith to John Armstrong, March 13, 1813, Smith Papers.

contested, and in the harbor area Fort McHenry mounted but a pitifully few guns manned by an insignificant number of army troops. As a United States Army post Fort McHenry was not even subject to General Smith's orders; and its commander, Major Lloyd Beall, proved more an adversary than a cooperative colleague. Although a major port, Baltimore was protected by only a single naval gunboat commanded by Captain Charles Gordon. As for the militia, the four brigades in Smith's division proved an uneven lot. The second and ninth brigades, drawn from inland rural counties, were practically worthless, lacking arms, training, and leadership. The eleventh brigade from Baltimore County and under the command of Brigadier General Tobias Stansbury was of better quality, but hardly ready for combat. The finest militia troops in Maryland filled the ranks of Baltimore's own third brigade led by Brigadier General John Stricker, an old friend and political supporter of Samuel Smith. Within an hour up to forty-five hundred men could be at their posts ready to protect the city from attack. The third brigade constituted the heart of Baltimore's defense force, but in March 1813 fully one-third of the troops lacked weapons.[14] Smith operated on two levels in his efforts to fill the gaps in the city's security protection. On one plane the general vigorously sought state and federal aid for Baltimore, while on another he systematically improved the efficiency of both the men and fortifications responsible for warding off assault.

Between March 13 and April 16, 1813, when the British fleet blockaded the Patapsco River, Samuel Smith succeeded in convincing officials in Annapolis and Washington to send a significant amount of material and technical assistance to Baltimore. Of the two sources, the national government was by far the more important. Besides the fact that the government of Maryland was strongly Federalist and anti-Baltimore in sentiment, the state itself was extremely susceptible to British raids and its resources had been stretched too thin to permit much aid to its largest city. The federal government, however, was in much the same situation. That so much assistance was indeed sent by the national government to Baltimore can only be attributed to Smith's official position in Washington. This idea is strengthened by the fact that both Secretary of the Army John Armstrong and Secretary of the Navy William Jones privately believed that Baltimore would not be attacked. Indeed, Jones described the port of Baltimore as "one of the most secure in the U.S." Yet, despite this view, the two secre-

14. S. Smith to Armstrong, March 13 and April 16, 1813, and S. Smith to Gov. Winder, March 27, 1813, Smith Order Book; *Niles' Weekly Register*, March 27, 1813.

taries could not or would not resist many of General Smith's demands for more and more of the scarce materials they felt would be of more use elsewhere.[15]

Federal aid to Baltimore, although helpful, was meager compared to the critical needs of the city. The approach of Cockburn's fleet and the brutal raiding expeditions of the British forces against defenseless American settlements reminded Smith and the citizens of Baltimore that they would be dependent on themselves for their own defense.[16] Smith, acting on the governor's order to prepare the militia to defend the city, initiated numerous programs to increase the effectiveness of his forces. Under an agreement negotiated with Major Beall, commander of Fort McHenry, the artillery companies of the third brigade received training in the use of the fort's big guns. Since Secretary Armstrong had ruled that no regular army artillerymen would be sent to the fort, these militia would help operate the cannon in case of attack. On March 24 Smith put the entire third brigade on full alert. Guards were posted around Fort McHenry, the equipment of the troops was inspected, and cavalry units were ordered to ride out along both sides of the Patapsco River in order to familiarize themselves with the terrain. Smith made sure that every man and every unit in the third brigade participated in the new duties by frequently rotating them. The purpose was twofold. Not only did it mean that all the troops of the third brigade received some training and experience, but also it required no money. Each militia man served for such a short time that it counted only as regular duty. Smith utilized this device because neither the federal nor state government had officially called out the Baltimore militia, and until this was done there was no one to pay the soldiers.[17]

While the general struggled with the difficult problem of getting his troops ready, he also took steps to improve his position with

15. Gov. Winder to S. Smith, April 23, 1813, Smith Papers; Reginald Horsman, *The War of 1812* (New York, 1969), p. 77; Armstrong to S. Smith, March 16, 1813, Smith Order Book; William Jones to Capt. Charles Gordon, March 15, 1813, Secretary of the Navy, Captain's Letters, 1813, National Archives, hereafter cited as SN,CL; William Jones to S. Smith, March 14, 1813, and Armstrong to S. Smith, March 16, 1816, Smith Order Book; see also Armstrong to Col. J. G. Swift, March 31, 1813, War Department, Secretary of War, Letters Received, Registered Series, National Archives; hereafter cited as WD,LR,RS.

16. Smith was aware of this fact from the beginning. See S. Smith to Armstrong, March 13, 1813, Smith Order Book.

17. S. Smith to Armstrong, March 17, 1813, Smith Order Book; Major Lloyd Beall to Armstrong, March 19, 1813, WD,LR,RS; S. Smith, order to the third division, March 24, 1813, Smith Order Book.

respect to Patapsco Neck and the works at Fort McHenry, the two places where Baltimore appeared most exposed. Smith had long expected that any attack on Baltimore would be a combined land-sea effort and that North Point, sixteen miles from the city at the tip of Patapsco Neck, was the logical place for a British landing. Here the water was deep enough for transports to land troops under the protection of heavily armed warships. To confirm his opinions, Smith dispatched Major William Barney and a small cavalry troop to North Point with orders to scout the area. Barney's report verified Smith's information about the possibility of a landing at North Point. The major, however, went further. He noted places where ambushes could be laid and lookouts placed to observe naval movements. Barney's observations were so thorough that he identified as the best defensive position on the peninsula the very place where the Battle of North Point would be fought over a year later. If Smith could not immediately station troops on Patapsco Neck, he at least knew where to put them when they became available.[18]

Fort McHenry continued to be Samuel Smith's most pressing problem during the spring of 1813. Located on Whetstone Point, where the Patapsco branched, the fort guarded the entrance to Baltimore's inner harbor. Should the British successfully sail past the bastion, nothing could save the city from a destructive bombardment. Major Beall, commander of this vital post, lacked energy and ability. Cautious, nervous, irascible, and chronically ill, the major seriously hampered General Smith's efforts to repair and expand the fort's facilities. As the weeks went by the conflict between the two men grew. One of Smith's chief complaints against Beall involved the quartering of militia units inside the fort. Beall allowed militia infantry to drill within the post during the day, but at night all the militia save a few artillerymen were evicted. Time and again Smith complained to Secretary Armstrong that Beall's extraordinary behavior endangered the safety of the post. Smith warned that an enemy force might easily sneak up in small boats and overpower the undermanned garrison. Beall's reasons for evicting the militia infuriated Smith. Fort McHenry had barracks to accommodate three hundred fifty men, yet Beall's force amounted to only fifty-two officers and men of the regular army. The soldiers, however, had brought their wives and children along. This circumstance, plus the fact that Beall and his officers requisitioned more quarters than they really needed, sup-

18. S. Smith to Walter Jones, March 13, 1813, Smith Order Book; Maj. William Barney to Gen. John Stricker, March 25, 1813, Smith Papers.

posedly exhausted available space. In other words, Beall put the comfort and convenience of his men ahead of Baltimore's security. Inexplicably, Armstrong never reprimanded Beall, and the unfortunate situation persisted for several months before Smith finally persuaded Armstrong to supersede Beall with a more competent officer.[19]

Smith's desire to make Fort McHenry secure took precedence over personal animosities. Since Beall had both the money and authority to build new works at Fort McHenry, the general wisely decided to cooperate with him when possible. Using plans drafted by Colonel Joseph Swift of the Corps of Engineers, Smith and Beall organized militia and civilian work gangs to rebuild the two massive fortifications in front of the fort known as the Upper and Water Batteries. But Fort McHenry's greatest weakness in March and April 1813 was lack of cannon. More precisely, the fort needed mounted cannon. Scattered about the post were literally dozens of guns, including fifty-six imposing ship cannon salvaged from a wrecked French man-of-war and donated by the French consul in Baltimore. Until carriages were built and the guns mounted on the batteries both inside and outside the fort, Baltimore's situation remained precarious. Gun carriages weighed several thousand pounds and had to be constructed by skilled craftsmen using oak or mahogany that had been seasoned for at least a year. Through unremitting labor over sixty large guns were made ready for action by the fall of 1813. In 1814 more artillery would be added, but the real work of preparing Fort McHenry had already been completed a year earlier.[20]

Impressive as Smith's accomplishments had been during his first month of command, his preparations were far from complete when the British fleet arrived in the middle of April. On April 13 the British, after weeks of aimless destruction, left the mouth of the

19. S. Smith to Armstrong, April 9, 21, and 23, 1813, WD,LR,RS; Smith, order to the third division, April 14, 1813, and S. Smith to Armstrong, April 23, 1813, Smith Order Book.

20. See, for example, Maj. Beall to Armstrong, March 19, 1813, WD,LR,RS; S. Smith to Armstrong, March 29 and April 17, 1813, and S. Smith to Mayor Edward Johnson, April 12, 1813, Smith Order Book; Swift to S. Smith, March 27, 1813, quoted in J. Thomas Scharf, *Chronicles of Baltimore* (Baltimore, 1874), p. 343; see also Armstrong to Beall, March 21, 1813, and Armstrong to Swift, March 31, 1813, Secretary of War, Letters Sent, Military Affairs, National Archives, hereafter cited as SW,LS,MA; S. Smith to Gov. Bowie, September 23, 1812; and S. Smith to John C. Calhoun, February 7, 1818, Smith Papers; S. Smith to Armstrong, March 18, 1813, WD,LR,RS; S. Smith to Committee of Public Supply, May 21, 1813, Smith Order Book; Maj. George Armistead to Armstrong, July 7, 1813, WD,LR,RS.

Potomac River and moved up Chesapeake Bay toward Annapolis and Baltimore. With the enemy less than thirty miles from the city, Smith frantically speeded preparation. In an effort to obtain additional federal support, he sent his personal aide, Major Isaac McKim, on a special mission to Secretary Armstrong. McKim outlined Baltimore's critical situation and asked that the national government call out part of the Maryland militia to defend the city. The evidence indicates that neither Armstrong nor his advisors shared Smith's concern over the intentions of the British. The secretary had long believed that the enemy's fleet had too few troops for such an enterprise.[21] This opinion was shared by Armstrong's representative in Baltimore, Colonel Decius Wadsworth, who had also told the secretary on the day McKim arrived in Washington that the Patapsco was too shallow at its mouth to permit the entrance of ships of the line. "On the whole," reported Wadsworth, "I cannot imagine there is any serious cause of alarm respecting the safety of that place."[22] Despite his personal reservations, however, Armstrong suspended his judgment and gave Smith at least part of what he desired.

The letter Armstrong sent Smith by way of McKim contained an ambiguous order. The secretary of war declared that the next day he would send a requisition to Governor Winder asking two thousand militia "for the defense of Baltimore." These troops would be paid and supplied by the United States government. Armstrong recognized that it would take time for this drafted militia to be organized and marched to Baltimore. Therefore, to meet the immediate threat, he authorized General Smith to call out two thousand soldiers of his division who would also become the responsibility of the government, but who would only serve until the drafted militia arrived. Armstrong's instructions, however, failed to specify exactly who was responsible for determining when the drafted militia were capable of replacing Smith's troops. Furthermore, the whole question of command at Baltimore was left unclear. Did Armstrong's order mean that Smith himself was in the service of the United States? And what of the drafted militia? Who would have authority over them when they arrived in the city? As he had before, Smith took advantage of such a slipshod, indecisive directive by defining his mandate as he saw fit and in the process unashamedly arrogated more power to himself than his superiors had intended.[23]

21. Walter Dorsey to S. Smith, April 13, 1813, S. Smith to Armstrong, April 13, 1813, and Armstrong to S. Smith, March 16, 1813, Smith Order Book.

22. Decius Wadsworth to Armstrong, April 13, 1813, WD,LR,RS.

23. Armstrong to S. Smith, April 13, 1813, WD,LR,RS.

As soon as Armstrong's letter reached Baltimore, Smith dispatched a flood of orders putting the entire third brigade of city militia in motion. A squad of cavalry galloped out of the city and along muddy roads toward North Point. Led by the Major Barney who had earlier reconnoitered the area, the troops were assigned the task of observing the enemy's activities. At the same time Smith directed Captain Charles Gordon of the navy, a man over whom he technically had no authority, to establish a post at North Point from which he could signal by flag the approach of the fleet. The small flotilla of guard boats earlier sent to Baltimore by Secretary of the Navy Jones was spread out from North Point to Fort McHenry. Each boat was to pass along Gordon's flag signals until the information reached the fort. Having established his security system, General Smith proceeded to organize his militia force. Ignoring Armstrong's call for two thousand troops, Smith, after consulting with his advisors, decided to call up only one regiment of the third brigade consisting of about eleven hundred soldiers. In addition the general dispatched some cannon and a company of infantry to North Point. Smith's actions were dictated by his wish to improve the training and efficiency of the city militia. His plan was to call up a different regiment to active duty each week so that every soldier could have the opportunity of being drilled and disciplined.[24]

The growing concern about the British intentions also led the city government of Baltimore to take additional steps to preserve the city's safety. On April 13 the mayor and the city council created a special governmental agency known as the Committee of Public Supply. Staffed by the mayor and other important citizens, including Smith's business partner, James A. Buchanan, the committee's job was to take all measures necessary for the city's defense. Later the committee's tasks would increase, but in the early days of its existence the group acted mainly as Smith's purchasing agent. Although the federal government was responsible for arming, feeding, and clothing the Baltimore militia called into temporary service, no supplies were on hand in Baltimore. Furthermore, despite Smith's pleas, Armstrong delayed appointing federal officials for Baltimore who would have the power and money to provide necessities for the troops. At Smith's suggestion the Committee of Public Supply assumed the duty of provisioning the militia with the expectation that the national government would

24. S. Smith, order to the third division, April 13, 1813, and S. Smith to Robert Brent, May 8, 1813, Smith Order Book.

reimburse the city for its expenditures. The arrangement was a good one and freed the general from the nagging problems of scrounging arms and food for his men.[25]

The Committee of Public Supply soon became the most important agency concerned with the defense of Baltimore. Composed of leading citizens, businessmen, and bankers, it could tap the physical and monetary resources of the city as no other group could. Beginning with only $20,000, the committee soon possessed over $500,000 loaned by city banks. Where state or federal aid was often slow and hesitant, the committee could act immediately and decisively to provide needed materials or men. The relationship between Smith and the committee, whose members were nearly all friends or associates, could not have been better. It solicited his recommendations and never failed scrupulously to carry them out. The total cooperation of the Committee of Public Supply unquestionably added a new dimension to Smith's command.[26]

On April 16 the dreaded moment finally arrived. The citizens of Baltimore awoke to find Admiral Cockburn's fleet positioned at the mouth of the Patapsco River. From Fort McHenry General Smith, alerted by his flag signals, watched British barges and schooners sweep up the river to within six miles of where he stood and capture an unfortunate sloop. The audacity of Cockburn's sailors and marines nearly brought them the prize of Captain Gordon's gun boat, which barely escaped under the guns of the fort. Inside the city Smith's contingency plans were put into operation. "On the alarm gun being fired 4,000 men assembled," he wrote Armstrong, but he added that many were unarmed. For the next three weeks Baltimore was blockaded and constantly in fear of attack.[27]

With the British fleet actually operating within sight of the city, Smith had little difficulty persuading national, state, and local authorities to hasten assistance. The navy department, for example, ordered Captain Gordon to lease four schooners at Baltimore and after

25. J. Thomas Scharf, *History of Maryland from the Earliest Period to the Present Day,* 3 vols. (Baltimore, 1879), 3: 35; S. Smith to Committee of Public Supply, April 13, 1813, Smith Order Book; S. Smith to Armstrong, March 29, 1813, WD,LR,RS.

26. Scharf, *History of Maryland,* 3: 39; S. Smith to Armstrong, April 15, 1813, WD,LR,RS.

27. *Niles' Weekly Register,* April 24, 1813; Baltimore *American & Commercial Daily Advertiser,* April 17, 1813; S. Smith to Armstrong, April 16, 1813, WD,LR, RS.

providing arms and crews to lead them against the smaller British vessels. For his part Secretary Armstrong sent additional muskets for the use of the city militia. Governor Winder cooperated by allowing Smith to buy arms in Baltimore at state expense. As expected, however, the major effort was mounted by the people of Baltimore themselves. Under Smith's directions the Committee of Public Supply purchased muskets, harness, horses, and numerous other articles for the use of the militia. Hulks were obtained and stationed between Whetstone Point and the north bank of the Patapsco. In case of attack they were to be sunk to prevent the British from sailing past the fort into the inner harbor. The Committee of Public Supply, again at General Smith's urging, hired additional laborers to hasten completion of the earth works and batteries at Fort McHenry.[28]

One of the most significant additions to General Smith's forces was the "Marine fencibles," an organization of one hundred fifty seamen created and supported by the Committee of Public Supply. No unit proved more useful and reliable. Composed of sailors beached by the British blockade, the fencibles performed numerous duties. Some were assigned the job of manning guard boats at night in order to prevent a surprise attack on the fort. Others mounted and prepared the big French guns designated for use on the vitally important Water Battery. The effectiveness of the fencibles in 1813 led Smith to reconstitute the corps in 1814, when they helped to repel the British assault on Fort McHenry.[29]

Although General Smith clearly felt that an assault against Fort McHenry was his greatest danger, he did not entirely neglect the possibility of an attack by land. A small start was made on fortifying Hampstead Hill, located east of the city, and within a few days of the fleet's arrival several hundred troops were stationed on Patapsco Neck. At first Smith ordered these troops to resist any attempt at a landing. It soon became apparent, however, that the force was too small for anything but intelligence work. Indeed, Smith eventually instructed most of the militiamen to retire toward Baltimore because

28. Walter Jones to Charles Gordon, April 15, 1813, Secretary of the Navy, Letters Sent, National Archives, hereafter cited as SN,LS; Armstrong to S. Smith, April 13, 1813, WD,LR,RS; Dorsey to S. Smith, April 13, 1813, and S. Smith to Committee of Public Supply, April 13, 15, 18, and 19, 1813, Smith Order Book.

29. S. Smith to Committee of Public Supply, April 18 and May 18, 1813, and S. Smith to Armstrong, April 21 and 24, 1813, WD,LR,RS; Scharf, *History of Maryland*, 3: 120–121; Irving Brant, *James Madison; Commander in Chief, 1812–1836* (New York, 1961), p. 324.

he feared boats full of British soldiers might sail up one of the broad creeks on the Neck and cut off their route of retreat. Obviously the general had underrated the difficulty of protecting the city from land attack.[30]

On April 24 the bulk of Cockburn's force moved away from Baltimore and up Chesapeake Bay, but the city remained blockaded and in a state of high tension. Unknown to Smith and the defenders of Baltimore, Cockburn and his superior, Admiral John Borlase Warren, had neither the force nor the orders to capture any American city. Their duty was to destroy American naval power in the Chesapeake, to create a diversion which, it was hoped, would draw troops away from American operations along the vulnerable Canadian border, and to bring the horror of war to the inhabitants of the Chesapeake. Admiral Cockburn performed this latter duty with gusto, and the destruction of Frenchtown and Havre de Grace made his name synonymous with evil among Americans. In early May Cockburn returned down Chesapeake Bay to Baltimore, where he again made menacing gestures. After burning a few villages on the Eastern Shore, however, the entire fleet dropped down to Hampton Roads and awaited reinforcements.[31]

While the British had plagued the upper Chesapeake, Smith perfected his defensive position. Using the authority of the Committee of Public Supply, he ordered construction of a small battery a mile behind Fort McHenry that would eventually be named Fort Covington. But Smith's most pressing problem in this period involved a challenge to his right to command. On April 13 Armstrong had promised to requisition two thousand militia from Maryland to defend Baltimore. For some reason this request was not transmitted to Governor Winder until April 16, and he in turn delayed acting until April 23. On that day the governor called up the detachment, over half of which was to be drawn from the third brigade already on duty in Baltimore. Aside from this latter force most of the drafted militia did not arrive in Baltimore until the fleet had already left two weeks

30. S. Smith to Lt. Col. McDonald, April 14, 17, and 19, 1813, Smith Order Book.

31. Benson J. Lossing, *The Pictorial Field-Book of the War of 1812* (New York, 1868), pp. 670, 673; Scharf, *History of Maryland*, 3: 41; Charles G. Muller, *The Darkest Day: 1814; The Washington-Baltimore Campaign* (Philadelphia, 1963), pp. 24–25; Horsman, *War of 1812*, pp. 73–79; J. W. Fortescue, *A History of the British Army*, 13 vols. (London, 1899–1930), 9: 322; Harry L. Coles, *The War of 1812* (Chicago, 1965), pp. 38–45.

later. As commander of the drafted militia Winder nominated Brigadier General Henry Miller of Baltimore. Predictably Miller was a Federalist; but since he was also a personal friend of Armstrong, the federal government did not delay issuing him a commission in the regular army.[32]

Confusion was now total. The vague and conflicting orders issued by Armstrong and Winder left it unclear whether General Miller or General Smith held supreme command. For his part Miller tried to persuade the Committee of Public Supply to recognize his authority, but it responded instead with a declaration of loyalty to Smith. Both men then appealed to Armstrong for a decision. The secretary answered that Miller was the legitimate commander unless Smith could prove he had already been called into active service by the Governor of Maryland, in which case he would be, as a major general, the ranking officer. Smith, of course, had in his papers Winder's orders of March 13 telling him to prepare the militia to defend Baltimore. That order, however, said nothing about the general being called into active service. Armstrong's ruling had put Smith in an embarrassing position of having to ask Winder to choose between himself, a political foe, and Miller, a personal friend and political supporter of the governor's. With understandable misgivings General Smith sent Major McKim to Annapolis to seek a final solution.[33] For twenty-four hours Winder deliberated before giving McKim his answer to Smith's inquiry. "The meaning of the order [of March 13]," said the governor, "was, that you would proceed to compleat the organization of the Militia under your command and place them in the best possible state for defence, of course your commission as Major General commenced from that period."[34] Winder's reply established Smith's authority beyond any doubt and the general wasted little time in passing along the governor's letter to Secretary Armstrong. Winder's motives remain unclear. His delay in answering Smith would seem to show that he at least considered alternatives to confirming the general's

32. Wadsworth to Armstrong, May 3, 1813, Gen. Henry Miller to Armstrong, April 29, 1813, and Armstrong to S. Smith, April 13, 1813, WD,LR,RS; Armstrong to Gov. Winder, April 16, 1813, and Armstrong to Wadsworth, May 13, 1813, SW,LS,MA; Gov. Winder to S. Smith, April 23, 1813, Smith Order Book; Gov. Winder to Armstrong, April 26, 1813, and Armstrong to Gov. Winder (copy), May 1, 1813, Smith Papers.

33. Gen. Miller to Armstrong, May 7, 1813, and S. Smith to Armstrong, May 6 and 10, 1813, WD,LR,RS; Committee of Public Supply to S. Smith, May 4, 1813, Smith Papers; Armstrong to S. Smith, May 7, 1813, SW,LS,MA; S. Smith to Gov. Winder, May 9, 1813, Smith Order Book.

34. Gov. Winder to S. Smith, May 10, 1813, Smith Order Book.

position. Perhaps the governor believed that removing Smith while the British sat before Baltimore would be neither wise nor politic.[35]

By May 10 Cockburn's departure from the Baltimore area could not be doubted. Under existing state and federal laws Smith had no choice but to dismiss the troops he had called into service under Armstrong's order of April 13. Miller's troops were finally straggling into Baltimore, where they would remain sullen and useless for the next month. A week after he had released his troops General Smith sent a detailed description of his accomplishments during the recent crisis to the Committee of Public Supply. He noted that because of the arms he had secured from the state and federal governments, the third brigade now had over thirty-seven hundred infantry and riflemen, seven hundred artillerymen, and four troops of cavalry completely equipped. Furthermore, he reported their discipline and morale as exceptionally good. Turning to the harbor fortifications, Smith described Fort McHenry in mid-March as being "little capable of opposition," but that now it presented a "formidable appearance." He emphasized with pride that the Water Battery now was completely manned by seamen in the pay of the city and that every cannon on that important work was mounted. Smith reminded the committee that Fort Covington was nearly complete, while on the Ferry Branch the army engineers had commenced building a battery that would later be named Fort Babcock. Even if these works should be silenced, Smith assured the committee that the British fleet could not reach the city because of the hulks that would have been sunk to block the channel and the long booms made out of ship masts that had been stretched across the various water passages to Baltimore.[36]

Smith's report to the Committee of Public Supply also contained a sharp warning of future danger. With British naval units still in Chesapeake Bay and over four months of fighting weather remaining, he urged the city not only to continue but to expand its preparations for defense. Smith pointed out that during the recent blockade small British barges and schooners easily won naval control of the Patapsco and seized numerous American vessels. He submitted a plan to build a fleet of gun boats powered by oars and mounting two large guns. "With such a force well-manned," Smith speculated, "I should believe that it would not only secure the rivers from insult, but enable us to render it extremely dangerous for the Enemy to water at Sus-

35. S. Smith to Armstrong, May 10, 1813, WD,LR,RS.

36. S. Smith, order to the third division, May 10, 1813, and S. Smith to Committee of Public Supply, May 18, 1813, Smith Order Book; see also Gen. Miller to Armstrong, July 7, 1813, WD,LR,RS.

que[hanna] or to lay off the [mouth of the] Patapsco."[37] In following days Smith urged the committee to purchase cannon and other types of war material that he vowed were necessary for the city's defense. The committee faithfully implemented the general's suggestions.[38]

Smith's increasing dependence on the Committee of Public Supply resulted from a reduction in federal and state assistance following the withdrawal of Cockburn's squadron. As the pressure on Baltimore eased there appeared less cause for concern; Governor Winder and secretaries Armstrong and Jones turned their attention to other more pressing problems. General Smith and the citizens of Baltimore, however, were more convinced than ever that Baltimore would be attacked and acted accordingly. Throughout June and July the city government pushed toward completion the construction of additional harbor fortifications and the gun boats Smith had recommended.[39]

After placing General Stricker in temporary command, Smith traveled to Washington in June and assumed his seat in the United States Senate. His position as chairman of the naval affairs committee and as a member of the military affairs committee gave him numerous opportunities to see Jones and Armstrong and lobby personally on behalf of Baltimore. Despite his persistence the Maryland senator gained little from the government until the end of the month. At that time the British fleet in the Chesapeake, greatly strengthened both in ships and troops, attacked Norfolk and Hampton, Virginia, and showed signs of once more moving up the bay.[40] The renewed threat to Baltimore gave Smith an opportunity to press harder for more federal support, and beginning on June 27 he deluged Secretary Armstrong with letters and personal visits demanding money, arms, and regular troops. On July 1 the general was joined in Washington by a delegation from the Committee of Public Supply, who seconded his application. The results of these meetings were mixed. Armstrong refused to hold General Miller's drafted militia any longer in the service of the United States, and they were accordingly dismissed. The secretary also denied Smith authority to call up the Baltimore

37. S. Smith to Committee of Public Supply, May 18, 1813, Smith Order Book.

38. S. Smith to Committee of Public Supply, May 18 and 21, 1813, Smith Order Book.

39. S. Smith to James Houston and William Banck, May 22, 1813, and S. Smith to Armstrong, June 27, 1813, Smith Order Book; *Niles' Weekly Register*, July 7, 1813.

40. S. Smith, order to the third division, May 25, 1813, Smith Order Book; S. Smith to Armstrong, June 27, 1813, WD,LR,RS; Coles, *War of 1812*, p. 92; Horsman, *War of 1812*, pp. 77–80. The fleet carried over four thousand soldiers.

militia and have them paid and supplied by the federal government. He did promise to seriously consider repaying the Committee of Public Supply for some of their expenses and to order fifteen hundred muskets to be delivered to Baltimore. Armstrong also dismissed Beall and named Major George Armistead to command Fort McHenry. The new commander was authorized to complete fortifications already in progress and to make other improvements.[41]

By July 12 the British fleet had moved up to the mouth of the Potomac River. After informing both Armstrong and Governor Winder that he firmly believed Baltimore to be the enemy's object, Smith raced back to Baltimore and put the third brigade on full alert. For two frustrating weeks Baltimore waited for the British to arrive. During this period there was little Smith could do. Until the fleet definitely menaced the city there was no chance that Armstrong or Governor Winder would approve the mobilization of the militia. On July 22 the general again journeyed to Washington and pleaded with Armstrong to give him more discretion in calling out the third brigade. But even as Smith met with the secretary the fleet finally weighed anchor and sailed slowly up the Chesapeake. Still without the powers he desired, General Smith returned to Baltimore to make what preparations he could.[42]

On August 1 the British fleet, fighting unfavorable winds, reached the vicinity of Annapolis and Smith finally felt justified in calling up on his own authority at least some militia troops to defend the city. He was soon supported by Armstrong, who ordered federal officials to feed and supply militia units mobilized at Smith's direction. In the previous alarm Smith had succeeded in making the city's third militia brigade as ready as was possible. He knew that if the British moved up the Patapsco to assault the fortifications these troops would easily have enough time to assemble. There was, therefore, no need to call them into service until the moment for battle arrived. Smith's real

41. S. Smith to Armstrong, June 27, 1813, and S. Smith to Gov. Winder, July 1, 1813, Smith Order Book; L. Sterret and H. Payson of the Committee of Public Supply to Armstrong, July 2, 1813, WD,LR,RS; Armstrong to S. Smith, July 6 and 8, 1813, Armstrong to Sterret and Payson, July 6, 1813, Armstrong to Paul Bentalou, July 6, 1813, and Armstrong to Maj. Armistead, July 6, 1813, SW,LS,MA; S. Smith to Armstrong, July 7, 1813, and Gen. Miller to Armstrong, July 7, 1813, WD,LR,RS.

42. Muller, *Darkest Day*, p. 38; S. Smith to Armstrong, July 7, 1813, and Bentalou to Armstrong, July 22, 1813, WD,LR,RS; S. Smith to Gov. Winder, July 15 and 22, 1813, Smith Order Book; Gen Stricker to S. Smith, July 22, 1813, Smith Papers.

problem was that he needed more trained men to defend the city. After all, the British had as many troops as did the third brigade. The British soldiers were also professionals. Wisely Smith decided to take advantage of the British threat by developing the military competence of the next best unit in his division, the eleventh or Baltimore County brigade. In August 1813 the eleventh was a rowdy, disorganized mob wanting nearly everything to become a first-rate fighting force. Yet, despite its shortcomings, Stansbury's brigade far surpassed any other militia outside Baltimore. General Smith had actually begun the job of rehabilitating the eleventh almost a month earlier when he had distributed among its troops the fifteen hundred muskets Armstrong had sent him. On August 1 Smith ordered up one regiment of the eleventh, about eight hundred men, and directed it to assemble on Patapsco Neck. By August 8 the fleet finally came into view of the barges and guard boats the general had stationed at the mouth of the Patapsco. The next day the general requisitioned yet another regiment from the eleventh and ordered General Stansbury to take command of all operations on Patapsco Neck. Smith obviously expected Stansbury to whip his men into shape and severely criticized his subordinate when it was discovered that he did not even post guards around his encampment. Nevertheless, at the end of August Smith could tell Armstrong that the brigade had "improved wonderfully."[43]

Smith's thinking on the best way to protect Baltimore from land attack had matured since April. Beset by other difficulties he had then relied on a few hundred militia troops to repel any landings, but the mobility of the British barges had forced him to realize that his small force could easily be cut off and destroyed. Given a second opportunity, the general readjusted his plans; now over fifteen hundred men camped near Bear Creek. They could not and would not contest a landing at North Point, although they might delay or even halt British columns attempting to approach the rear of Baltimore. If all four thousand English soldiers should strike at Stansbury, Smith had no illusions about the result. On Hampstead Hill, with the cooperation of the Committee of Public Supply, a line of breastworks was thrown up and an artillery park containing perhaps fifty cannon

43. S. Smith to Armstrong, August 1, 1813, WD,LR,RS; Armstrong to S. Smith, July 6, 1813, SW,LS,MA; Baltimore *American & Commercial Daily Advertiser,* August 9, 1813; S. Smith, orders to the third division, July 15 and August 1, 1813, S. Smith to Gov. Winder, August 8 and 11, 1813, and S. Smith to Gen. Stansbury, August 21, 1813, Smith Order Book; S. Smith to Armstrong, August 31, 1813, Smith Papers.

was established. This was the line of defense Smith counted on to stop an assault, just as he would in September 1814.[44]

The second visit of the British fleet brought few changes in the arrangements made in April and May for the protection of the harbor area. Forts McHenry, Covington, and Babcock were virtually complete and the hulks stood ready for sinking. Aside from an additional boom placed between Moales Point and Ferry Point, the chief improvement in river defense was the aggressive patrolling of the Patapsco by the city-owned barges that Smith had asked be built. Their presence prevented the possibility of sneak attack and made it dangerous for the smaller British ships to venture far from the men-of-war and frigates of the fleet. Altogether, Baltimore's response was thoroughly professional. The miscalculations and improvisations that had characterized the city's reaction two months before simply were not present. Once again, however, the British chose not to attack and by August 24 had set out for winter quarters in the West Indies. Smith and the citizens of Baltimore were left to wonder whether their ordeal had ended.[45]

44. Scharf, *History of Maryland*, 3: 49; S. Smith to Armstrong, August 1, 1813, WD,LR,RS; S. Smith, order to the third division, August 16, 1813, Smith Order Book.

45. S. Smith to Gov. Winder, July 30 and August 8, 1813, and S. Smith, orders to the third division, August 9 and 24, 1813, Smith Order Book; S. Smith to Armstrong, August 1, 1813, WD,LR,RS.

13

Defender of Baltimore

WHEN GOOD fighting weather returned in 1814, the American military position had deteriorated. Emperor Napoleon had finally been crushed by England and its allies, thus freeing thousands of British troops and hundreds of ships to descend on the United States. In London plans were laid to invade America at three different points along the northern frontier, while at the same time coastal cities were to be harassed with amphibious assaults. An especially ambitious expedition was planned for Chesapeake Bay, around which a large portion of the American population lived. Under the joint command of Admiral Alexander Cochrane and General Robert Ross, the fifty ships and seven thousand troops of the Chesapeake force reached the American coast in August. The objectives of these sea-borne invaders were left indefinite by the British high command. They were told to attack targets of opportunity but were given special orders to occupy Washington and destroy Baltimore, a center of privateering activity, if it could be done "without too much risk."[1]

The huge British fleet sailed up the Patuxent River and landed forty-two hundred troops at Benedict, Maryland, on August 19. Five days later the veterans of countless European engagements smashed a larger American army composed almost entirely of militia at the misnamed Battle of Bladensburg. While the terrified militiamen

1. Earl of Liverpool to the Duke of Wellington, September 27, 1814, printed in the *Maryland Historical Magazine* 2 (1909): 112.

scattered over the countryside, General Ross led his men into Washington and leisurely burned most of the public buildings. From a distance President Madison and his advisors observed the nation's capital go up in smoke. Following the destruction of the city, Ross retreated to his shipping, and after a prolonged delay the entire expedition moved back down the Patuxent to Chesapeake Bay. Already the senior officers had decided in private consultations that Baltimore would be next. If its defenses proved as weak as those of Washington, then it too would be put to the torch.

Reports of the massive American defeat at Bladensburg and its aftermath shocked but did not panic Baltimore. There was great pride that those elements of the third division fighting under General Stansbury had acquitted themselves honorably during the battle and concern that the survivors would find their way back to the city in time to meet the British asault everyone expected. For over a year the city's inhabitants had been preparing for what now seemed certain: a British invasion. Samuel Smith certainly had not relaxed his efforts to improve Baltimore's security. As early as June 20 he had ordered Major Armistead at Fort McHenry to close the booms during the night to prevent ships from entering or leaving the harbor under cover of darkness and thereby to lessen chances of a surprise attack. The marine fencibles were once again ordered to train on the big guns, and directions were given to the city barges to resume patrols on the Patapsco. The general was also able in July to persuade the federal government to repair some of the booms stretched across the front of Fort McHenry that had been damaged during the winter. After official word arrived that war had ceased in Europe Smith redoubled his exertions, putting men to work making 320,000 cartridges for the five thousand men he anticipated it would take to defend Baltimore.[2]

From long experience Smith had known exactly what to do when, on August 18, he received messages telling of a large British fleet ascending the bay toward Washington, Annapolis, and Baltimore. Using the emergency powers vested in him as commanding general of the third division, he called out the third brigade the next day and ordered it to appear fully equipped on the parade ground. Even as the well-disciplined citizen-soldiers of Baltimore moved to their posts, the

2. S. Smith to Maj. George Armistead, June 20 and July 11, Smith Order Book, and S. Smith to John C. Calhoun, February 7, 1818, Samuel Smith Papers, Library of Congress; John Armstrong to the Governors of the United States, July 4, 1814, and Armstrong to S. Smith, July 8, 1814, Secretary of War, Letters Sent, Military Affairs, National Archives; hereafter cited as SW,LS,MA.

general dispatched orders to those regiments of the eleventh brigade not at Bladensburg. They were instructed to "march without delay by Companies & Half companies" to Baltimore and meet on Hampstead Hill as they had the year before. On August 23, the day before the Bladensburg fiasco, the Committee of Vigilance and Safety began operations. The successor to the Committee of Public Supply, this new organization was even stronger and more efficient than its predecessor. Its records reveal that it had total responsibility not only for defending the city but also for administering it during the crisis. Among other duties it raised money, built barracks, arrested suspected spies, purchased supplies of all sorts, and made provision for the city's sick and poor. It also undertook to represent the city's interests before the state and federal governments. Like the Committee of Public Supply, the Committee of Vigilance and Safety was the indispensable mechanism necessary to free the city's resources and effectively utilize them. It differed, however, in that the committee members were elected by the citizens of Baltimore rather than appointed by the mayor as had been the case in 1813. It thus had a broad popular constituency that insured its decisions would be respected. Although elected, the committee members were still drawn from the merchant-business classes and consequently had access to those groups in Baltimore controlling the wealth. In practice the Committee of Vigilance and Safety was as loyal an ally to Smith as the Committee of Public Supply had been.[3]

Following the "Bladensburg Races," as one wit described the American rout on August 24, and just as Baltimore appeared in the greatest danger, Samuel Smith's right to command was contested. The situation was analogous to his dispute with General Miller a year earlier save that Smith's case was far weaker, and for a few anxious days at the end of August it seemed possible that the general would be relegated to a secondary status. Smith's challenger was Brigadier General William H. Winder, nephew to the governor of Maryland and the unfortunate commander of the American forces at Bladensburg. Winder began his military career as a captain in Samuel Smith's third militia division. When war began he enlisted in the regular army and rose rapidly through the ranks. On July 2, 1814, he was named by

3. Gov. Levin Winder to S. Smith, August 18, 1814, and Gen. William Winder to S. Smith, August 18, 1814, Smith Papers; S. Smith, orders to the third division, August 19, 20, and 23, 1814, Smith Order Book; Minutes of the Committee of Vigilance and Safety, August 25, 1814, in William D. Hoyt, Jr., ed., "Civilian Defense in Baltimore, 1814–1815," *Maryland Historical Magazine* 39 (September 1944): 204.

Secretary of War Armstrong as commander of the newly created tenth military district that included Maryland, the District of Columbia, and northern Virginia. It was in that capacity that he found himself at the head of a ragged, frightened mob of militia at Bladensburg.[4]

Samuel Smith had sensed immediately that Winder's appointment might conflict with his own. On July 20 he had written Secretary Armstrong asking for the same broad powers he had been given the previous year to call all militia troops into actual service that he deemed necessary. Armstrong, however, had not responded. A week before the British landed at Benedict, General Winder had made inquiries as to whether he could on his own authority call out the Baltimore militia. Smith had firmly replied that under the laws of Maryland only he could do that.[5] The question of command became even more acute after enemy troops had debarked. In the same letter in which he informed the governor that he had mobilized the third brigade, Smith pleaded for orders "to govern my conduct & to designate the nature of my authority in the event of an invasion or threatened invasion of my Military District."[6] The governor replied that he had long been concerned with the possibility of conflicting commands but felt only the federal government could make a final determination. He reminded Smith that in the past Armstrong had ruled that a regular army officer was superior to all ranks of militia officers unless they were in the actual service of the United States. By that interpretation General Winder was clearly the legitimate commander of Baltimore and its defenses. But Samuel Smith was not one to step aside because of nice legal distinctions.[7]

For a few days the momentous events at Bladensburg and Washington pushed the quarrel between Smith and Winder into the background. Winder's defeat and the British threats against Baltimore again made the dispute one of primary importance. Unless one man or the other achieved undisputed control, the defense of Baltimore would be made infinitely more difficult. Smith's claims were strengthened on August 25, when the Committee of Vigilance and Safety publicly supported him. On that day the committee received a personally delivered petition from Brigadier General John Stricker;

4. Armstrong to Gen. Winder, July 2, 1814, SW,LS,MA.

5. S. Smith to Armstrong, July 20, 1814, and S. Smith to Gen. Winder, August 14, 1814, Smith Order Book; Gen. Winder to S. Smith, August 12, 1814, Smith Papers.

6. S. Smith to Gov. Winder, August 19, 1814, Smith Order Book.

7. Gov. Winder to S. Smith, August 19, 1814, Smith Papers.

Commodore Oliver Hazard Perry, the hero of Lake Erie, who was waiting to take command of a new ship in Baltimore; Major George Armistead, the regular army officer in charge of Fort McHenry; and Master-Commandant Robert T. Spence of the United States navy. As the top military officers in the city these men took the highly unusual step of telling the city government that it was their "wish" that Smith command all forces stationed at Baltimore. The only explanation for such a procedure is that in the unusual circumstances that prevailed, with national authority temporarily neutralized, these officers felt that they must take some initiative to avoid serving under the incompetent Winder. It was also a tribute to Smith that their confidence in him was such that they would risk future official reprisals in order to keep him in command. There is no evidence Smith himself instigated the officers' petition, but there does appear to be some collusion between the authors and the Committee of Vigilance and Safety. Only some previous understanding could explain why they made their plea to a quasilegal governmental body in Baltimore rather than to the governor of Maryland or even the secretary of war.[8]

Upon hearing the officers, the Committee of Vigilance and Safety voted to send a three-man delegation headed by Colonel John Eager Howard to Smith's headquarters. The general undoubtedly savored the sight of his old enemy Howard, the man who had tried to end his political career in 1798, arriving to convey the committee's request that he "take upon himself the command of the Forces that may be called out for the defense of our city." Howard reported back to the Committee of Vigilance and Safety that Smith was "willing and would" accept the command if the governor of Maryland "sanctioned" it. Thereupon the committee drafted a letter to Governor Winder asking him to "invest Maj. Genl. Smith with powers in every respect commensurate to the present exigency."[9] Conceivably all that occurred was honest and aboveboard, but in the context of the long-standing contest for command the episode seemed contrived. It had been made to appear, rightly or wrongly, that the people of Baltimore and the chief military officers on duty at that place were unanimous in their feelings that General Smith rather than General Winder was the man they trusted to defend the city, regardless of military etiquette. It would have been very difficult for Governor Winder or the national government to disregard the opinions of Baltimore on this matter.

8. Declaration of the Committee of Vigilance and Safety, August 25, 1814, Smith Papers.

9. Minutes of the Committee of Vigilance and Safety, August 25 and 26, 1814, in Hoyt, ed., "Civilian Defense," pp. 204–206.

To force Winder on an unwilling city might have meant catastrophe in the event of an attack.

In response to the communication of the Committee of Vigilance and Safety, Governor Winder awarded Smith the position of major general of the Maryland troops called into actual service by the federal government. Winder protested to his nephew that in giving Smith the post he had not made him the overall commander at Baltimore, maintaining that only the national administration could make that determination. Technically he was probably correct, but with Smith now on active duty in the service of the United States, the government would be less likely than ever to subordinate him to an officer of a lower rank. In its general outline the entire incident was very similar to Smith's conflict with General Miller in 1813. At that time Secretary Armstrong had decided in Smith's favor as soon as it was made clear the governor had indeed called the general into active duty. With precedent on his side Smith hastened to solidify his authority. To General Winder, who was marching toward Baltimore with the remains of his army, Smith sent a copy of the governor's letter and informed him that he had "in consequence assumed the command agreeably to my rank." Winder was ordered to report on the number of troops he had and to send ahead tents and other camp equipment belonging to Stansbury's brigade. A day later Smith informed Armstrong that he was in control. General Winder, he commented to the secretary of war, was now in Baltimore, but "I have not yet seen him." Suddenly without men or power William Winder was a pathetic figure, and an appeal to his friend James Monroe, who had taken over the war department as well as his duties as secretary of state, brought no satisfaction. The national government was hardly more than a group of refugees and in no position to displace the popular and firmly entrenched soldier-politician of Baltimore. Winder was politely advised to obey Smith's orders.[10]

Having survived yet another test of his durability, Smith focused his full resources on the military situation in Baltimore. Fortunately, he did not have to give much attention to the harbor fortifications. The labors of 1813 had put them in good order and the only major decision left was when to sink the hulks to block the ship channel. For advice on this and many other matters the general relied on Captain John Rodgers, victor over the *Little Belt* and a tough naval

10. Gov. Winder to S. Smith, August 26 and 27, 1814, Smith Papers; S. Smith to Gen. Winder, August 26, 1814, Smith Order Book; S. Smith to Armstrong, August 27, 1814, Smith Papers; James Monroe to S. Smith, September 2, 1814, Smith Order Book.

veteran who knew how to handle men and cannons. Smith concentrated his energies on preparing for a land attack against the city, for he had not changed his opinion that the British would land at North Point. With the prospect that he would be facing perhaps seven thousand enemy troops, the general gave orders that additional trenches and breastworks be added to the Hampstead Hill fortifications. The Committee of Vigilance and Safety responded swiftly and efficiently. Picks and shovels were requisitioned, most of the city's Negro population, both slave and free, was pressed into service, and huge sums of money were borrowed to hire white laborers and craftsmen. The city was arbitrarily divided into four sections, each being responsible for providing work crews one day out of four. Baltimore was literally digging for its very existence.[11]

While the British dallied in the Patuxent, Baltimore's fortifications grew and fresh troops streamed into the city. At Smith's call every able-bodied man enrolled in the third division, with the exception of the third brigade, was marched to Hampstead Hill and there joined by thousands of militia troops from Pennsylvania, Delaware, and Virginia. Rather than the five thousand soldiers he had predicted, the general found himself in charge of fifteen thousand men by early September. At sixty-two years of age, the general showed more stamina than most of his subordinates. He seemed to be everywhere, inspecting the harbor fortifications, supervising the work on Hampstead Hill, or meeting with the Committee of Vigilance and Safety. Each day he penned scores of orders creating hospitals, setting up horse relays to key points, disciplining recalcitrant militiamen, and distributing arms and ammunition. Through it all he carefully followed intelligence reports on British movements sent to him by Major William Barney, who had performed the same service in 1813. If discipline, planning, and hard work could save Baltimore, then Samuel Smith and the city's inhabitants had already won the battle.[12]

On September 6 the British finally left their anchorage in the Patuxent, and four days later Barney reported that the fleet was moving up the bay. But Smith had received information from other

11. S. Smith, orders to the third division, August 27, 29, and 30, 1814, S. Smith to Committee of Vigilance and Safety, August 28, 30, and 31, 1814, and S. Smith to Thomas C. Worthington, August 29, 1814, Smith Order Book; Minutes of Committee of Vigilance and Safety, August 29 and 31 and September 1 and 3, 1814, in Hoyt, ed., "Civilian Defense," pp. 209, 211, 212–213, 215–216.
12. S. Smith to Monroe, September 3 and 9, 1814, and S. Smith to Committee of Vigilance and Safety, September 3, 1814, Smith Order Book; William Barney to S. Smith, September 10, 1814, Smith Papers.

sources contradicting Barney's observations and delayed sounding the alert. Sometime on Sunday morning, September 11, a messenger from the observation post Smith had established at Herring Bay far to the south of Annapolis and Baltimore arrived, confirming that the British were sailing rapidly northward. Almost immediately other outposts flashed warnings of the approaching invaders. Despite his superb intelligence service the general was surprised at the speed of the British ships and ordered the alarm guns fired in order to assemble the troops as soon as possible. By late afternoon the third brigade had formed up. A token force was sent to cover the south bank of the Patapsco, but, following through on the experience he had gained in 1813, the general ordered his friend General Stricker and the bulk of the third brigade to march to Patapsco Neck, where he anticipated the enemy would land. Stricker had spent a good deal of time on Patapsco Neck during the spring and summer of 1813 and was thoroughly conversant with William Barney's survey of the terrain. In obedience to a battle plan he and Smith had worked out months before, Stricker positioned his men at the narrowest part of the Neck between Back River on the north and Bear Creek on the south. The site had the additional advantage that the enemy could not easily get behind it in small boats.[13]

The British army, led by General Ross, debarked on Monday morning, September 12, at North Point, precisely where Smith expected it would. The British column moved slowly west along Patapsco Neck, while the fighting ships maneuvered toward Fort McHenry. The four thousand soldiers of Ross' command encountered little resistance until midday when advance units of the two armies met and exchanged gunfire. When General Ross rode forward to investigate, he received a fatal wound; Colonel Arthur Brook, the next senior officer, assumed the command. Between 2 P.M. and 3 P.M. the two armies came into view of each other and an artillery duel ensued. The spectacular but quite ineffective Congreve rockets that had frightened the American militia at Bladensburg failed to panic the Baltimore troops Samuel Smith had spent years training. For nearly one and a half hours Stricker's men behaved like regulars, standing their ground against a superior force and taking a terrible toll of the enemy. Stricker was finally forced to order a retreat when large numbers of British troops threatened to turn his left flank by wading through a marsh. In attempting to counter this move the American

13. Barney to S. Smith, September 10, 1814, and Monroe to S. Smith, September 11, 1814, Smith Papers; S. Smith to Monroe, September 23, 1814, Smith Order Book.

general had ordered one regiment to execute a difficult maneuver that proved too complex under fire. Confusion swept its ranks and the men finally broke and ran. Of more importance, however, the other regiments maintained their discipline. Stricker had performed his assigned mission better than anyone had a right to expect. He had not been ordered to hold his position at all costs but merely to delay the enemy's advance as long as it was feasible to do so. His men had never been in a battle before and yet they had withstood with honor an attack by troops who had helped defeat Napoleon's legions.

The third brigade marched back along Patapsco Neck in good order and formed around the second line of defense. British casualties had been numerous and the army was in no shape to pursue the Americans. Observing this, Stricker, still adhering to the original plan of battle, led his command back to Hampstead Hill, posting them in advance and to the left of the entrenchments. It was another proof of Smith's foresight that he had kept his best troops mobile and filled the earthworks on Hampstead Hill with the thousands of militiamen who were less well trained and more likely to act like soldiers if given some protection. To support Stricker, whose responsibility was to prevent the British army from marching around the left end of the American fortifications, Smith sent forward General Winder and a force of Virginia militia. If he could not lead, Winder would have an opportunity to show that he could follow.[14]

At 10 A.M. on September 13 the British line moved out of the woods and faced the Americans at a distance of two miles. Stationing himself at the highest point along the American position, Smith could see a breathtaking panorama. To his right and left, concealed in skillfully built trenches and earthworks studded with cannon, crouched eleven thousand men. A half mile ahead and to the left stood the massed ranks of Stricker's and Winder's commands, while in the distance he could make out the red uniforms of the enemy. As the Americans waited, Colonel Brook and Admiral George Cockburn, who had accompanied the troops, argued over strategy. Cockburn, known as the "incendiary" to the people of Chesapeake Bay, urged that the army be immediately launched against the American positions. Brook maintained that a frontal assault would fail because, he believed, at least twenty thousand men had to be manning the extensive works he observed. Furthermore, the ground was wet from a recent rain and the footing on the side of the ridge would be treacherous. Although neither

14. Col. James Biays to S. Smith, September 12, 1814, and S. Smith to Monroe, September 19, 1814, Smith Papers; Gen. John Stricker to S. Smith, September 15, 1814, printed in the *Baltimore Patriot and Evening Advertiser,* September 23, 1814.

Brook nor any other British officer verbalized it, there must have been some feeling that if the troops before them fought like Stricker's men had the day before, there was little likelihood that a victory could be won. In the end Brook rejected Cockburn's advice and decided to try a less risky plan.

About midmorning Brook moved his army toward his right in an obvious effort to flank the American left. The most significant moment in the defense of Baltimore had arrived. Should the American units under Winder and Stricker fail to block this effort the battle would be lost; the fortifications would be useless, the American army easily defeated, and Baltimore defenseless. But Winder and Stricker did not fail. On orders from Smith the two generals adapted "their movements to those of the enemy." Instead of a clear road into Baltimore, Brook faced two brigades and a third in reserve. Worse yet the British army now ran the risk of having its line of retreat cut should the Americans sally forth from their fortifications. Reluctantly but prudently Brook marched his army back to his original position but now at a distance of only one mile from Hampstead Hill. Having tried his way and not succeeded, Brook was apparently about to yield to Cockburn's scheme of storming the American fortifications.

For a man who had never commanded large bodies of men in battle before, Smith was displaying remarkable ability. Not waiting for the British to strike, the general ordered Stricker and Winder to arrange their troops in a line at right angles to the left end of the American entrenchments. Now if Brook attacked, his troops would be exposed to fire not only from Hampstead Hill, but also from their right flank. In that deadly crossfire the attackers would surely be cut to pieces and Brook knew it. With orders that told him not to attack Baltimore if the price was too high, heading an army smaller than its adversary and dispirited at the death of its leader, and confronted by an unknown but astute American general, Brook could only retreat. His decision came none too soon, as Smith already was contemplating an attack of his own the next morning. At 1:30 A.M. on September 14 the British army slipped quietly away in the midst of a rain storm. At daylight when the British maneuver was discovered, Smith dispatched General Winder to harass the rear guard. No major American attack could be mounted because of the poor physical condition of the troops, who were thoroughly soaked and had enjoyed little sleep in the past three days. Undisturbed, the British returned to North Point and boarded their transports.[15]

15. Gen. Stricker to S. Smith, September 15, 1814, printed in the *Baltimore Patriot and Evening Advertiser,* September 23, 1814; S. Smith to Gen. Cad-

While the British army was being frustrated, the British navy was having its own troubles. Admiral Cochrane had hoped to smash through the defenses into the inner harbor from where the city of Baltimore could easily be shelled. Should this prove impossible he at least intended to get near enough to the scene of the land operations to support Brook's army with his big naval guns. If the cannon at Fort McHenry and on the Lazaretto could be silenced, it would be an easy matter to wipe out the whole right flank of the Hampstead Hill line anchored at Fell's Point. But none of this could take place until the star-shaped bastion at the tip of Whetstone Point was destroyed. Cochrane's task was complicated by the fact that his very largest vessels, the gigantic seventy-four-gun ships-of-the-line, were too big to enter the Patapsco. The British admiral thus had to rely on his frigates and bomb vessels. The latter carried two guns, each capable of firing a projectile thirteen inches in diameter and weighing two hundred pounds. Cochrane could also see that a mad rush past the fort would fail because of the booms and sunken hulks clogging the ship channel. The only course open to the British fleet was to stand off at a distance just beyond the range of the American cannon and bombard the fortifications in the hope of neutralizing them.

Cochrane opened his attack from two miles below Fort McHenry on the morning of September 13. From couriers who dashed between the fort and his Hampstead Hill command post Smith learned that hundreds of bombs and rockets had hit the fort and that Major Armistead, along with his thousand-man garrison, could do nothing but huddle in their shelters. Around two in the afternoon, about the time Colonel Brook's men prepared to attack, Cochrane sent his frigates in toward the fort to test its condition. Armistead's gunners quickly manned their forty-two-pounders and the frigates veered away. The most serious threat to McHenry came on the night of the 13th even as Brook's men were about to retreat. Under cover of rain and darkness several smaller British vessels and barges carrying two hundred men sailed into the Ferry Branch just south of the fort. Cochrane was planning to land troops behind McHenry and capture it, but once again the arrangements Smith had made in 1813 frustrated the British. The general had foreseen this very possibility and had prepared. Two batteries, Forts Covington and Babcock, had been constructed along the Ferry Branch behind Fort McHenry. Operated by experienced gun-

wallader, September 17, 1814, and S. Smith to Gov. Winder, September 15, 1814, Smith Order Book; William M. Marine, *The British Invasion of Maryland, 1812–1815* (Baltimore, 1913), pp. 130–170; J. W. Fortescue, *A History of the British Army*, 13 vols. (London, 1899–1930), 9: 146–149.

ners of the United States navy, these batteries blasted the British flotilla, along with those guns that could be brought into play from Fort McHenry and the Lazaretto. At least one of the barges was sunk (with the loss of all hands), and the surviving vessels fled back to the main fleet.[16]

Both on land and sea the British had been repulsed. On September 14 the fleet lifted its bombardment and drifted down the Patapsco to North Point where they rejoined the troop transports. Before sailing for the West Indies Cochrane released several American civilians he had been holding, including Francis Scott Key, who carried with him some lines of poetry scribbled on an envelope, the future national anthem. News of the victory at Baltimore lifted the spirits of many Americans still shocked by the burning of Washington. More substantively, the Battle of Baltimore, when coupled with the simultaneous victory at Plattsburg on the northern frontier, improved the bargaining position of the American negotiators at the peace talks in Ghent. No longer could the British seriously contend that the United States should accept a loss of territory as the price of ending hostilities. For Samuel Smith the events of September 13–14 were the high point of his life. He had accomplished many things in sixty-two years and he would do more, but none could compare in his own mind with the successful defense of Baltimore in 1814. Unfairly, Smith's achievement has frequently been obscured by some, who have stressed the parts played by John Rodgers or George Armistead. These and others of Smith's subordinates fought hard and well, but he was the chief architect of victory, the man whose energy, stature, and personal prestige made Baltimore capable of resisting the British. From first to last it was his triumph.

16. S. Smith to Monroe, September 19, 1814, printed in the *Baltimore Patriot and Evening Advertiser*, September 23, 1814; Gen. Winder to S. Smith, September 14, 1814, Smith Papers; S. Smith to unknown recipient, September 14, 1814, Smith Order Book; Report of British Officers on the Battle of Baltimore Made in Halifax on September 28, 1814, and reprinted in the *Baltimore Patriot and Evening Advertiser*, October 25, 1814.

14

A Second Congressional Career

As THE chief defender of Baltimore Samuel Smith received the applause of a grateful and relieved nation. Only a few, principally Joseph Hopper Nicholson, dissented from the view that the battle for Baltimore had been brilliantly directed by the general. Nicholson, who was present at Fort McHenry during the shelling, had hated Smith for years and had been one of those who had tried to defeat the general's bid for reelection to the Senate in 1809. Now in 1814 he tried the same tactics that had almost worked then. To his friend Nathaniel Macon, Nicholson wrote long, bitter letters condemning Smith and urging an investigation into his conduct during the battle. Macon, although sympathetic, rejected the scheme as impractical because in Washington "the affair near Baltimore is highly spoken of."[1] A few days later Macon relayed other information to Nicholson that was even more disturbing. "The reputation of the commanding general," the North Carolinian commented in reference to Smith, "has unquestionably I think gained much, taking the whole affair into view."[2]

Ultimately the September events in Baltimore did revive Samuel

1. Nathaniel Macon to Joseph Hopper Nicholson, October 19, 1814, Joseph Hopper Nicholson Papers, Library of Congress.
2. Macon to Nicholson, October 24, 1814, Nicholson Papers.

Smith's political career from the setback of 1811, when Madison had tried to cast out the Marylander from the Republican party. But in the fall of 1814 the general, now a hero in two wars, could not but believe that his twenty-year political career was about to end. In August of 1814, only a few weeks before the British landed, Smith had learned that the Federalist majority in the state legislature would not reappoint him to a third term in the United States Senate. Since his friend Nicholas Moore occupied his old seat in the House of Representatives, it looked as if Smith would be without political employment after Congress adjourned in the spring of 1815. In October 1814 the general suffered another blow that was both personal and political. General Winfield Scott, a popular and successful veteran of the military campaigns on the northern frontier, was appointed William Winder's successor as commander of the tenth military district and specifically given authority over the militia of Baltimore in case of attack. Smith suspected, and friends in Washington confirmed, that the appointment of Scott was an effort by the administration to embarrass Smith by superseding him. Whether this rumor was true or not, the proud Marylander would not serve under a man of lesser rank and promptly resigned his commission as major general.[3]

The decision to retire from a position he had held for over thirty-five years and through two wars deeply affected the aging Smith. "I think that Genl. S—— has rather a melancholy and mortified appearance," Nathaniel Macon observed shortly after the resignation, "I am sorry to see it, I cannot see such appearance without feeling sorrow."[4] Loss of his military position also deprived Smith of one of his principal political strengths. No longer would he be able to mobilize the city brigade to back his political ambitions; the days when the general harangued militia gatherings and freely distributed liquor to his troops on the eve of elections had come to an end. For two decades Smith had set the tone of, if indeed he had not controlled, Baltimore politics. An era ended in 1814, and the city of Baltimore entered into a new political age destined to be influenced by younger men and new forms of party organization. As for Samuel Smith,

3. J. Thomas Scharf, *History of Maryland from the Earliest Period to the Present Day*, 3 vols. (Baltimore, 1879), 3: 142; *Niles' Weekly Register*, October 27, 1814; S. Smith to Gov. Levin Winder, October 18, 1814, Gov. Winder to S. Smith, October 18, 1814, and John Spear Smith to S. Smith, October 22, 1814, Samuel Smith Papers, Library of Congress.

4. Macon to Nicholson, October 27, 1814, Nicholson Papers.

even as he receded as a figure of local and national power, he was about to begin a second congressional career in many ways even more eventful than his first.

The spring of 1815 found the war with Britain ended and Samuel Smith's prospects improving. Nicholas Moore had opportunely resigned his seat in the House, and the city of Baltimore had voted overwhelmingly to return the general in his place. Before leaving the Senate, however, Smith performed an act of signal importance. Ever since the Jay Treaty he had expressed strong disapproval of the system of discriminating duties that gave American vessels a near-monopoly of the import trade. While these duties had been useful and even necessary in the decade after the Revolutionary War, Smith had argued as early as 1795 that they would inevitably produce results unfavorable to American trade. Pointing to the provision of the Jay Treaty pledging the United States to freeze the level of duties on incoming British vessels while allowing the English government to lay countervailing duties against American ships, he had warned that soon all maritime nations would retaliate against the United States with discriminating duties of their own. Smith's motives can be described as enlightened self-interest. He continued to believe that American merchants and ships could successfully compete with foreigners in a free-trade environment and that a reciprocal lowering of discriminating duties was the best way to expand America's mercantile opportunities. In 1796, 1802, and 1803 he had proposed resolutions or legislation authorizing the president to negotiate with foreign nations for a mutual reduction of such taxes. In each attempt he had been stymied by conservative merchants and shipowners who failed to see his logic and tenaciously clung to their domination over the import trade. The war in Europe had forced those nations to postpone their plans to discriminate against American shipping since most of them relied on the United States as a neutral carrier to supply goods they could not otherwise obtain. Even Great Britain had relaxed its regulations before 1812 and permitted American ships to trade with its West Indian colonies. But after Waterloo sealed the fate of Napoleon and Europe returned to a peacetime economy, it was only a matter of time until these open doors were closed.[5]

In a speech to the Senate in late February 1815 Smith revealed the growing threat to the nation's commercial welfare. He showed that

5. U.S., Congress, *The Debates and Proceedings in the Congress of the United States . . . 1789–1824*, 42 vols. (Washington, D.C., 1834–1856), 13th Cong., 3d sess., 1815, p. 163; hereafter cited as *Annals of Congress*.

new British countervailing duties had gained for English shipowners complete control over the transport of many vital American products. Because of the duties it was simply cheaper to use British vessels than the more highly taxed American ships. Fish oil, tobacco, cotton, rice, pearlashes and many other exports formerly carried in American vessels now found their way to Britain in English bottoms. In addition to Great Britain Smith found that Spain, France, Sweden, Denmark, and Holland also had recently imposed discriminating duties against the United States. "If we continue our discriminating duties," Smith's long and fact-filled speech concluded, "the result must be that our ships will be rendered useless."[6] While acknowledging that raising American duties higher was a possibility, he noted that other nations would only follow suit. Smith deduced there was but one solution: "Is it not, therefore, Mr. President, for us to agree to meet the nations of Europe on equal terms—the ships of each to be admitted into the ports of the other on the same terms with their own ships?"[7] Reaffirming his faith in the better designed and manned ships of the American merchant marine to outdistance their rivals in a fair contest for trade, Smith asked the Senate to pass the reciprocity bill he had submitted, a bill very similar to that which he had proposed in 1803.[8]

Shipowners, already beginning to feel the pinch, and Americans generally were more receptive to a freer trade than they had been a decade before. Smith's reciprocity bill easily passed through Congress and helped lay the groundwork for a commercial convention negotiated with the British a few months later. Within three years all of Smith's confidence in the efficacy of the measure was rewarded as American vessels rapidly achieved preeminence in the carrying trade both ways across the Atlantic. The reciprocity act of 1815 stands as Samuel Smith's most significant legislative accomplishment. It did not end, however, his struggles for the freest commercial intercourse possible. The commercial convention with Britain did not extend the principle of reciprocity to all trade within the British empire, particularly to the West Indian possessions. During the next fifteen years the Marylander directed more and more of his energies toward the goal of complete reciprocity.[9]

After an absence of thirteen years Samuel Smith took his seat in

6. Ibid.
7. Ibid.
8. Ibid.
9. Ibid.; Bradford Perkins, *Castlereagh and Adams; England and the United States, 1812–1823* (Berkeley, 1964), pp. 169, 223.

the House of Representatives on December 4, 1815, as the Fourteenth Congress began its first session. The general listened closely as James Madison's seventh presidential address to Congress was read by the clerk. In his speech, which many felt had old Federalist overtones, Madison hinted at the necessity of reestablishing a national bank, called for a protective tariff to preserve American manufacturing begun during the war from being ruined by foreign imports, and asked Congress to consider the construction of roads and canals under national supervision. The overture to the great age of American nationalism, Madison's address outlined the three issues which would shape the nation's politics for many years to come: the Bank of the United States, the tariff, and internal improvements. Over these matters parties would form and presidents would be elected or defeated. Smith, however, would approach them as he always had, basing his judgments of them on their relation to commerce, Baltimore, and national security.[10]

The first of the Madisonian proposals to come before the House was a plan for a new national bank. Debated by the House in January 1816, the scheme envisioned an institution far larger than its predecessor. Smith, of course, had been instrumental in preventing recharter of the first Bank of the United States in 1811, arguing then that the bank was dangerous politically and performed no functions that state banks could not do as well. This latter opinion was sadly disproved by experience during the war. State banks had not demonstrated that they were responsible or that they were sufficient to the needs of the government. In many areas of the country state banks had issued far more notes than their capital justified, with the result that most state bank notes declined in value and the notes of one bank often were not accepted by another. As far as collecting taxes, transferring funds, and making loans, the state banks were of little help to the United States government. After Washington was burned in 1814 the state banks totally suspended the payments of specie in redemption of their notes, thus adding to the depreciation in their value. Even by the end of 1813 the absence of a stable and accepted medium of exchange had harmed the American economy. Keenly aware of all business conditions, Smith had confronted the financial malaise spreading across the country and determined that only strong

10. James D. Richardson, ed., *A Compilation of the Messages and Papers of the Presidents, 1789–1897*, 10 vols. (Washington, D.C., 1896–1899), 1: 565–566.

centralized leadership could reverse the alarming trend toward total economic dislocation. Many months before Madison's speech he had become convinced that a new national bank had to be established. In January 1815, while still a member of the Senate, he had been chairman of a select committee considering a bank proposal and had pressed successfully for amendments that strengthened the charter. Madison, however, had vetoed the plan, objecting that the capital of the new bank should be larger and that there should be more government control.[11]

The Marylander did not change his mind about the necessity of a national bank, and when the House considered a new plan in 1816, he gave it strong support. Only on one section of the bank bill did he raise any real objections. He asked, futilely, that the deadline for state banks to resume specie payments be pushed back in order to avoid inflicting hardship. Smith insisted that no legislation would be so effective in restoring specie payments as having the Bank of the United States begin exchanging specie itself. Once that happened, he reasoned, the state banks would as a matter of course also resume payments. As finally approved by Congress and the president the second Bank of the United States had a capital of $35,000,000 and was permitted to conduct operations for a period of twenty years.[12]

Having dispensed with the first item in Madison's program, Congress next turned its attention to the question of a protective tariff. The tariff issue confronted Samuel Smith with a profound dilemma. On the one hand he knew that without a government subsidy the thriving industries of America would be washed away in a tidal wave of cheaper products imported from Britain. More specifically, failure to adopt a protective tariff would expose the important iron and distilling industries in Maryland to a ruinous competition. Should American manufacturing enterprise be crippled or retarded, then the United States would slip back into that neocolonial subservience to Great Britain that had been so galling in the years before the war. On the other hand, a protective tariff was potentially harmful to the shipping interest. Its object was to reduce or eliminate the importa-

11. Bray Hammond, *Banks and Politics in America from the Revolution to the Civil War* (Princeton, 1957), pp. 229–234; *Annals of Congress,* 13th Cong., 3d sess., 1815, pp. 164–166.

12. *Annals of Congress,* 14th Cong., 1st sess., 1816, pp. 1071–1072, 1120–1121, 1127, 1133; Macon to Nicholson, April 2, 1816, Nicholson Papers; Hammond, *Banks and Politics,* p. 244; George Dangerfield, *The Awakening of American Nationalism, 1815–1828* (New York, 1965), p. 12.

tion of certain goods, and it necessarily followed that the profits of American shipowners would suffer. There was also the possibility that foreign nations would retaliate with tariffs against American products and reduce the export carrying trade. Caught in this web of conflicting loyalties, Smith anxiously sought a suitable compromise.[13]

In 1816 the tariff was not yet the divisive question it would be after 1824. The great majority of Americans both in and out of Congress favored somewhat higher duties to protect manufactures and to help pay off the national debt. The contest was over what should be protected, the level of that protection, and the duration of the tariffs. Smith's concern with the tariff bill began when Secretary of the Treasury Alexander Dallas submitted an extensive report on the subject to the Committee on Ways and Means, of which the general was a member. With his approval a bill was reported to the House which placed an average duty of 25 percent on those imports that competed with American-made goods but which the domestic industry did not produce in quantities sufficient to satisfy local demands. It was assumed that within a period of three years American industry would be competitive with that of Europe, and so a provision in the bill reduced the duties yearly until by 1819 they would stand at a uniform 20 percent. The job of guiding the bill through the House fell upon William Lowndes of South Carolina, chairman of the Ways and Means Committee. He soon suffered a serious illness, however, and the burden of defending the legislation shifted to Smith, who was the second-ranking member of the committee. Throughout late March and early April 1816 the general was constantly on his feet, beating back all efforts to postpone the bill or seriously weaken its provisions. Twice he spoke for significant changes in the bill. On the first occasion he gained House approval for an amendment increasing the specific duty on some types of manufactured iron, an obvious effort to benefit his Maryland constituents.[14] A few days later he unsuccessfully opposed a motion limiting the duration of the tariff bill to four years because of "the injurious effect on commerce, as well as manufactures, that the constant apprehension of change would produce."[15] A moderate yet permanent tariff,

13. F. W. Taussig, *The Tariff History of the United States* (New York, 1892), pp. 18–19.

14. Edward Stanwood, *American Tariff Controversies in the Nineteenth Century*, 2 vols. (New York, 1903), 1: 140–141; Dangerfield, *American Nationalism*, pp. 13–16; Charles M. Wiltse, *The New Nation, 1800–1845* (New York, 1961), p. 57; *Annals of Congress,* 14th Cong., 1st sess., 1816, pp. 1236–1361 passim.

15. *Annals of Congress,* 14th Cong., 1st sess., 1816, p. 1288.

he believed, was the best policy. The Marylander in later years looked back to the tariff of 1816 as the best act on the subject ever passed by Congress because it not only helped manufacturing, but also the duties were low enough so as not to harm the commercial interests of the nation. He viewed the act as a reasonable and sensible response to the crisis in American industry and the debt-ridden treasury. He had, at least temporarily, taken a position on the tariff that harmonized the various interests he represented.

The third and last of Madison's recommendations to Congress for attaining national self-sufficiency and rapid economic growth was a system of roads and canals to be built under the auspices of the federal government. Like the bank and the tariff the roots of the movement to improve communications and transportation within the United States went back many years before the war. But the war had underlined the critical need for more and better transportation systems, especially in the northwest, where much of the fighting had occurred. Moreover, both during and after the war a swelling tide of emigrants had flowed into the trans-Allegheny west and were demanding that the government open up routes over which commerce and settlers might move. It was not only the West, however, that desired internal improvements. Most states from New York southward were anxious to create new avenues to the interior in order to tap the growing wealth of those areas. In some cases the greatest pressure for building roads and canals came from the commercial cities along the Atlantic coast, which vied with each other to become major entrepôts through which western crops would pass on their way to the outside world. Certainly this was the case in Maryland, where Baltimore, the fastest growing city in the nation, was trying to stand off Philadelphia's challenge to its control of the commerce of central Pennsylvania and at the same time extend its sphere of influence to the Ohio valley. Maryland had long been most aggressive in financing internal improvements, and in Samuel Smith the state had a spokesman who knew well the value of good roads and would champion Maryland's interests in Congress.

Actually Smith had been actively supporting federally directed internal improvements long before Madison had mentioned it in his annual address and even before Albert Gallatin, as secretary of the treasury, had unveiled a national plan for roads and canals in 1808. In 1806 the Marylander had determined that a "good turnpike road to the Ohio" was needed and along with others proposed the plan in Congress. During the debates over where the eastern terminus of the road should be, the general had obtained the assistance of Senator

Thomas Worthington of Ohio, and together they convinced Congress to begin construction at Cumberland, Maryland, rather than at Washington. The Maryland legislature quickly seized on the great prize Smith had achieved and commenced building a turnpike linking Baltimore and Cumberland. Paid for from the proceeds of land sales in Ohio, the Cumberland or National Road was begun in 1811 and reached Wheeling in 1818 and Columbus, Ohio, in 1833. It helped to give Baltimore a fast start in the race for the riches of the West.[16]

Despite this record of favoring national assistance to internal improvement projects, the Marylander opposed a bill drafted by John C. Calhoun of South Carolina and submitted to the House on February 4, 1817. The Calhoun scheme simply resurrected Gallatin's old report of 1808 and provided that the various projects were to be paid for out of a fund into which the bonus the Bank of the United States had agreed to pay the government for the privileges granted in its charter and the dividends due the government from the bank stock it held would be placed. Smith's reasons for demurring from the support of this legislation are not at all clear. Since he always had acted on the assumption that the national government had whatever powers were necessary to fulfill its responsibilities, he could hardly have had qualms about the constitutionality of the measure. Furthermore, a year later he voted for a resolution in the House stating that Congress had the power under the Constitution to appropriate funds for roads, canals, and the improvement of waterways. The general's complaint against the Calhoun program seems to have been directed at the timing of the bill. On February 7 he declared that the United States was not financially ready to commit itself to the huge expenditures the bill contemplated. The general asked that the matter be postponed until the next session of Congress. Although this might be interpreted as a tactic to kill the bill, Smith's later behavior indicates that he was sincere. As a member of the Ways and Means Committee he was sensitive to the problem of reducing the national debt, and he may have felt the income from the bank would be better used in redeeming government bonds. The Marylander's vote against the internal improvements bill proved to be one of only a very few exceptions to his record of voting for all such legislation.[17]

16. S. Smith to James Noble, March 4, 1825, and S. Smith to J. T. Chauncey, January 25, 1823, Smith Papers; George Rogers Taylor, *The Transportation Revolution, 1815–1860* (New York, 1951), p. 22.

17. Charles M. Wiltse, *John C. Calhoun: Nationalist, 1782–1828* (New York, 1944), p. 133; Dangerfield, *American Nationalism*, p. 18; *Annals of Congress*, 15th Cong., 1st sess., 1817, p. 1386, 14th Cong., 2d sess., 1817, pp. 819–885. Although this bill passed both houses of Congress, President Madison exercised his veto power on constitutional grounds.

On March 4, 1817, James Monroe assumed the presidency and the misnamed Era of Good Feelings began. The general had neither supported nor opposed the secretary of state's candidacy. His only participation in the election seems to have been in the Republican presidential nominating caucus held in March 1816. Smith had issued the official call for the caucus and had been elected chairman, proof that he had come a long way since 1811 in rehabilitating his position in the Republican party. The change in administration was most important for Smith, as it removed a major barrier to his resuming friendly relations with the executive branch. Since 1811 the Marylander had been excluded by Madison from the higher councils of government, but now Madison was in retirement and Smith's other antagonist, Albert Gallatin, was in Europe on diplomatic assignment. Neither Smith nor the new administration felt any hostility for each other, and there was a strong disposition to bury the old prewar conflicts. Monroe and his Cabinet had many reasons for wishing to rally the general to their support. Nearly sixty-five years old, he had certainly reached that stage in life when most people regarded him as a venerable figure who had contributed much to the nation and to his party. Moreover, the administration needed his unmatched knowledge of commercial and financial affairs, that expert knowledge which had made him one of the most valuable members of Congress since he had first entered that body twenty-four years before. And though Smith no longer controlled Baltimore politics, he remained a prominent leader in the city and could certainly help encourage local sentiments favorable to the administration. Finally, Smith's appointment in 1818 as chairman of the influential Ways and Means Committee, the body which practically dictated decisions to the House in financial affairs, made his friendship even more desirable to appropriations-conscious administrators. For his part, the Marylander seemed happy once more to be consulted and listened to by those in power.[18]

The years 1818–1824 were generally satisfying ones for Samuel Smith, at least from a political point of view. In relation to the administration he found that the treasure-chest of patronage was again open to him, and his recommendations for deserving friends soon began cluttering the desks of the president and the departmental heads. Even more gratifying were the letters soliciting his opinions. In June of 1817, for example, Richard Rush, who was temporarily handling state department affairs while the new secretary of state, John Quincy Adams, was traveling to Washington, inquired of the

18. Washington, D.C. *National Intelligencer,* March 19, 1816.

general his views on a British proposal concerning American trade with the West Indies. In a lengthy reply Smith attacked the plan as contrary to American interests.[19] Rush thanked him fulsomely for his essay in words that surely gladdened an old heart too long in political purgatory: "Its facts and opinions will I am persuaded, be prized by the government in a manner due to your high-character throughout the country for comprehensive knowledge and enlightened views upon subjects of so much interest."[20] Although Smith and the administration had their differences, especially over the long-running negotiations with Britain, his standing with the president continued to rise throughout Monroe's two terms. Unknown to the Marylander, the president twice proposed to send him on important diplomatic missions. The first occasion was in 1818, when Monroe wished to dispatch two representatives to Constantinople and Naples to conclude commercial agreements. Four years later Smith was seriously considered as minister for one of the four new Latin and South American nations recently established by anti-Spanish revolutions. Long cherishing the idea of a diplomatic career, the general might well have accepted one of these posts. In both instances, however, Secretary of State Adams, who had disliked Smith since their days together in the Senate many years before, prevented the offers from being made.[21]

Until he returned to the Senate in 1822, Smith continued to play an active part in the House of Representatives. Maintaining his posture as a moderate nationalist, he voted for internal improvements bills and several tariff measures that were in keeping with the mild protection principle embodied in the tariff act of 1816. On the explosive issue of Missouri, which John Quincy Adams described as "a titlepage to a great tragic volume," the Marylander followed an erratic but generally middle-of-the-road course. As a representative of a slave state and an owner of domestic slaves himself it was not surprising that he should vote to admit Missouri without banning slavery from it. Nor was it unusual that he supported the great compromise of 1820

19. S. Smith to Secretary of the Navy Benjamin Crowninshield, May 29, 1817, Smith Papers; S. Smith to Secretary of War John C. Calhoun, August 28 and September 30, 1818, in W. Edwin Hemphill, ed., *Papers of John C. Calhoun*, 3 vols. (Columbia, S.C., 1967), 3: 78, 175; Charles Francis Adams, ed., *Memoirs of John Quincy Adams*, 12 vols. (Philadelphia, 1874–1877), 5: 56, 6: 28, 232; Richard Rush to S. Smith, June 13, 1817, and S. Smith to Rush, July 1817, Smith Papers.

20. Rush to S. Smith, July 13, 1817, Smith Papers.

21. Adams, ed., *Memoirs of Adams*, 4: 72, 73, 77–78, 5: 496.

which admitted Maine as a free state and Missouri as a slave state, and prohibited slavery anywhere else in the old Louisiana Purchase territory, nor that he voted for the lesser compromise of 1821 permitting the entrance of Missouri into the Union with the understanding that the state would never pass laws contrary to the rights of American citizens. What must have raised a few eyebrows among his constituents were positions he took on two subordinate votes. The first occurred in February 1819, when he deserted other southerners and voted in favor of the second part of the famous Tallmadge amendment that called for freeing all slave children born in Missouri when they reached age twenty-five. In a second vote, in January 1821, Smith joined with only five other representatives in supporting a resolution demanding that before Missouri became a state it expunge from its constitution that section preventing free Negroes from entering its boundaries. Adding to the confusion, the general, in his only lengthy speech during the Missouri debates, unequivocally asserted the power of Congress over the territories in all matters, presumably including whether or not to allow slaves in them. But he added quickly that once a territory became a state, federal authority ended and that state could admit slaves if it chose.[22]

There is nothing in Smith's papers to explain these inconsistencies and no evidence that he ever gave any systematic thought to the great issues involved in the Missouri Compromise. His actions certainly reveal in him an ambivalent attitude toward slavery, but they also reflect an effort on his part to preserve the Union intact and uphold the power of the central government. In a period when sectional interests were beginning to predominate over those of the nation, Samuel Smith had rejected the strong states' rights position of other southerners and intended to stand four-square with the national government he had helped create. However significant the Missouri controversy was in the larger pattern of American history, it held little interest for the Marylander. Missouri belonged to the new emerging America of westward expansion and sectionalism while he remained preoccupied with trade and defense, problems that were gradually being displaced as the primary interests of the American people and their government.

In the area of commerce Smith was indefatigable in his labors to extend the reciprocity principle contained in his act of 1815. Begin-

22. *Annals of Congress*, 15th Cong., 1st sess., 1818, p. 1657, 17th Cong., 1st sess., 1822, pp. 1480–1481, 15th Cong., 2d sess., 1819, pp. 1214–1215, 16th Cong., 2d sess., 1821, p. 944, 16th Cong., 1st sess., 1820, pp. 941–942; Adams, ed., *Memoirs of Adams*, 4: 502.

ning in 1817, Smith sponsored or supported a number of bills which he hoped would force the British to open the West Indian possessions to American vessels on the same terms British ships enjoyed. The general was equally active in looking after the interests of the army. As chairman of the House Ways and Means Committee from 1818 to 1822 he had ample opportunity to assist the military. Indeed, from the army's point of view it was a fortuitous circumstance that the friendly Smith held this post during these difficult years. The great economic collapse of 1819 made retrenchment of government expenditures necessary, and the military establishment was a prime target for congressional economizers. Feeling was so strong that drastic reductions should be made in the army that an administration plan to reduce its size by half was rejected at least in part because many congressmen felt it did not go far enough. For four years it became the general's self-appointed duty to mediate between the budget-conscious Congress and the welfare of the army. While he probably wished that no cuts at all would be made, he bowed to the inevitable and usually reported military budgets to the House that were slightly less than the war department requested. When the appropriations were debated, he vigorously defended them against any moves to shrink them further. Overall he was markedly successful. Among other things he was able to save the military academy at West Point, much of the coastal fortifications program, and pensions for veterans. Despite his best efforts he could not prevent Congress from slicing the strength of the army from twelve to six thousand men.[23]

A useful and honored senior politician in Washington during the Monroe years, Smith was not so favored by fate back in Baltimore, where events combined to annihilate his business and his personal fortune. The instrument of the general's downfall was his business partner of more than thirty years, James A. Buchanan. Smith had long since surrendered the operations of S. Smith & Buchanan to his partner, and Buchanan had maintained the company as the largest and most prosperous in Baltimore. When the second Bank of the United States had been chartered in 1816, Buchanan had been appointed president of the Baltimore branch and a member of the cen-

23. Adams, ed., *Memoirs of Adams*, 4: 61, 5: 342; Wiltse, *Calhoun: Nationalist*, pp. 223–225; *Annals of Congress*, 14th Cong., 2d sess., 1817, p. 695, 16th Cong., 1st sess., 1820, pp. 1603–1615, 1620–1625, 1634, 17th Cong., 1st sess., 1822, pp. 626–633; Thomas Hart Benton, *Thirty Years' View*, 2 vols. (New York, 1886), 1: 11.

tral board of directors in Philadelphia. Caught up in the post-war speculative fever and unchecked by the incompetent president of the bank, William Jones, Buchanan had engaged in a veritable orgy of financial mismanagement. Along with James W. McCulloch, cashier of the Baltimore branch, and George Williams, one of the branch's directors, Smith's partner wildly speculated in the stock of the Bank of the United States. The three conspirators freely lent themselves funds from the branch bank without collateral and purchased the stock on margin, hoping that it would go up in price so they could sell the shares and make a sizable profit on a minimal investment. Buchanan had conducted much of this operation in the name of S. Smith & Buchanan, thus implicating the company in his frauds and through it all revealed nothing of his dealings to Smith. At the height of their manipulations the three bank officials had illegally spent about three million dollars of the institution's funds.[24]

The panic, which began in 1818, ultimately brought to light the incredible state of affairs in Baltimore. To save the Bank of the United States its directors began to curtail credit and generally exert closer supervision over the branches. Samuel Smith may have received his first inkling of approaching calamity when a congressional committee investigating the bank reported in January 1819 that there were irregularities in the Baltimore branch's operations.[25] At almost the same time Jones resigned as president of the bank and was succeeded shortly thereafter by Langdon Cheves of South Carolina. By the end of April the conspirators had been entirely exposed; McCulloch was removed from office while Buchanan resigned. Within a few weeks S. Smith & Buchanan failed. "The House of Smith and Buchanan, which has been these thirty years one of the greatest commercial establishments in the United States," John Quincy Adams confided to his diary, "broke last week with a crash which staggered the whole city of Baltimore and will extend no one knows how far."[26] In an instant the general had lost the fruits of a lifetime of labor. Montebello, the town house, the magnificent household possessions, and most of his landholdings were swept up by the Bank of the United States to help cover the gigantic deficit. Buchanan, however, knowing long in advance what was coming, had transferred owner-

24. Hammond, *Banks and Politics*, pp. 261–263.
25. Ibid., pp. 258–259; *Annals of Congress*, 15th Cong., 2d sess., 1819, pp. 552–573.
26. Adams, ed., *Memoirs of Adams*, 4: 382.

ship of much of his property to relatives. He even arranged to retain his home in Baltimore.[27]

Throughout May and June of 1819 Smith bordered on insanity or suicide. His condition was not helped when his brother Robert flatly refused to add his name to those who agreed to secure the debt of $300,000 for which Smith was personally responsible. By the end of May the shattered old man was confined to his bed.[28] "It is impossible for him to continue to feel as he does and live or retain his senses," reported his daughter-in-law, Cary Ann Smith, "I never saw anyone so broken down in my life."[29] In the same letter she noted that Smith had ceased eating, sleeping, or behaving rationally. "The dread of disgrace," she continued, "the stings of ingratitude, the loss of fortune, altogether is too much for his sensibility and pride."[30] A week later Cary Anne saw no improvement in the general's health. Although the rest of the family were bearing the tragedy well, she observed that Smith's "mind and body appear to be sinking under it." Much of his grief, she believed, was caused by a concern that he would be blamed for what Buchanan had done.[31]

Even as the distracted Smith suffered through this intense personal crisis his friends and relatives, with the notable exception of his ungracious brother Robert, offered their sympathy and help. Several merchants, among them his brother-in-law William Patterson, joined John Spear Smith, Samuel's son, in securing the debt.[32] Secretary of the Treasury William H. Crawford, a close friend of many years, expressed his deep concern and that of many others in Washington for Smith's situation. Crawford assured the general that no one had "even whispered a doubt of your being in any degree a participant in the highly improper acts of some of the officers of the branch bank," and offered his friend whatever help he could give.[33] Much later General Lafayette, with whom Smith had kept up a sporadic correspondence

27. See Buchanan's deposition, June 1, 1821, Smith-Carter Papers, University of Virginia Library; S. Smith to John Spear Smith, December 10, 1819, Smith Papers, Maryland Historical Society (all other references to the Smith Papers in this chapter are to those papers found at the Library of Congress).

28. Adams, ed., *Memoirs of Adams*, 4: 382; Jonathan Hollins to Wilson Cary Nicholas, May 20, 1819, Wilson Cary Nicholas Papers, University of Virginia Library.

29. Cary Anne Smith to Peggy Nicholas, June 8, 1819, Nicholas Papers.

30. Ibid.

31. Cary Anne Smith to Peggy Nicholas, June 16, 1819, Nicholas Papers.

32. Nelly Carr to Mrs. Thomas Jefferson Randolph, May 27, 1819, Nicholas Papers.

33. W. H. Crawford to S. Smith, June 11, 1819, Smith Papers.

since the Revolution, wrote that the Marylander's misfortunes had deeply affected "your old Companion in arms and constant friend."[34]

Smith had recovered sufficiently by the end of the summer to begin reorganizing his life. After prolonged legal wrangling he was able to retain in his wife's name some land in Kentucky, a few lots in Washington, and a handful of Bank of the United States stock. With the help of his son he rebought his house in Baltimore, but he was forced to sell off all but three of his slaves and his well-stocked wine cellar as well. John Spear Smith pleased the family in 1822 when he purchased Montebello. To keep up the payments, however, he turned it into a working farm, which he managed full-time. Once the richest family in Baltimore, the Smiths now went to extraordinary lengths to save money. For several years Samuel and Margaret lived together with their son and daughter-in-law, alternating between Montebello and the city house in order to cut living expenses. This arrangement did not always please Cary Anne, who was none too happy being cooped up with the "old folks." The general's government pay, the per diem that every congressman swore was not nearly enough to pay living costs in Washington, became an important source of income. In 1823 Smith commented to his daughter in England that he and Margaret lived so frugally in Washington that they returned to Baltimore with a surplus of $300.[35]

The years between 1819 and 1826, when Smith was finally released by the bank for the balance of the debt, were in many ways cruel ones for the proud old man. In 1822, for example, he was not able to travel to England because of the possibility one of his creditors would have him arrested there for debt on the expectation his daughter's husband would pay. He was also galled by the appearance of his name as a defaultor in the annual statement of the bank, a report published in many newspapers. By the arrangements made in 1819 he was not even technically in debt to the bank and he greatly resented the embarrassment these yearly reports caused him. Finally, in 1824, the bank agreed to correct the error which, wrote the general, "will greatly relieve my feelings." Dark though they were, the bankruptcy years were not hopeless. Smith learned to accept his fate philosophically. He took a professional interest in his wife's few assets and delighted in parlaying them into a small but respectable for-

34. Gen. Lafayette to S. Smith, August 24, 1820, Smith-Carter Papers.

35. See list of Margaret Smith's belongings, 1839, Smith Papers; S. Smith to Mrs. Mansfield, May 3, 1823, and June 6, 1822, Smith-Carter Papers; Cary Anne Smith to Peggy Nicholas, June 16, 1819, Nicholas Papers.

tune.[36] Best of all he remained in Congress, where he was respected not only for his knowledge but also for his experience. "I have lost nothing in the opinion of the people and the nation," he told his family after being reelected to the House of Representatives in 1822, "I have more consideration paid to me in Congress than I ever had and have as admitted rendered special service since I have been at the head of the Ways and Means."[37]

Age and misfortune were taking their toll on the general. Although still wondrously resilient, he was beginning to lose the toughness and drive that had made him both a successful merchant and politician. His letters show greater introspection than ever before, a more reflective approach toward his own life and the world about him. Smith had always been a concerned and proud family man, but after the bankruptcy he took increasing interest in his many children and grandchildren. In short, Samuel Smith was not only an old man but was beginning to feel like one as well. This new note of mellowness so obvious in his private life was also reflected in his public career. The catastrophe of 1819 nearly completed his transition from an active, interested politician to a revered hero and elder statesman. Without the militia organization and his wealth he could not influence Baltimore politics to any great extent. While his own position in Congress was guaranteed by the great affection Baltimore's citizens had for him, he could not transfer that support to others. This evolution in Smith's life was perfectly illustrated by the part he played in the presidential election of 1824, his last fling at partisan politics.

What made the contest of 1824 so interesting was the number of candidates; no less than five men were in contention. From Kentucky there was Speaker of the House Henry Clay, sometimes referred to as the dashing "Harry of the West." South Carolina's legislature nominated its favorite son and Monroe's secretary of war, John C. Calhoun, architect of the nationalistic American system but soon to become an ardent states' rights champion. The candidate of New England and John Quincy Adams, America's leading diplomat and currently secretary of state. The most underrated of the five proved to be Andrew Jackson of Tennessee, "the hero of New Orleans," whose politics were unknown but whose popularity was nationwide. The last of the candidates, William H. Crawford of Georgia, was also a member of Mon-

36. S. Smith to Crawford, December 17, 1820, and S. Smith to Mrs. Mansfield, November 13, 1822, and June 6, 1824, Smith-Carter Papers; S. Smith to Gales & Seaton, March 22, 1822, and S. Smith to Crawford, December 20, 1820, and October 13, 1825, Smith Papers.

37. S. Smith to Mrs. Mansfield, November 13, 1822, Smith-Carter Papers.

roe's Cabinet, filling the position of secretary of the treasury. Since all five were Republicans the campaign was conducted by personal factions rather than political parties. The disintegration of the old Jeffersonian party that was visible as early as 1806 was now complete. The coalition of southern aristocrats with the big-city political machines and the small landholders of the north and west had ended.[38]

Samuel Smith knew each of the candidates personally and well. All had served with him in Congress, and he had observed and worked with Adams, Calhoun, and Crawford during their years in the Cabinet. The available evidence would indicate that he decided to back Crawford at an early date, perhaps by 1818, and he never wavered in that determination. At first glance Crawford and Smith would seem to have had little in common. Twenty years younger than Smith, Crawford had migrated with his family from Virginia to Georgia as a boy and had there been educated as a lawyer. In Georgia politics he had sided with the rich landed elite and his entire later career in government was characterized by strong conservative leanings. He had been a competent secretary of the treasury, his evident talents attracting the favorable attention of Jefferson, Madison, and Gallatin as well as other leading Republicans. With their blessing he became the candidate of orthodox Republicanism, the man they felt who could best carry on the old policies. Together with his numerous congressional supporters, who called themselves "Radicals," Crawford became a leading exponent of frugal and limited government, moderate tariffs, and a small but efficient military establishment. Smith came out of an urban-commercial milieu, and the interests he represented had naturally favored a strong central government capable of defending trade and protecting Baltimore from attack. Although he could agree with Crawford on the tariff issue, the two men most definitely differed in theory over defense policies and internal improvements.[39]

Despite these conflicting opinions Smith was closer to Crawford ideologically than to any of the other candidates—save perhaps Jackson, whose views were still a mystery. The Crawfordites were not throwbacks to the John Randolph school of Republicanism for they

38. See Phillip Jackson Green, *The Life of William Harris Crawford* (Charlotte, N.C., 1965), pp. 199–226; Samuel Flagg Bemis, *John Quincy Adams and the Union* (New York, 1956), pp. 11–31; Dangerfield, *American Nationalism,* pp. 212–213.

39. Green, *Life of Crawford,* pp. 1–8; Dangerfield, *American Nationalism,* pp. 212–213; *Annals of Congress,* 18th Cong., 1st sess., 1824, pp. 738–739; Benton, *Thirty Years' View,* 1: 33; Wiltse, *Calhoun: Nationalist,* p. 291.

recognized that some flexibility had to be exercised on such issues as the tariff and internal improvements if the election was to be won. In practice Smith and Crawford got along quite well before 1824, although the general steadfastly opposed Radical efforts to trifle with the military. A variety of reasons separated Smith from the other presidential hopefuls. For one thing, he recoiled from the extreme positions Adams, Clay, and Calhoun took on the tariff. In the debates over the tariff of 1824, the Marylander had declared his enmity toward any further increases in duties. Clay had taken the lead in pushing the measure through Congress and Calhoun did not disapprove the measure. Personal feelings also kept the general from having a close relation with several of the contenders. Smith and Adams had disliked each other for fifteen years, and, more recently, the Marylander had been critical of Adams' handling of the negotiations with Britain on the West Indies trade question. He got along no better with Henry Clay, who had frequently attacked the operations of the Ways and Means Committee and its chairman. Toward Andrew Jackson, Smith had nothing but good feelings. He admired the Tennessean for his military accomplishments and had defended on the House floor Jackson's sweep into Florida in 1818. Nevertheless, Smith never took the Jackson campaign for the presidency seriously, a blindness shared by many professional politicians on the eve of the election.[40]

Even had his policy differences with Crawford been greater, the general would undoubtedly have given Crawford his support out of friendship. He had known the Georgian since 1807, when Crawford entered the Senate. After Crawford became secretary of the treasury their warm feelings for each other grew and they carried on a regular and frequent correspondence with each other when not in Washington. Part of their relationship was professional, since the treasury department necessarily had to keep in close touch with the Ways and Means Committee. But Crawford went out of his way to seek the Marylander's counsel on financial matters, and, as John Quincy Adams' diary reveals, carried those views to the president and Cabinet. In 1819, when Smith was at the nadir of his fortunes, the Georgian had stood by him, offering solace and encouragement. A year later, when the Marylander had campaigned unsuccessfully to become Speaker of the House in place of Clay (who had resigned), Crawford again gave him every assistance. As long-time colleagues and close friends,

---

40. See Adams, ed., *Memoirs of Adams*, 5: 345, 4: 173; Benton, *Thirty Years' View*, 1: 124–126; *Annals of Congress*, 15th Cong., 2d sess., 1819, pp. 446–453, 17th Cong., 1st sess., 1822, p. 612.

it was natural that Smith should try to aid Crawford in his ambitions to become president.[41]

But the amount of assistance Smith rendered to Crawford during the campaign was almost negligible. In Congress he did on occasion speak out against efforts to harass the secretary, but he refused to engage in retaliatory machinations against Calhoun or Adams. In January 1821, for example, the Crawfordites tried to embarrass Calhoun by cutting away large parts of the war department's budget. When Smith defended the appropriations and even attempted to add to them, a fellow Crawford supporter in exasperation demanded that he desist for it was vital to maintain "discipline in [our] ranks." Replying that he had "never heard so broad a declaration in the House," the Marylander denounced the idea that he should support or oppose a bill without first judging its merits.[42] Unspoken was the assumption, one he had always made, that the national interest took precedence over partisanship. This political rectitude, evident through thirty years in Congress, made him a responsible public official but lessened his value as a party politician. The same dogged independence had caused him to challenge the policies of three presidents, even though he nominally belonged to the same party as they did.

Outside the walls of Congress Smith did what he could to further Crawford's interests. As the chief Crawford supporter in Maryland he busied himself with writing newspaper articles defending the Georgian from his many enemies. But so weak were the Crawford forces in the state that there were no newspapers Smith could count on to get his pieces published.[43] Over seventy years old, the general could not hope to stir enthusiasm by personally stumping the state. From the comfort of his home he dutifully kept in touch with Crawford leaders in other states, especially Martin Van Buren in New York, exchanging information with them and issuing over-optimistic statements about how well their man was doing in Maryland. On February

41. See, for example, Crawford to S. Smith, July 1, 1817, May 5 and 23, 1818, July 3 and 29, 1820, and June 25, 1821, Smith Papers; Adams, ed., *Memoirs of Adams,* 4: 324, 173, 5: 332. Smith's effort to become Speaker may have been related to Crawford's campaign. As Speaker, Smith might have helped the Georgian through his power to appoint committees.

42. *Annals of Congress,* 16th Cong., 1st sess., 1820, pp. 912–913, 917, 2d sess., 1821, pp. 902–903.

43. Washington *Gazette,* July 5 and 15, and September 11, 12, and 13, 1823. Drafts of other articles may be found in the Smith Papers. For additional evidence of Smith's campaign activities in Maryland, see William R. Stewart to S. Smith, January 20, 1823, Vertical File, Maryland Historical Society; S. Smith to Stevenson Archer, 1823, and Crawford to S. Smith, July 18, 1823, Smith Papers.

14, 1824, the general, now back in the Senate, disregarded explicit instructions from the Maryland legislature and attended the last of the controversial presidential caucuses. Only a handful of the eligible congressmen were present and most of them were Crawford men. The Georgian's opponents had already mounted a publicity campaign against the caucus that convinced many Americans the institution was undemocratic, and in the end the caucus nomination cost Crawford much support. Along with the two paralytic strokes he suffered in 1823 and 1824, it was one of the major reasons for his defeat.[44]

In the fall elections of 1824 Crawford received only forty-one electoral votes and 46,618 popular ballots, finishing far behind Jackson and Adams. In Maryland the Georgian was given one of the state's eleven electoral votes.[45] Smith had not even been able to carry Baltimore for his friend, as the city's electorate gave Andrew Jackson a large majority. Possibly nothing could have been done to put Maryland in the Crawford column, but Smith certainly had not conducted a vigorous or effective campaign. Never before had he been so out of touch with the political leanings of the citizens of his city and state. The truth of the matter was that he really did not care a great deal who would be elected president. He hinted at this view in January 1825, when the House of Representatives was deciding whether Jackson, Adams, or Crawford should be president, since none of them had gained a majority of electoral votes. "Who ever he may be," he wrote his daughter, Mary Mansfield, "he will find our finances and all our institutions in excellent order."[46] Six weeks after Adams had been sworn in as president, the general commented that, although he didn't think the new administration as good as the last one, the government was so well organized "that it can move on of itself." Just as revealing was a letter he sent to his grandson in England which styled the presidential election of 1824 as a foolish game with few practical consequences. But Smith's detachment from the passion of the contest went beyond words. In 1822 he had given up his seat in the House and returned to the Senate, filling a vacancy caused by the death of William Pinkney. The move was unquestionably dictated by his age and his financial problems, since the pace in the Senate was less hectic than in the House, while the longer tenure of a Senate seat

44. Robert Carter Nicholas to S. Smith, February 21, 1822, and Martin Van Buren to S. Smith, August 7, 1824, Smith Papers; S. Smith to Van Buren, May 6, 1823, Martin Van Buren Papers, Library of Congress; Washington, D.C. *National Intelligencer*, February 16, 1824.

45. Bemis, *Adams and the Union*, pp. 30–31.

46. S. Smith to Mrs. Mansfield, January 16, 1825, Smith-Carter Papers.

meant that his governmental salary was more secure.[47] He left the House, however, knowing that the presidential election would almost certainly be deadlocked. As a representative he might conceivably have done Crawford some good, perhaps repeating in some measure the role he had played in 1800. In the Senate he was of no use at all to the Georgian. Nothing but personal convenience led him to abandon the House when he did. Only four years remained in Pinkney's term and the general could then have campaigned for the office, as he had to do anyway. That he did enter the Senate under such circumstances plainly showed the relative value he had assigned to the presidential campaign. He seemed to have reached the conclusion that, like himself, the basic institutions and principles of the American government had finally transcended political partisanship and were now beyond challenge.

47. S. Smith to Mrs. Mansfield, April 28, 1825, and November 13, 1822, and S. Smith to his grandson, Samuel Smith Mansfield, July 16, 1824, Smith-Carter Papers; Joseph Anderson to S. Smith, October 10, 1822, Smith Papers.

15

Elder Statesman

"I AM now among the oldest residents being 73 years of age," Samuel Smith proclaimed from Baltimore in March 1825, "in perfect health, active, and walk and talk as well as I ever did."[1] The old general was, of course, venerated by the citizens of Baltimore for reasons far more substantial than his advanced age. A hero in that now distant war for independence, twice the defender of the city from attack, a major contributor to Baltimore's economic prosperity, and long the city's most famous political representative, Smith was an object of civic pride, an ornament to be displayed on all important occasions. In the fall of 1824 the general had been most prominent in welcoming to Baltimore another aged veteran of the Revolution, the Marquis de Lafayette. The Frenchman had returned to America for the first time since the war and had been greeted with hysterical acclaim in the cities he had passed through on his way to Washington. In his role as president of the Baltimore chapter of the Cincinnati, a club originally restricted to Continental Army officers and their sons, Smith had been part of the welcoming committee which met Lafayette at Frenchtown on his way from Philadelphia. On the long steamboat trip to Baltimore he had enjoyed an emotional reunion with the French aristocrat, who had once asked him to join his staff during the Revolution. On reaching the city Smith escorted Lafayette on an inspection of Fort

---

1. S. Smith to Mrs. Mansfield, March 19, 1825, Smith-Carter Papers, University of Virginia Library.

McHenry and then together they drove in a carriage through the streets followed by the entire complement of the city's cavalry units. A tremendous multitude lined the parade route, cheering these two heroes of a struggle most of them were too young to remember. While in Baltimore Lafayette attended an intimate dinner at the general's house and a much grander banquet sponsored by the Cincinnati at which Smith presided.[2]

In following years the general repeatedly was called upon to be the city's spokesman on public occasions. Among his saddest duties was to deliver a funeral oration in July 1826, commemorating the deaths of Jefferson and John Adams who, with remarkable coincidence, had both passed away on July 4, 1826, the fiftieth anniversary of the Declaration of Independence. Cary Anne Smith, John Spear Smith's wife, reported that the old man was nearly overcome with grief but "the people were very much pleased with his speech." She added that the only complaint had been that he had spoken for too long a time.[3] In 1827 Smith was invited to participate in a Civic Festival in memory of the American victory at the battle of Baltimore in 1814. At about the same time he represented the city in entertaining President John Quincy Adams, who visited Baltimore to attend the funeral of John Eager Howard and viewed Fort McHenry and the battlefield on Patapsco Neck. Year after year the general attended public celebrations and the funerals of important men. As with many famous public figures who live extraordinarily long lives, Samuel Smith was becoming in the eyes of the citizens of Baltimore more a symbol than a human being. The general undoubtedly enjoyed the compliments and the attention paid him, but his days of service had not yet come to an end. Despite his age his mind was clear and his capacity for work had only slightly diminished. Unlike other old men in Congress, such as Nathaniel Macon or Rufus King of New York, he was unwilling to restrict his activities to an occasional pronouncement on the events of the day.[4]

After John Quincy Adams became president in March 1824, Smith and most other Crawfordites switched their political allegiance to Andrew Jackson; the general made plain to one and all that he favored

2. S. Smith to Gen. Lafayette, September 1, 1824, and Committee of Arrangements to S. Smith, September 3, 1824, Samuel Smith Papers, Library of Congress.

3. Cary Anne Smith to Jane Randolph, July 24, 1826, Edgehill-Randolph Papers, University of Virginia Library.

4. Grand Marshall James Mocher to S. Smith, September 10, 1827, Smith Papers; Charles Francis Adams, ed., *Memoirs of John Quincy Adams,* 12 vols. (Philadelphia, 1874–1877), 7: 334–335.

the Tennessean for the chief executive's post in the election of 1828. But beyond declarations he did not go. Indeed, he was not pleased to see Van Buren and other Jacksonian leaders try to embarrass President Adams by opposing his programs and appointments for partisan reasons.[5] The Marylander saw no contradiction in favoring Jackson and at the same time seeking close relations with the Adams administration. What others might call fence-straddling was for him living up to the principle that the conduct of public business should be carried on rationally and independent of political motives. "I never did, I never will, and I never can oppose measures because of the man," the Marylander declared to Crawford, "you know my disposition on that point."[6] Until the day he retired from Congress he faithfully conformed to that creed.

As a senator and chairman of the Senate Finance Committee, Smith proved very friendly to Adams. Unlike some other Jacksonians he did not vote against Henry Clay's controversial nomination as secretary of state nor did he oppose Adams' plan to send representatives to the Panama Congress in 1826, an issue the president's opponents made a party matter. Smith's attitude nettled the more extreme Jackson men in the Senate, and, as a result, he lost a bid to become president pro tem in December 1826. Also damaging to his standing with "Old Hickory's" supporters was the fact that he asked for and received patronage favors from the administration. Working through Henry Clay, Smith obtained a diplomatic appointment for one of his sons-in-law, Christopher Hughes, an incredibly obtuse individual who would cause the general much pain. Party lines were reforming in the middle years of the 1820s, and the pressures for political discipline were increasing. As in the 1790s many were confused by Smith's nonconformist behavior.[7]

In no area did the general try harder to cooperate with Adams and Clay than over the West Indies trade question. For thirty years he had

5. Isaac Munroe to S. Smith, October 29, 1826, and S. Smith to W. H. Crawford, October 13, 1826, Smith Papers.

6. S. Smith to Crawford, October 13, 1826, Smith Papers.

7. Henry Clay to S. Smith, March 17, 1825, and S. Smith to Crawford, October 13, 1826, Smith Papers; U.S., Congress, *American State Papers. Documents, Legislative and Executive, of the Congress of the United States,* 38 vols. (Washington, D.C., 1832–1861), vols. 1–6, *Class I. Foreign Relations* (Washington, D.C., 1832–1859), 5: 877; John C. Fitzpatrick, ed., *Autobiography of Martin Van Buren, Annual Report of the American Historical Association, 1918,* 2 vols. (Washington, D.C., 1920), 2: 201, note 2; Adams, ed., *Memoirs of Adams,* 6: 520, 525; S. Smith to Mrs. Mansfield, March 19, 1825, Smith-Carter Papers; Clay to S. Smith, March 17 and May 4, 1825, Smith Papers.

championed the cause of commercial reciprocity, and the Reciprocity Act of 1815 had been one of his major triumphs as a legislator. Backed by this act American diplomats had managed to negotiate reductions in the level of discriminating duties with many nations, including Great Britain. The British, however, steadfastly refused to include their imperial possessions as part of the reciprocity arrangements and virtually prohibited American ships from entering the salt-water ports of Canada and the West Indies. The chief losers by this policy were New England shipping interests; American produce continued to flow into the English colonies but aboard British vessels. Since 1815 it had been a major objective of American diplomacy to open the colonial ports to American ships on the same basis British ships were admitted. In 1817, 1818, and 1820 legislation, some of it drawn up by Smith, had been passed by Congress as retaliatory measures against the British exclusionary policy. The early laws levied additional duties on British ships coming from ports not open to American vessels, while the act of 1820 closed United States' ports to British ships from the West Indies except under certain specified conditions. Exports from the United States to the West Indies sharply dropped, causing a massive depression in the colonial economy in that area.[8]

The economic dislocation plus the accession to power in Britain of a more liberal ministry produced a parliamentary act in 1822 that seemingly gave the United States most of what it had demanded. The law opened many colonial ports to American ships, although it restricted imports to items that would not compete with similar products from Canada. American ships were allowed to carry colonial products back to the United States on the same terms as British vessels. These privileges were made contingent on the United States granting equal treatment to British ships in American ports. Moreover, the act carefully reserved for Britain the right to lay additional tariffs on goods being brought from America, while exempting from those tariffs the same kinds of products imported from other parts of the Empire. Smith felt the act of 1822 represented a total capitulation by the British, and that despite the restrictions the United States would quickly monopolize the carrying trade to the colonial possessions. He dismissed the preferential tariffs as meaningless in practice and justified legally. Charging British ships duties when sailing from one port in the Empire to another would be the equivalent of taxing the

8. Samuel Flagg Bemis, *John Quincy Adams and the Foundations of American Foreign Policy* (New York, 1965), pp. 457–458. Bemis is inclined to view favorably Adams' handling of the West Indian trade dispute.

American coastal trade. Therefore he pleaded with President Monroe to accept the offer defined in the law, but Monroe and Secretary of State Adams disagreed, hoping to drive even a harder bargain and force England to give up the preferential tariffs. Monroe did issue a proclamation in 1823 opening American ports to British ships, essentially a suspension of the American law of 1820, but the treasury department ordered port collectors to continue collecting discriminating duties on British vessels coming from the colonies. The British replied with matching duties, and although American vessels were still at a disadvantage, they were admitted to the colonies and for several years there was an open trade.[9]

Shortly after Adams became president the British mounted another effort to force the Americans to accept reciprocity. Parliament passed four acts in late June and early July 1825 that invited countries in Europe, Africa, and western Asia to help supply the West Indies and again offered the United States a chance to participate in the West Indian trade if it admitted British ships into American ports on a most-favored-nation basis. The acts, which experts in diplomatic history find very confusing, also prohibited American ships from carrying any but American goods to the West Indies, a blow to the carrying trade, and totally banned United States' ships from the West Indian ports after July 25, 1826. The implication was that unless the American government reached a reciprocity agreement with Britain by July 25, 1826, the open trade with the West Indian colonies would come to an end. Tardily Adams and Clay realized that they had overreached themselves and instructions were sent to the American minister in England, Albert Gallatin, to reach an agreement based on the more generous act of 1822. But British patience was exhausted; the ministry refused to bargain, and an order-in-council was issued peremptorily interdicting American ships from sailing to the West Indian colonies.[10]

Samuel Smith had now had his fill of what he regarded as Adams' incompetence and decided to take matters into his own hands. Early in January 1826 he contacted Clay and asked why the president had not issued a proclamation abolishing the discriminating duties and allowing British and American ships to enter United States' ports on equal terms. By doing this the government would have met the condi-

9. Ibid., p. 458; U.S., Congress, *Register of Debates in Congress 1825–1837*, 29 vols. (Washington, D.C., 1825–1837), 19th Cong., 1st sess., 1826, p. 582; hereafter cited as *Congressional Debates*.

10. George Dangerfield, *The Awakening of American Nationalism, 1815–1828* (New York, 1965), pp. 259–263.

tions of the parliamentary acts of June and July and preserved the West Indian trade. Clay, seemingly confused by recent events, said something about negotiations.[11] Surprised, Smith inquired what could be gained by talks. "For what will you negotiate," he remembered asking Clay, "we have nothing to do but assent and the trade is at once opened."[12] Having gotten nowhere with the secretary of state, the angry senator visited the president. He pressed Adams to release a proclamation at once or he threatened to introduce legislation that would accomplish the same goal. Adams remarked that legislation was a good idea, and if a law was passed eliminating the duties, "he would not only sign it, but sign it with pleasure." After drafting a bill Smith presented it for Clay's inspection and the secretary gave his approval. Even though Clay changed his mind a few days later, insisting that negotiation was preferable to legislation, Smith determined to proceed with his plans with or without the administration's support.[13]

Almost certainly at Smith's suggestion a group of Baltimore merchants sent Congress a petition in April 1826, asking that the discriminating duties he dropped so as to preserve and expand trade with the West Indies. The petition was referred to the Senate Commerce Committee, whose chairman gave an unfavorable report. Reflecting Clay's thinking, he urged that Congress do nothing and allow the administration to work through diplomatic channels. Smith had expected this result; the purpose of the petition was merely to bring the question before Congress. No sooner had the Commerce Committee's report been read than the general was on his feet arguing that the Baltimore petition should not be thrown out but rather recommitted, this time to Smith's own Finance Committee. In a major speech the Marylander lucidly reviewed the history of reciprocity and explained why he thought the United States had acted against its own best interests when it refused to accept the British offers. Negotiation would take too long, he contended. Only a law passed immediately could revive the West Indian trade and keep American shippers, wheat growers, and flour producers from suffering ruinous losses. The Senate agreed with Smith and the petition was given over to his committee.[14]

11. *Congressional Debates*, 19th Cong., 2d sess., 1827, p. 407, 22d Cong., 1st sess., 1832, p. 1363.

12. *Congressional Debates*, 22d Cong., 1st sess., 1832, p. 1363. See also S. Smith to John Spear Smith, February 20 and 21, 1832, Smith Papers.

13. *Congressional Debates*, 22d Cong., 1st sess., 1832, p. 1363; C. C. Cambreling to S. Smith, February 11, 1832, and S. Smith to John Spear Smith, February 25, 1832, Smith Papers.

14. *Congressional Debates*, 19th Cong., 1st sess., 1826, pp. 576–589.

On April 19 Smith presented to the Senate the bill he had earlier drawn up and shown to Clay. It was short and to the point. British vessels arriving in American ports from the colonies would be treated exactly the same as American ships if the same courtesy was extended in colonial ports. The proposed law was to take effect on June 30, less than a month before the British-set deadline. The president was given authority to suspend the law's operation if the British continued their discriminating duties in the colonial ports. Smith's bill would have ended the long contest over the West Indian trade, but administration opposition proved too formidable, and the bill was tabled on May 9 by a margin of two votes. By the time Congress reassembled in December 1826 the whole country was aware of the administration's mismanagement of the colonial trade dispute. American ships were now prohibited entirely from entering colonial ports while vessels of other nations were welcomed.[15]

Adams and Clay had won their chance to negotiate, but in London Albert Gallatin found the ministry intransigent. The president finally turned the problem over to Congress in his annual message. Not surprisingly, the colonial question had now become a matter of political dispute between the Jackson men and the president's supporters in Congress. As the loudest critic of Adams' previous policy Smith found himself reviled by the administration press and suffered the indignity of a tongue-lashing by Henry Clay during a party held at the secretary of state's house. Clay accused him of interfering in executive matters and contributing to the closing of the West Indian ports. The general denied both publicly and privately that he was an opponent of the administration and pointed out that his efforts to reciprocally abolish discriminating duties through legislation were known to and approved by the president. There was no doubt, however, that Smith felt he had been badly treated by Adams and Clay and his relations with the administration rapidly deteriorated.[16]

In response to the president's message, the Senate Commerce Committee presented a bill concerning colonial trade that obviously had Adams' and Clay's blessing. The measure provided that after a certain date the ports of the United States would be closed to all British ships sailing from colonial ports and prohibited British vessels from clearing

15. Ibid., pp. 589–590, 709.

16. Dangerfield, *American Nationalism*, p. 263; Clay to Albert Gallatin, December 28, 1826, Martin Van Buren Papers, Library of Congress; Adams, ed., *Memoirs of Adams*, 7: 174; S. Smith to Crawford, October 13, 1826, and S. Smith to Peter Force, December 17, 1836, Smith Papers; *Congressional Debates*, 19th Cong., 2d sess., 1827, pp. 406–410.

from America for the colonies. A complicated system of bonds was to be established in order to enforce compliance, and the president could suspend the law's operation if he had evidence that American ships were again being allowed into the colonial ports on the same terms as British vessels arriving from the United States. Although reciprocity was the object of the scheme, Smith disapproved of it as being "too antagonistic" toward the British and therefore likely to be rejected by them. Thus when the bill came to the Senate floor, he moved to strike out everything but the enacting clause and substitute the bill he had proposed the year before. Again Smith gave a lengthy address explaining the virtues of his bill. Supported by the Jacksonians, Smith's motion succeeded. But when the House refused to assent, the measure was lost and Congress adjourned having taken no action. The president, obeying a law passed in 1823, had no choice but to close American ports to all British vessels arriving from colonial ports in the Western hemisphere.[17]

The president and secretary of state had committed themselves on the colonial trade issue to the point that there remained no hope that a settlement could be reached with the British while they remained in office. When Andrew Jackson took over the presidency in 1829 and appointed Martin Van Buren to the state department, both were anxious to end the dispute, and Smith's hopes for reopening the trade with the colonial possessions were renewed. He was especially encouraged when Jackson named his old friend Louis McLane of Delaware to be the American minister in London. McLane was influenced by Smith's views on reciprocity, and the two men worked closely together to conclude a successful negotiation. Despite the American government's willingness to help matters by abandoning many of the points Adams and Clay had insisted upon, notably on the right of England to levy preferential tariffs, the talks did not progress smoothly. It began to appear that the previous administration's actions had made any agreement on colonial trade nearly impossible. At this critical juncture Smith introduced a bill in Congress that allowed the president to reopen American ports to British vessels going to or from the colonies on the basis of complete reciprocity. In essence the Smith bill said to Great Britain that the United States was now willing to accept the terms offered in the parliamentary acts of June and July 1825. Congress passed the bill on May 29, 1830, and shortly thereafter

17. *Congressional Debates*, 19th Cong., 2d sess., 1827, pp. 399, 403–462, 486, 495–496, 501, 504–505; Dangerfield, *American Nationalism*, p. 264; Clay to Gallatin, March 20, 1827, Van Buren Papers; Adams, ed., *Memoirs of Adams*, 7: 235–238.

McLane was able to reach a settlement. On October 5, 1830, President Jackson issued a proclamation lifting restrictions on the West Indian trade, American ships were again admitted to colonial ports, and an issue as old as the nation itself had finally been laid to rest. The achievement of reciprocity within the British empire was the natural extension of the Reciprocity Act of 1815, and together they constitute Smith's chief claim to legislative statesmanship.[18]

Closely related to the reciprocity issue in Smith's mind was the problem of tariffs. He had never been a staunch defender of this aspect of the American System. In 1816 he did vote for a modest tariff bill, and even as late as 1820 he raised no serious objections to tariff legislation. But in 1824 he had sharply condemned a tariff bill that drastically raised the general level of protection. "There must, Mr. President," he had then declared to the Senate, "be some point at which to stop."[19] He had argued that the proposed bill unfairly taxed millions to benefit only a few, although he admitted the need for some protection. What lay behind his opposition was the fact that high tariffs adversely affected American shipping and commercial interests. By their very nature high duties on imports interfered with the free exchange of goods between the United States and other nations. "One reason . . . that our commerce was so depressed," he had asserted in 1824, "was, that we were, by our own unwise policy, depriving ourselves of all foreign markets."[20] Four years of experience with the tariff of 1824 had strengthened the Marylander's belief that the system was wrong and had to be combatted. On February 5, 1828, he bluntly told his fellow senators where he stood: "a free and open trade is the only true American system."[21]

The proposed tariff of 1828 was even more offensive to the Marylander than that of 1824. Either from design or merely ignorance the measure not only increased duties on many manufactured items, but also placed ridiculously high rates on some of the raw materials imported into the United States. While manufacturers would receive greater protection, their costs of production would also rise. Furthermore, by generally raising the level of protection the new tariff

18. Louis McLane to S. Smith, May 11 and 13, October 29, November 28, and December 5, 1829, and March 6, May 22, and August 19, 1830, Smith Papers; Thomas Hart Benton, *Thirty Years' View*, 2 vols. (New York, 1886), 1: 128; Fitzpatrick, ed., *Autobiography of Van Buren*, p. 274.

19. U.S., Congress, *The Debates and Proceedings in the Congress of the United States . . . 1789–1824*, 42 vols. (Washington, D.C., 1834–1856), 18th Cong., 1st sess., 1824, pp. 738–739.

20. Ibid., pp. 661–662.

21. *Congressional Debates*, 20th Cong., 1st sess., 1828, p. 243.

promised to create an additional barrier to trade and thus further harm merchants and shipowners. Southerners, too, resented the rate increases. Lacking manufacturing in their own region, they were being forced to pay more for essential goods in order to keep northern industry prosperous and growing. Although he saw to it that Maryland's manufacturing interests were protected in the bill, Smith attacked the measure at every opportunity. When a New Jersey senator offered an amendment to protect vermicelli because a man in his state made it, Smith commented sarcastically that the protectionists "will not even let us have our soup in peace" and that they would "be taxing the air we breathe next." When the final vote on the tariff measure was taken on May 13, it passed by a vote of 26 to 21, with Samuel Smith joining the minority.[22]

Smith did not make his opposition to the tariff on legal grounds. He considered the tariff of 1828 to be contrary to the public interest and the whole principle of high protection to be bad policy. But unlike other southerners who voted against the tariff bill, he did not think that tariffs were unconstitutional. He adamantly opposed those southerners who were willing to use extreme means to frustrate the federal government. When John C. Calhoun anonymously published the antitariff *South Carolina Exposition and Protest* in 1828, the general wrote the vice president condemning the statement's principles and its implications of disunion. Informing Calhoun that he had thoroughly proved to his own satisfaction the legality of the tariff, Smith warned him that South Carolina's actions were already being looked upon as a counterpart to the Hartford Convention. Nevertheless, as the issue of the tariff grew in importance during the next few years, the general added to his list of objections to higher protection the injustice that was being done to the South and the necessity of making concessions to save the Union.[23]

While matters of trade took up much of Smith's time during John Quincy Adams' presidency, he did not neglect other areas. He continued, for example, to give unwavering support to internal improve-

---

22. Benton, *Thirty Years' View*, 1: 95–102; Edward Stanwood, *American Tariff Controversies in the Nineteenth Century*, 2 vols. (New York, 1903), 1: 243–290; F. W. Taussig, *The Tariff History of the United States*, 8th ed. (New York, 1931), pp. 68–108; Dangerfield, *American Nationalism*, pp. 281–287; Robert V. Remini, "Martin Van Buren and the Tariff of Abominations," *American Historical Review* 63 (1958): 903–917; Charles M. Wiltse, *John C. Calhoun: Nationalist, 1782–1828* (New York, 1944), p. 371; *Congressional Debates*, 20th Cong., 1st sess., 1828, pp. 725, 736, 727.

23. S. Smith to John C. Calhoun, July 5, 1828, Smith Papers.

ments. The Cumberland Road drew his particular attention. Even though Congress had been making appropriations for the repair and extension of the road for years, opposition to further expenditures was always strong. In session after session the Marylander led the fight to obtain funds.[24] Baltimore had benefited greatly from the road, but Smith was also alive to its importance to national unity. He came to see the project as an antidote to sectionalism, as a "great national work, which was to join the Western with the Atlantic States," which would bind those areas together "by the ties of mutual advantage."[25] For the same reasons, he voted for every canal and road bill that came before Congress, many of which would not be of any value to his home state. Smith had always been a nationalist, if by that is meant a loyalty to and concern for the whole country. In the 1820s, however, he became a conscious nationalist, preoccupied with defining the role of nationalism in a time of sectional disintegration.

As Adams' tenure as president drew to a close, Smith could take some satisfaction in the role he had performed. He had generally avoided political controversy, preferring to stake out areas where he could work with the administration. Although his heart was with Jackson, the general behaved in a nonpartisan manner. His was the path of the statesman: pursuing the national welfare as he saw it without regard for political consequences. And he was not without power. He had, for example, used his position as chairman of the Senate Finance Committee to promote his views on reciprocity. In 1828 his colleagues had elected him president pro tem of the senate, an office in which he could influence legislation through the judicious selection of the committees that drew up bills. But his real authority was in himself. Not only his great age and honorable career, but also his encyclopedic knowledge of commercial affairs affected those about him. Never a gifted speaker, Smith was yet closely attended when he argued on any question involving commerce or finance. Because he was above politics, his words carried greater weight with senators of all political persuasions.[26]

In the presidential campaign leading up to the election of 1828, the general was nothing more than an interested observer. "When your election was lost," he explained to Crawford, "I made a determination . . . 'that I never would take an active part in any future Presidential Election,' to which, I have rigidly adhered, and from which

24. *Congressional Debates,* 19th Cong., 1st sess., 1826, p. 350, 2d sess., 1827, pp. 488–489, 20th Cong., 1st sess., 1828, pp. 104–105.
25. Ibid., 19th Cong., 2d sess., 1827, pp. 488–489.
26. Ibid., 22d Cong., 1st sess., 1831, p. 1.

(in respect for myself and my own tranquility), I feel no inclination to depart."[27] Realistically he added: "I am now too old to be active and am rather inclined to live quietly—if I was otherwise disposed I could render no service."[28] Smith did assist the Jacksonians by reporting on the progress of the campaign in Maryland, but aside from letting it be known in Baltimore that he favored the Tennessean, there was nothing more he could or would do. Jackson's victory pleased him, and he was proud to help in the planning of the inauguration ceremonies as chairman of a joint congressional committee. In his capacity of president pro tem it was his duty to swear in Vice President Calhoun.[29]

From the beginning the new administration lavished attention on the general. He found patronage was made available to him on a scale comparable to what he had enjoyed during Thomas Jefferson's administration. Through his close friends Louis McLane, who became secretary of the treasury on his return from London, and Secretary of State Martin Van Buren, Smith was assured of having his opinions conveyed to the president. Van Buren, and his successor at the state department, Edward Livingston, regularly flattered him with requests for his views on pending negotiations. Jackson himself told the Marylander that he had been seriously considered as the next minister to England but it was felt he could do far more for the administration in the Senate. The old man realized that Jackson was merely complimenting him and that no such offer had ever been contemplated. Still, he was delighted that the president had taken the trouble to single him out for praise. Although Smith and Jackson had their differences during the president's first term, mainly over the spoils system and the Bank of the United States, the Marylander had not been accorded such attention by any administration since Jefferson's.[30]

As a member of the Senate during Jackson's first term Smith's pace

27. S. Smith to Crawford, November 1, 1828, Smith Papers.

28. Ibid.

29. Martin Van Buren to S. Smith, July 5 and September 24, 1827, Smith Papers; Wiltse, *Calhoun: Nationalist*, p. 12.

30. Unknown person to S. Smith, June 9, 1829, S. Smith to Van Buren, July 8, 1829, Van Buren to William Wright, September 10, 1829, Van Buren to S. Smith, November 3, 1829, and October 15, 1830, Wright to S. Smith, November 24, 1829, Lewis Cass to S. Smith, October 31, 1831, and McLane to S. Smith, April 5, 1833, Smith Papers; S. Smith to Van Buren, May 11 and 14, and July 8, 1829, and October 20, 1830, Van Buren Papers; S. Smith to Edward Livingston, November 3 and 8, 1831, and June 30 and July 22, 1832, and Livingston to S. Smith, July 1 and September 9, 1831, Smith Papers; S. Smith to Mrs. Mansfield, March 16, 1829, Smith-Carter Papers.

did not noticeably slacken from earlier years. Approaching his eight-ieth birthday, he refused to allow occasional bouts of lumbago and arthritis to interrupt seriously his work in Congress. Rare was the issue before the Senate upon which the general did not speak. His major efforts as a legislator, however, were reserved for two questions which particularly concerned him: tariff policy and the future of the Bank of the United States. Of the two, the tariff was by far the most impor-tant; the discontent throughout the South against the high rates of the 1828 bill threatened the very existence of the Union. The tariff of 1828 was also unpopular with northern protectionists who wished to see its objectionable features removed. This growing sentiment for revision of the tariff led to some changes in the law in 1830, and when President Jackson called for general reductions in the tariff as part of his annual address to Congress in December 1831, some kind of re-form was assured. But if most legislators could agree that the level of duties should be cut, the size of the reduction and what articles were to be affected remained controversial.[31]

No man in Washington was more anxious to see tariffs reduced than Samuel Smith. Besides his concern about the deleterious effects of a high protection policy on commerce and shipping, he was becoming more and more disturbed by Calhoun's extremism. Shortly after Congress had assembled in December 1831, the vice president had given the general an ultimatum. The South, said Calhoun, would only accept a tariff bill that would bring in revenues less than those needed to pay off the national debt on schedule. Moreover, he de-manded that all imports be taxed at the same rate rather than con-tinuing the system of setting a duty on each individual item. Controlling his anger, Smith told the South Carolinian that neither he nor the administration would accept any delay in the redemption of the public debt. As for the rest of Calhoun's scheme, the Marylander called it impractical. Privately Smith was outraged. "His plan is dictatorial, and folly in the extreme," the general fumed, "and can meet with no support."[32] Smith might dislike Calhoun and his politics, but he could not be blind to the legitimate grievances of the southern states. He recognized that reduction of the tariff was vital to the nation's welfare as well as to that of the shipping and commercial interests.[33]

Filled with determination, the general convened a meeting of the

31. Taussig, *Tariff History*, pp. 102–104; Charles M. Wiltse, *John C. Calhoun: Nullifier, 1829–1839* (New York, 1949), p. 134.

32. S. Smith to John Spear Smith, December 10, 1831, Smith Papers.

33. S. Smith to John Spear Smith, December 30, 1831, Smith Papers.

Senate Finance Committee early in the session and presented to the members his ideas on what a new tariff measure should contain. The basic principle of his plan was that any tariff should be based on the government's revenue needs and not on the wishes of northern industrialists. The practical result would have been, in his opinion, a return to the moderate level of protection provided for in the tariff of 1816. The other members of the committee rejected the proposal. Although they all wanted a compromise tariff, some felt the general had gone too far in lowering the level of protection, while others held out for even greater reductions. With such drastic divisions among the committee members, Smith was unable to obtain any consensus, and no bill at all was reported out to the Senate.[34]

The tariff question did not formally come before the upper chamber until January 9, 1832, when Henry Clay submitted a resolution to eliminate the duties on those foreign imports that would not compete with American manufactures. Clay's resolution was hardly a compromise as far as the South was concerned. The hated principle of protection was retained and southerners would still be taxed for the benefit of northern manufacturers. Robert Y. Hayne, the brilliant senator from South Carolina, stated the southern position when he called all protective tariffs unconstitutional.[35] It was left for Samuel Smith to steer the middle course, and so he rose on January 20 to address the Senate. "We have arrived at a crisis," he began solemnly, "yes Mr. President, at a crisis more appalling than a day of battle." The crowded chamber listened attentively as he enumerated the reasons why the tariffs of 1824 and 1828 had been so oppressive to the southern states. Common sense and fair play dictated that the tariff must be substantially reduced: "I want nothing that shall injure the manufacturer. I only want justice." He denounced Clay's resolution as offering too little. But even the few concessions the Kentuckian was willing to make, Smith pointed out, were being challenged by the lobbyists for special interest groups. Smith feared that these individuals would block not only Clay's plan but all meaningful changes in the tariff law. Their influence, he charged, was very great with the Committee on Manufactures, which had the responsibility of devising a tariff bill. "Those interested men," snorted the old senator, "hang on the Committee on Manufactures like an incubus." Fixing his eyes on the members of that committee, the general urged them to "discard sectional interest" and to "relieve the oppression of the South."[36]

34. S. Smith to John Spear Smith, December 24, 1831, Smith Papers.
35. Wiltse, *Calhoun: Nullifier*, p. 136.
36. *Congressional Debates*, 22d Cong., 1st sess., 1832, pp. 186–187.

To this point, Smith's speech sounded much like others made by southerners against the protective tariff system. The last half of his address, however, showed that he was still an ardent nationalist. Having scourged the protectionists as being greedy and unpatriotic, he now spoke boldly to the southerners. He denied Hayne's claim that the protective tariff was unconstitutional. Not only did the government have the power to lay protective duties, but also it was in the national interest that it do so since tariffs produced needed revenue and promoted manufactures. The general then enlarged on his own views of what America's tariff policy should be. What the country needed, he argued, was a just and rational tariff law. Just in that it would not unduly penalize the South nor give northern capitalists too high a rate of return on their investments. A just tariff, he said, should be primarily based on the revenue needs of the government with protection only a secondary consideration. A rational tariff meant that only those items should receive protection that could not stand up to competition from foreign imports. Currently, he asserted, heavy duties were being laid on many imported goods that were not being manufactured in this country, thus raising their cost unnecessarily. Furthermore, a rational tariff should not, like the law of 1828, tax raw materials. If American industry was ever going to be truly competitive, the government must allow it to keep costs low by purchasing needed raw materials as cheaply as possible.[37]

Smith's speech on the tariff was perhaps the best in his long career, and certainly one of the most lucid delivered during the debate. It was at once informed, conciliatory, and statesmanlike. If there was a fault, it was his overly optimistic expectation that manufacturers could be made to accept a level of protection as low as that of the tariff of 1816. Jacksonian senators congratulated Smith on the speech and even Hayne came by to compliment him on his "strong" remarks. Administration papers in Virginia, Maryland, and New York reprinted the speech, and Smith purchased five hundred copies to distribute among the members of the Maryland legislature.[38] Henry Clay attested to the speech's importance by attacking the general on the floor of the Senate as an enemy of manufactures. Maliciously he quoted to Smith a short rhyme:

> Old Politicians chew on wisdom past
> And totter on in business to the last.[39]

37. Ibid., pp. 187–194; Benton, *Thirty Years' View*, 1: 268.
38. S. Smith to John Spear Smith, January 13, February 2 and 3, 1832, and Van Buren to S. Smith, March 25, 1831, Smith Papers.
39. *Congressional Debates*, 22d Cong., 1st sess., 1832, p. 296.

Statesman or not Smith was not going to let such impudence remain unanswered: "Totter, sir, I totter [?] Though some twenty years older than the gentleman, I can yet stand firm, and am yet able to correct his errors."[40] For a few moments pandemonium swept the Senate as it appeared that the two men might come to blows or even issue challenges to a duel. Finally, repeated cries of "order" from other senators restored calm in the chamber.[41]

The tariff bill that eventually came before Congress in the spring of 1832 was not to Smith's liking. Although it removed many of the worst features in the act of 1828 and decreased the protective duties back to the level of 1824, he did not believe the reductions were sufficient to halt the nullification movement in South Carolina. Despite his stand against the measure, it was passed and signed into law on July 14. Four months later a special convention met in South Carolina and passed an ordinance declaring the tariff law null and void; after February 1, 1833, the convention decreed that federal officials would not be permitted to collect the duties. As an indication of South Carolina's determination to stand fast, the state legislature provided funds for arms and called for volunteers. To frustrate the nullifiers President Jackson asked Congress to pass two pieces of legislation: one further reducing the tariff and another, called the Force Bill, giving the government additional powers to collect import duties.[42]

Smith had no quarrel with the Force Bill and urged its immediate passage. He solidly backed the president's efforts to crush disunion. The new compromise tariff, largely Clay's work, was something else again. The bill called for gradual reductions of all tariffs to the level of 20 percent, but this would not be reached until the year 1842.[43] Smith assaulted the measure as fiercely as he had the tariff of 1832. On February 22, 1833, he told the Senate that most duties were too high and should be lowered immediately rather than over an eight-year period. "The people," he asked, "are they to be saddled with these enormous duties for eight years? What for, sir?"[44] The answer, of course, was protection. Yet, if that was the case, he wondered why Hayne, Calhoun, and other South Carolinians had agreed to the bill. By doing so Smith declared they were "completely relinquishing the principle against which South Carolina stands ready to go to the death

40. Ibid., p. 297.
41. S. Smith to John Spear Smith, February 3, 1832, Smith Papers.
42. *Congressional Debates*, 22d Cong., 1st sess., 1832, p. 1185; Glyndon G. Van Deusen, *The Jacksonian Era: 1828–1848* (New York, 1959), pp. 61–67.
43. *Congressional Debates*, 22d Cong., 2d sess., 1833, p. 693.
44. Ibid., p. 705.

against the Government and has actually prepared for war."[45] Smith next challenged the idea that Clay's bill was conciliatory. If, indeed, the bill was really a conciliatory gesture, then Congress was guilty of disgraceful behavior. It would be passing a bad law to gratify the demands of a state behaving in a rebellious and illegal manner. But the Marylander was not willing to admit that the tariff bill was truly a compromise. Whatever South Carolina's representatives said, the convention as well as the state legislature of South Carolina had taken the position that protective tariffs were unconstitutional. Congress might well be passing a law that would not be acceptable to the nullifiers. He pleaded with his colleagues to throw out the Clay bill and replace it with a "fair and permanent" tariff. The Senate, however, passed the bill by a vote of 29 to 16 on March 1. Contrary to the general's fears, South Carolina was satisfied with the compromise tariff, and although the state convention nullified the Force Bill, the crisis had ended. [46]

During the tariff battles of 1832 Smith had also become deeply concerned with another issue: recharter of the second Bank of the United States. Since its creation in 1816 the bank had demonstrated its usefulness to the economy and the government. As a central bank it had provided a stable currency not only by issuing notes of its own, but also through its ability to restrain local banks from circulating depreciated bills. Loans obtained from the Bank of the United States had helped finance the economic development of the country. The treasury department also benefited from the bank: the central office in Philadelphia and the many branches served as collection and disbursement agencies for federal revenues. Moreover, the government owned 20 percent of the stock in the bank, and the interest was a welcome source of income. But the bank, despite its utility, had a troubled and turbulent history. In 1818 and 1819 the institution, as a result of President William Jones' unfitness and the frauds in the Baltimore branch, had curtailed credit and called in loans in order to keep itself from insolvency. The bank had succeeded in preserving itself, but at a ruinous cost to the economy. Thousands went bankrupt and an already bad depression became worse.[47] "The Bank was saved,"

45. Ibid.
46. Ibid., p. 708.
47. Bray Hammond, *Banks and Politics in America from the Revolution to the Civil War* (Princeton, 1957), pp. 251–325; Robert V. Remini, *Andrew Jackson and the Bank War* (New York, 1967), pp. 15–66; Van Deusen, *Jacksonian Era*, pp. 61–67.

one contemporary ruefully observed, "and the people were ruined."[48] Although the bank was expertly directed during the 1820s by the suave and talented Nicholas Biddle, it always was widely distrusted. Andrew Jackson had come to the presidency vowing that the bank was unconstitutional and harmful in its present form. He called for changes in its charter when Congress should get around to discussing renewal. Biddle, however, was determined to have the charter remain unchanged. The conflict between Jackson and Biddle, which was both personal and political, came to a head in 1832 when Biddle asked Congress to decide the bank's future.[49]

Samuel Smith had been a friend of the second Bank of the United States from its inception. Indeed, he had been a prime mover in its creation and even his bankruptcy in 1819 had not changed his opinion of the bank's value to the country. As chairman of the House Ways and Means Committee and later of the Senate Finance Committee, the general knew better than most men the importance of the institution to the financial operations of the government. The confrontation between Biddle and Jackson placed him in an awkward position. On the one hand he considered himself a Jacksonian and therefore was reluctant to openly disagree with the president. On the other hand, he genuinely believed the bank to be essential to the nation's prosperity and that Jackson's hostility to it was based on ignorance and prejudice. During the first two years of Jackson's presidency, Smith was able to avoid abandoning either the president or the bank. In this he was helped by Jackson's uncertainty over what policy to follow in regard to the institution.

Jackson's first official pronouncement on the bank had come in his annual message of December 1829. In vague terms the chief executive questioned the bank's constitutionality and whether it had really served its principal function of generating a stable economy for the country. The message also asked Congress to consider changes in the charter to meet these objections, but no specific suggestions were offered. That part of the president's message concerning the bank was referred in the Senate to Smith's Finance Committee. As part of its deliberations the committee conducted hearings at which Nicholas Biddle was the chief witness. The committee members, already predisposed to support the bank, were favorably impressed

48. William M. Gouge, *A Short History of Paper Money and Banking in the United States*, 2 vols. (Philadelphia, 1833), 2: 109.

49. Remini, *Jackson and the Bank War*, pp. 49–66.

by the Philadelphian's testimony and their report to the Senate was influenced by his thinking. The report, written by Smith, defended the bank's constitutionality and showed that Jackson's assertions about the currency were wildly inaccurate. Smith closed by defending the present structure of the bank as the very best one possible. In short, the Finance Committee had entirely vindicated Biddle and the Bank of the United States.[50]

Throughout 1830 and early 1831 Jackson and Biddle sniped at each other. Biddle especially was very active in propagandizing for the bank. He saw to it, for example, that Smith's Finance Committee report was distributed in all parts of the country. With an election on the horizon, the president sensed that an all-out fight with the bank might be politically harmful. Therefore, through Secretary of the Treasury Louis McLane, he offered Biddle a deal: if Biddle would refrain from asking Congress for a new charter until after the 1832 election, the administration promised that it would not oppose the bank's continuance. McLane's conversation with Biddle precipitated an important debate among the bank's friends in Congress. The National Republican party and its presidential candidate, Henry Clay, pressed Biddle to disregard the president's offer and move at once to bring the recharter question before Congress. Clay's motives were transparent. His campaign was not going well and he desperately needed an issue on which Jackson was vulnerable. The bank's charter, he felt, was such an issue.[51]

On the other side of the debate were those congressmen who were both supporters of Jackson and friends of the bank. The chief spokesman for this group was Smith.[52] Their aim was to persuade Biddle to accede to the president's wishes, for if the recharter matter was brought forward before the election, they would be placed in the dilemma of choosing between political loyalty and an institution they believed must be saved. Consulting closely with McLane, Smith wrote letter after letter to Biddle urging him to delay his request for another charter. "I had last night a long conversation with McLane," Smith wrote the bank's president on one occasion, "and I am authorized by him to say it is his deliberate opinion and *advice* that a renewal of the Charter ought not to be pressed during the present

50. Ibid., pp. 61–64; Senate Finance Committee Report, March 29, 1830, Smith Papers.

51. Remini, *Jackson and the Bank War*, pp. 72–73; Van Deusen, *Jacksonian Era*, p. 65.

52. Benton, *Thirty Years' View*, 1: 227.

session in which I concur *most sincerely.*"⁵³ The general insisted that
the president's word was good and that putting off recharter for a
year would save the bank. But if the president was pushed into a
corner, Smith added ominously, "neither McLane nor myself will
answer for the consequences."⁵⁴

As matters developed, it became apparent that Biddle's final decision would depend on the reports of Thomas Cadwallader, a director
of the bank and Biddle's personal representative in Washington.
Throughout the final days of December 1831 Cadwallader met almost
daily with Smith, McLane, and representatives of Henry Clay. His
letters to Biddle indicate that by December 21 Cadwallader had
decided that the bank should go ahead and make its application.⁵⁵
Although he continued to talk with Smith and McLane, his real
interest was to determine how Congress would act. While there was
little doubt that the recharter bill would pass the House, its fate in
the Senate was more uncertain. In one final effort to change Cadwallader's mind, Smith told him that if recharter came up now, he
and other Jacksonian senators who favored the bank would vote
against it. Their votes, the general advised Cadwallader, would tip
the balance and kill the Bank. "Smith failing us, you will think the
question settled *for this session,*" Cadwallader reported to Biddle,
"& so it is, unless we can turn the administration men from their objections to a present movement on it."⁵⁶ The Marylander's stand earned
the pro-bank Jacksonians one more chance to persuade Cadwallader
to their point of view. On December 30 Smith, McLane, and George
McDuffie, a South Carolinian who was chairman of the House Ways
and Means Committee, met with Cadwallader in McLane's office
in the treasury department. McDuffie, a Calhoun supporter, argued
for an immediate application, and McLane took the lead in opposing
such an action. According to Smith's account, the secretary gave
Cadwallader fair warning of the consequences: "I have staked myself.
So has General Smith. If you succeed in both houses, I will do nothing

53. S. Smith to Nicholas Biddle, December 7, 1831, in Reginald C. McGrane,
ed., *The Correspondence of Nicholas C. Biddle Dealing with National Affairs,
1807–1844* (Boston 1919), pp. 138–139.

54. Ibid.

55. S. Smith to Biddle, December 17, 1831, and Thomas Cadwallader to Biddle,
December 21 and 23, 1831, in McGrane, ed., *Correspondence of Biddle,* pp. 143–
145, 148–151, 152–153; S. Smith to John Spear Smith, December 16, 21, and 30,
1831, Smith Papers.

56. Cadwallader to Biddle, December 23, 1831, in McGrane, ed., *Correspondence of Biddle,* pp. 152–153.

to induce the President to sign the Bill . . . . Press the subject now & [the President] will unquestionably apply his veto."[57] Again McLane emphasized that Jackson was inclined to deal amicably with the bank if it waited until after the election to apply. In the end, however, McDuffie won out. By the end of the meeting Cadwallader had made clear his intention to recommend that Biddle initiate a request for recharter at once. Less than a week later Smith received a long letter from Biddle explaining why the general's advice had been ignored. The Philadelphian claimed that the convenience of the bank rather than politics had determined that he ask for a new charter now; if the bank was not to be continued, he would need four years to wind up its business. But Biddle was not as apolitical as he pretended. He confessed his belief to Smith that Jackson would be less likely to veto recharter before rather than after the presidential election for fear of losing popular support. In conclusion Biddle expressed his sorrow that Smith would not likely give his support to the bank.[58]

The memorial from Biddle asking Congress to recharter the bank was presented to the Senate on January 6, 1832, by George M. Dallas of Pennsylvania. Normally this would have been Smith's responsibility as chairman of the Finance Committee, but since he might well vote against the bank Biddle understandably reasoned that the task of leading the pro-bank forces should be entrusted to someone more friendly.[59] After much contemplation, Smith decided that he could not carry through on his threat to vote against recharter. "You may be assured that I shall pursue the even tenor of my way," he informed John Spear Smith, "and act as I always have done agreeably to the dictation of my own judgement regardless of consequences and I now know the Pt. does not expect that I shall vote agt. the Bank."[60] Even if the president should disapprove of his actions, Smith told his son that he "should act as I think proper."[61] Having made this most difficult choice, one quite in keeping with his whole career, the general committed all of his energies to the battle. During the debates he delivered two extensive speeches that concentrated on proving the economic importance of the bank, one of which was published in a number of newspapers. On June 11, 1832, the Senate passed the

57. S. Smith to John Spear Smith, December 31, 1831, Smith Papers.
58. Ibid.; Biddle to S. Smith, January 4, 1832, in McGrane, ed., *Correspondence of Biddle*, pp. 161–165.
59. *Congressional Debates*, 22d Cong., 1st sess., 1832, p. 943.
60. S. Smith to John Spear Smith, January 12, 1832, Smith Papers.
61. Ibid.

recharter measure by a vote of 28 to 20,[62] and, as he had said he would, Jackson vetoed the bill in spite of a half-hearted appeal from Smith to "disappoint those who have pressed the subject, who expect and count on your Veto, as a means to injure the party in public opinion."[63] When the Senate voted on whether to override the negative, the general absented himself from the chamber.[64]

The bank and the tariff were the last chapters in the general's long career in national government. After forty continuous years in Congress, eighteen of them in the House and twenty-two in the Senate, he retired to Baltimore in the spring of 1833 at the age of eighty-three. Few men have ever been privileged to serve so long a time in the national legislature, and fewer still have combined longevity with such a distinguished record. At some time during the presidencies of George Washington, John Adams, Thomas Jefferson, James Madison, James Monroe, John Quincy Adams, and Andrew Jackson, he had held every important position in Congress save Speaker of the House. His list of legislative accomplishments was lengthy and impressive. He had sponsored innumerable bills dealing with commerce, defense, banking, and internal improvements, many of which found their way into law.

The Marylander was not the type of man who philosophized about his principles, but his actions had clearly revealed what they were. He believed in a strong national government able to protect American interests abroad and to foster economic development at home. Early in his congressional career he had been a nationalist but only for the most provincial reasons. Nationalism to him had then meant a national effort to free American commerce from the decrees of France and Britain. After the War of 1812 his horizons widened considerably. As he grew older he came to see that the welfare of one part of the Union was organically related to the conditions existing in all the other parts. Although he never forgot his loyalty to Baltimore and American commerce, Smith had evolved into an advocate of genuine national interests by the end of his congressional career. Nowhere was this more plain than in his support for internal improvements, but his positions on reciprocity within the British empire, the tariff, and the bank can also be seen as those of an enlightened nationalist.

Smith's congressional experience was also characterized by a rugged individualism, and, with one or two exceptions, an admirable integ-

---

62. *Congressional Debates,* 22d Cong., 1st sess., 1832, p. 1045.
63. S. Smith to Andrew Jackson, June 17, 1832, Smith Papers.
64. *Congressional Debates,* 22d Cong., 1st sess., 1832, p. 1296.

rity. No matter whether or not he approved of the administration currently in office, he had made his own judgments on the issues. Nor had he ever been afraid to tell presidents when he thought they were wrong. It would not be accurate to place Smith in the first rank of legislative leaders during the history of the early Republic. His inability to compromise on major questions kept him from enjoying the confidence that a president must have in his spokesmen in Congress, and at the same time unsuited him for the political log-rolling that allows a representative assembly to function. Yet he was influential, largely because he possessed knowledge and understanding of the complex commercial and financial problems that monopolized the attention of Congress during his tenure. His unexcelled ability to translate these problems into terms understandable to lawyers and planters also made him a valuable advisor to every administration from Jefferson's to Jackson's. He was not a philosopher like Jefferson or Calhoun, nor an orator like Webster or Clay, nor even a charismatic politician like Jackson, but his career was as honorable as theirs and his accomplishments entitle him to an important niche in American history. He had earned a peaceful and honored retirement, but within a few years he would again be called upon by the citizens of Baltimore, as they had done so often before, to serve in a public capacity.

16

Return to Baltimore

AFTER FORTY years on the public payroll Samuel Smith returned to Baltimore without a job. During the last few months of his term in the Senate he had lobbied on his own behalf for an appointment that would ease his chronic financial plight. Jackson and Van Buren had been most sympathetic, but they had declined to honor his request that he be sent as the new minister to Great Britain. Instead they offered him the post of collector at the port of Baltimore, which he declined, considering the position too taxing for a man of his age. He added that it was also a job without power. Having failed to obtain an acceptable government position, he and Margaret settled back in their home near Exchange Place to enjoy each other and their numerous children and grandchildren. Nearby were John Spear Smith and his family, who still lived at stately Montebello. John had risen to prominence in Baltimore, having been appointed a brigadier general in the Maryland militia. Along with a cousin, John had started a sugar plantation in Louisiana which had proved lucrative, and together with the money made by his farming operations at Montebello, his fortune had reached modest proportions.[1]

Much less happy for Samuel and Margaret were their relations with Christopher Hughes, who had married their daughter Laura. For

1. Martin Van Buren to S. Smith, December 19, 1832, Louis McLane to S. Smith, February 25, 1834, and S. Smith to Andrew Jackson, March 11, 1834, Samuel Smith Papers, Library of Congress.

no other man, not even his son John, had the general done so much. Since before 1824 he had exerted himself to promote Hughes' diplomatic career and had successfully obtained for him several minor missions. This was no mean feat considering Hughes' reputation for arrogance and sheer foolishness. John Quincy Adams had once described him as a man who believed that the "whole science of diplomacy consists in giving dinners . . ." Yet Adams had, at Smith's request, appointed Hughes to be chargé d'affaires to the Netherlands. Van Buren and Jackson had even a lower opinion of Smith's son-in-law than Adams, but, as the secretary of state freely admitted, the administration would allow Hughes to serve as chargé in Stockholm out of respect for the man who nominated him. Hughes, however, considered the Stockholm position beneath his dignity and became increasingly hostile toward Smith, whom he seemed to believe was the cause of his failure to progress in the foreign service.[2] When Laura died late in 1832, the bond between the two men was broken. Waiting until the general was retired and able neither to help nor harm him in Congress, Hughes spilled out his hatred toward his former patron. In a letter to the general dated June 9, 1834, he expressed his "disgust and rage" and talked of the "uninterrupted series of wrongs, of injustice and cruel persecutions that I have suffered at your hands, and those of your family, ever since I had the misfortune . . . of marrying your daughter."[3] After placing the letter in his papers, marking it "A Ridiculous letter from Christopher Hughes," the old man sadly and temperately replied, denying Hughes' charges. The younger man later apologized but Smith refused to have any further communication with him.[4]

Though in retirement, Smith kept up his correspondence with friends still in the government. He displayed growing disenchantment with Jackson, believing that through his use of patronage the president had centralized power in his own hands at the expense of Congress. He was particularly disturbed when his friend Louis McLane was forced to resign from the treasury department after refusing to obey Jackson and remove federal funds from the expiring Bank of the United States. By the summer of 1834 he was suggesting that McLane should be nominated by the Democratic party to replace Jackson in

2. Charles Francis Adams, ed., *Memoirs of John Quincy Adams,* 12 vols. (Philadelphia, 1874–1877), 6: 539, 520; Van Buren to S. Smith, November 3, 1829, and Christopher Hughes to S. Smith, October 26, 1829, Smith Papers.

3. Hughes to S. Smith, June 9, 1834, Smith-Carter Papers, University of Virginia Library.

4. S. Smith to Hughes, June 10, 1834, Smith-Carter Papers.

the presidency rather than Van Buren, whom he suspected would only continue the present policies.[5] But Smith's interest in national politics was in reality hardly more than academic, and he devoted most of his time to his family and his own financial affairs.

Like most citizens of Baltimore, the general was perturbed by the sudden financial panic that began in the spring of 1834 and produced much economic distress. The basic cause of the numerous bank failures in the city, and for that matter around the country, was a sudden contraction of credit by the Bank of the United States. As part of a plan to force President Jackson to reverse himself and accept a new charter for the bank, Nicholas Biddle had tried to mobilize public support by purposely creating a monetary crisis. In demanding that local banks redeem their bills immediately in specie the bank had pushed many financial institutions to the wall. Under this pressure a number of banks and insurance companies in Baltimore collapsed, among them the prestigious Bank of Maryland, of which Smith had once been a director. Subsequent investigation of the bank of Maryland's affairs uncovered a sordid story of irresponsible speculation on the part of the president and several directors. Among other things, these officials had freely used the bank's assets to buy control of other businesses in the city but without furnishing adequate security.[6]

After the Bank of Maryland closed down, its affairs were put in the hands of trustees, who were responsible for eventually distributing its remaining assets to the depositors. Thousands of Baltimoreans who had placed funds in the institution waited patiently for seventeen months as legal technicalities prevented the trustees from making public an accounting of the bank's condition. Meanwhile, they were treated to a prolonged controversy in which the president, directors, and trustees published pamphlets blaming each other for the fiasco. This paper warfare served only to fan resentment among the many small depositors who had been ruined by the bank's failure. Moreover, only the former president of the Bank of Maryland had surrendered his mansion and personal possessions to pay off the debt he had incurred as part of the speculations. The directors, Reverdy Johnson,

5. S. Smith to unknown recipient, August 11, 1834, and McLane to S. Smith, August 23, 1834, Smith Papers.

6. Bray Hammond, *Banks and Politics in America from the Revolution to the Civil War* (Princeton, 1957), pp. 429–440; Glyndon G. Van Deusen, *The Jacksonian Era, 1828–1848* (New York, 1959), pp. 83–84; Matthew Page Andrews, *History of Maryland* (Garden City, N.Y., 1929), p. 49; J. Thomas Scharf, *History of Maryland from the Earliest Period to the Present Day*, 3 vols. (Baltimore, 1879), 3: 176–179; Annapolis *Maryland Gazette*, August 27, 1835.

John Glenn, Evan Ellicott, David Perine, and Hugh McElderry, continued to live in splendor. Predictably tensions grew, and in August 1835 the city erupted into violence.[7]

What would become one of the worst riots in American history up to that time began on the morning of Thursday, August 6, when a small group of men began breaking the windows in Reverdy Johnson's home on Monument Square. Mayor Jesse Hunt arrived on the scene and peacefully disbursed the crowd. Then, in an effort to head off further acts of vandalism, he called for a town meeting that afternoon to rally public opinion. With Hunt acting as chairman, the well-attended gathering resolved that the present trustees of the Bank of Maryland should surrender its books and papers to a committee made up of the bank's creditors, who would then report on what they found. It was already too late. Some of those attending the town meeting went back to Johnson's house and resumed hurling stones. Although Hunt once again was able to restore order, rumors abounded that an attempt would be made the next night to destroy the Johnson home. On Friday Hunt deputized five hundred citizens to seal off Monument Square and that night, armed only with sticks, they fought a pitched battle with a mob numbering in the thousands. While able to keep the crowd from entering the square, the hard-pressed deputies could not save John Glenn's mansion on north Calvert Street. Wielding brickbats, another mob sacked and burned the Glenn house despite repeated charges by mounted police.[8]

Save for a crowd that pulled down the walls of the Glenn house, Saturday was deceptively quiet as both sides regrouped. On Sunday, however, violence resumed on a much larger scale. Police and deputies were now carrying guns, and, when swarms of rioters again stormed Monument Square, the order was given to fire. At least ten but probably dozens more were killed and an unknown number wounded. Still, it was apparent that the city government had been overwhelmed, and the property belonging to the directors of the Bank of Maryland was systematically demolished. Even Reverdy Johnson's house finally was taken and pulled down. By Sunday night the rioters had seized control of the city and freed those who had been arrested earlier. In despair Mayor Hunt resigned after disbanding the special force of deputies which he feared would be massacred if it remained in the streets. After watching public authority

7. Baltimore *Gazette*, August 7, 1835, reprinted in the Annapolis *Maryland Gazette*, August 13, 1835; Scharf, *History of Maryland*, 3: 179.

8. Baltimore *Gazette*, August 8 and 10, 1835, reprinted in the Annapolis *Maryland Gazette*, August 13, 1835; Andrews, *History of Maryland*, p. 460.

vanish and seeing parts of the city put to the torch, a newspaper reporter wrote that Baltimore had returned to its "original elements."[9]

On Monday morning, August 10, large numbers of the nonrioting citizens of the city came together at the Exchange, where town meetings were usually held. There seemed to be no particular organization behind the gathering, but before long a general feeling that something must be done led to a demand for leadership and action. Very soon, according to the newspapers, Samuel Smith appeared and was chosen to be chairman of the meeting. Though eighty-three, the general still walked firmly and stood straight. Facing the crowd he told them that the time for resolutions had passed and it was necessary to act. Then, clutching an American flag, he began marching through the streets. By the time he had reached Howard Park several thousand people had rallied behind him ready to follow his instructions. At the park Smith was joined by the president of the first branch of the Baltimore city council, General Anthony Miltenberger, who had legally assumed the duties of mayor, and his own son, General John Spear Smith, commander of the militia. The three men addressed those present, telling them to arm themselves and then report to the mayor's office for orders. Within an hour Smith and his son dispatched armed parties to key points within the city, and large patrols were sent to march through the riot areas. Either because they had achieved their goals or feared the show of force, the rioters had fled and no resistance was met.[10] "The moment the citizens marched from the Exchange, under the veteran General Smith," the Baltimore *Patriot* reported, "and the American standard was seen moving in the air, riot and rebellion ceased."[11]

Because he had once more saved the city by providing leadership when it was most needed, the general became a natural candidate for the vacant office of mayor. Baltimore's newspapers led the movement to have him elected. The *Chronicle* insisted that the choice was logical since the "present tranquility" in the city was entirely due

9. Baltimore *Gazette*, August 11, 1835, reprinted in the Annapolis *Maryland Gazette*, August 13, 1835; Baltimore *Patriot*, August 10, 1835, reprinted in the Washington, D.C. *National Intelligencer*, August 12, 1835; Scharf, *History of Maryland*, 3: 181.

10. Baltimore *Chronicle*, August 11, 1835, and Baltimore *American*, August 11, 1835, reprinted in the Washington, D.C. *National Intelligencer*, August 12, 1835; Baltimore *Patriot*, August 10 and 12, 1835, reprinted in the Washington, D.C. *National Intelligencer*, August 12 and 13, 1835; A. Miltenberger to S. Smith, August 10, 1835, Smith Papers; Scharf, *History of Maryland*, 3: 181–182.

11. Baltimore *Patriot*, August 10, 1835, reprinted in the Washington, D.C. *National Intelligencer*, August 12, 1835.

to the "energetic and manly stand taken by this venerable patriot at the Exchange on Monday, in the first instance, and subsequently in the park."[12] The editors of the *Patriot* were just as emphatic: "From the first moment that the question was then brought up, until the period of our writing this paragraph, we have heard but one name mentioned in connection with this office: it is that of General SAM-UEL SMITH."[13] Baltimore's voters obviously shared these sentiments, for they turned out in unprecedented numbers on September 7 to give him their support. A day later he took the oath of office and began yet another chapter in his connection with the city he loved so deeply.[14]

Being elected mayor of Baltimore was an appropriate culmination of Samuel Smith's political career. He had contributed personally to the city's development as a merchant, defended it as a soldier, and championed its interests in Congress as a politician. Now he had the opportunity as mayor to directly administer its affairs. Baltimore had changed a great deal since he had first seen it from his father's wagon in 1759. Then it had been nothing more than a village, but in the mid-1830s it was the third largest city in the United States, and its population, over one hundred thousand, was the fastest growing in the country. It was also one of the most beautiful cities in America, if the accounts of foreign travelers can be believed. Uniformly they praised its white marbled public buildings, the splendid fountains and monuments, and the tasteful red brick mansions which abounded within the city limits.[15]

Although some thought the job of mayor would be too much for the aged Smith, he in fact turned out to be an energetic and competent chief executive. Within the city he used the power of his office to improve streets, marketplaces, and harbor facilities. During his administration the ship channel in the Patapsco was substantially deepened. The general went to great lengths to maintain public peace, the chief reason he had been elected to office in the first place. Although there were no major riots, Baltimore was plagued with

12. Baltimore *Chronicle*, August 12, 1835, reprinted in the Washington, D.C. *National Intelligencer*, August 13, 1835.

13. Baltimore *Patriot*, August 13, 1835, reprinted in the Washington, D.C. *National Intelligencer*, August 14, 1835.

14. Nathaniel F. Williams to S. Smith, August 31, 1835, Smith Papers; "The Mayors of Baltimore," *The Baltimore Municipal Journal* (Baltimore, 1919), p. 47.

15. Andrews, *History of Maryland*, pp. 456–458; S. Smith to Mrs. Mansfield, August 31, 1837, Smith-Carter Papers; Raphael Semmes, *Baltimore as Seen by Visitors* (Baltimore, 1953), pp. 103–136.

gangs of teenagers, both white and black, who fought with each other and annoyed other citizens. Smith ordered the police authorities to patrol the streets and break up the gangs, arresting those carrying concealed weapons. Reflecting the general prejudices of the age, the mayor was especially vigorous in punishing Negroes who misbehaved. Under his administration there was a double standard of justice. Negroes received twice the punishment, usually administered with a lash, that whites were subjected to for committing the same crime. Whatever the ethics of his conduct, Smith succeeded in maintaining law and order. "Never was a city of 100,000 more quiet or more peaceable than Baltimore," he confided to one of his daughters.[16]

Smith also used the mayor's office to seek outside aid for the city. Working closely with his former military aide, Isaac McKim, the holder of his old seat in the House of Representatives, the general obtained federal funds to rebuild the Lazaretto, which had burned down in 1836. A combination warehouse and quarantine facility, the Lazaretto was vitally important to the conduct of business at the port of Baltimore. In convincing the government to provide funds for a new building, Smith saved the city a great deal of money. He also did what he could to persuade the state government to appropriate funds to complete or expand the extensive system of canals and railroads that were beginning to make Baltimore a major entrepôt for the agricultural products of western Pennsylvania and the Ohio valley. In 1836 he took the lead in calling for a state internal improvements convention, which was held in Baltimore. Representatives from every county in Maryland met and passed resolutions asking the state legislature to support major transportation projects. Partly in response to the convention's requests the General Assembly did authorize the state to grant appropriations to the Baltimore and Ohio railroad, the Chesapeake and Ohio canal, and several other corporations.[17]

The general proved to be a strong mayor during his three years in office. His annual messages to the city council resembled those that a president might send to Congress. In them he explicitly suggested what measures he wished to see passed, and the city records indicate

16. "Mayors of Baltimore," p. 47; see Smith's messages to the City Council on January 4, 1836, January 2, 1837, and January 1, 1838, in "Mayor's Messages, 1832–1860," Baltimore City Records, City Hall, Baltimore; S. Smith to Mrs. Mansfield, August 31, 1837, Smith-Carter Papers.

17. S. Smith's message to the City Council of January 2, 1837, "Mayor's Messages," Baltimore City Records; Isaac McKim to S. Smith, February 1, 1836, Smith Papers; S. Smith to McKim and Benjamin Howard, January 18, 1837, Smith-Carter Papers; Scharf, *History of Maryland,* 3: 184–186.

that the city council usually followed his lead. Smith was also not afraid to be innovative. He proposed major changes in the organization of the city government which led to the creation of the Deputy City Register's office, a post adding to the efficient conduct of business. In two of his annual messages Smith proposed that the mayor's term of office be changed from two to three years, but this was never acted upon. To cut Baltimore's rising welfare costs he urged the city council to follow the precedent of the English poor law and send paupers back to the countries from which they came. Although this scheme was not implemented, it, together with his other ideas, indicated an effort to deal with urban problems that are still present over a century later.[18]

Smith positively enjoyed being mayor. Nothing pleased him more than to report to the city council on such matters as the number of houses that had been built, the amount of tonnage entering the harbor, or the progress of the Baltimore and Ohio railroad. And by all accounts the city believed he was doing a good job. After two years in office he could tell his daughter Mary Mansfield that "I perform all my duties as Mayor to the satisfaction of the good people."[19] He was still much in demand for such ceremonial celebrations as the fashionable military ball held in January 1836. According to the Baltimore *Republican* the general was the chief guest of honor at the ball and headed the grand march: "our venerable Mayor, who had brushed up his regimentals for the occasion, led the way, supported by the Masters of Ceremonies. The undimmed eye of the old patriot flashed with all the ardour of his youthful days as he marched round the spacious arena, the proud leader of the fairest and bravest of the city."[20] In all likelihood this adulation in Baltimore, the city that had been so central to his life, meant as much if not more to him than any other triumph in his career.

In November of 1838 Smith stepped down as mayor and six months later, on April 22, 1839, he died, apparently of a heart attack. "Another Patriot gone!", mourned *Niles' Weekly Register*, commenting that the general had died "full of years and honors."[21] Most of the Baltimore papers printed the editions announcing Smith's death with heavy black lines around the borders of the pages. All included long

18. "Mayors of Baltimore," p. 47; S. Smith's messages to the City Council of January 4, 1836, January 2, 1837, and January 1, 1838, "Mayor's Messages," Baltimore City Records.

19. S. Smith to Mrs. Mansfield, August 31, 1837, Smith-Carter Papers.

20. Baltimore *Republican,* January 8, 1836.

21. *Niles' Weekly Register,* April 27, 1839.

editorials praising him and recounting the major events of his life, usually stressing his military service in the Revolution and the War of 1812. Relatively little was said about his political career. His great success as a merchant was emphasized, with one editor styling him the "founder of the commerce of our city."[22]

Smith's funeral was by all accounts the grandest Baltimoreans had witnessed to that time. With great care the Baltimore city council supervised the spectacle, which took place on April 25.[23] Hours before the funeral procession began its slow progression through the city's streets, crowds had already assembled. Along every avenue through which the hearse would pass thousands of citizens jostled each other for a better view. Every window that overlooked the route contained eager spectators anxiously straining for the first glimpse of the cortege. Finally, at half past four o'clock in the afternoon, the long, somber parade began.

The commercial, military, and political aspects of Smith's long life were all well represented in the procession. Leading the mourners were units of the Baltimore militia. After the hearse followed carriages containing the general's family and innumerable dignitaries. Of particular interest to the vast crowds was the presence of almost every important official in the city, state, and federal government. The mayor of Baltimore, the governor of Maryland, and the president of the United States, Martin Van Buren, all shared the same coach. Van Buren's participation in the ceremonies undoubtedly stemmed not only from respect for a deceased elder statesman but also from genuine grief at the loss of a friend he had known for many years. Next in line were the carriages containing members of the president's cabinet, including Secretary of State John Forsyth, Secretary of War Joel Poinsett, Secretary of the Navy James K. Paulding, and Attorney General Felix Grundy. The line of notables stretched back for many blocks. Representatives, senators, diplomats, city councilmen, and members of the state legislature mingled with the merchants, bankers, and industrialists of Baltimore. Following the great and near great marched a seemingly endless column of militia formations and the city fire brigades.

The very last group in the cortege proved the most interesting. Thousands of plain citizens spontaneously joined the procession. Unlike the others these people had no official reason to be present; only genuine sorrow and respect could explain their actions. As one

22. Baltimore *Republican*, April 24, 1839; Baltimore *Sun*, April 25, 1839; Baltimore *American*, April 23, 1839.
23. A copy of the funeral plans is in the Smith Papers.

newspaper pointed out, the people were reacting to the loss of a symbol as well as a man; the children of the third generation after independence grieved at the death of a co-patriot of the founding fathers as well as the loss of Samuel Smith.[24]

The hearse, drawn by four white horses and flanked by mounted dragoons, passed through Baltimore's streets amid signs that the city attached great significance to the event of the general's funeral. Bells slowly tolled, stores were closed, and in the crowded harbor, activity ceased, as every ship, regardless of nationality, lowered its flag to half-mast. Each minute a cannon at Fort McHenry boomed a salute to the man who had saved the city from invasion a quarter-century earlier. But it was the crowds that impressed observers, both because of the numbers and the intensity of feeling many individuals manifested. It was not an uncommon sight to see both adults and children crying as the cortege passed. The procession ended at the cemetery of the First Presbyterian Church, of which Smith had been a lifelong member. There, after the appropriate prayers and eulogies, the casket was placed in the Smith family vault and the mourners slowly dispersed.[25]

24. John Spear Smith to unknown recipient, April 29, 1839, Smith-Carter Papers; J. Thomas Scharf, *Chronicles of Baltimore* (Baltimore, 1874), pp. 497–499.

25. Baltimore *Sun*, April 26, 1839; S. C. Larkin to Margaret Spear Smith, May 7, 1839, Smith Papers.

Selected Source Material and Index

Selected Source *Material*

Samuel Smith lived through eighty-seven eventful years. His life spanned the Revolution, the early national period, the War of 1812, the Era of Good Feelings, and the Jacksonian years. Each of these periods in the American past has attracted the interest of many historians, and the literature is consequently of mountainous proportions. In the bibliographical material that follows I have included pertinent manuscripts and printed primary sources. References to the secondary works used in this study are located in the footnotes. Readers seeking more information on a certain topic should consult the notes and bibliographies in the appropriate volumes I have cited.

MANUSCRIPTS

There are major collections of Smith manuscripts at the Library of Congress, Washington, D.C., and in the Smith-Carter Papers at the University of Virginia, Charlottesville. A small but valuable collection of Smith letters is located at the Maryland Historical Society, Baltimore. Large numbers of Smith letters can be found in the papers of William Eustis, Thomas Jefferson, James Madison, Wilson Cary Nicholas, and Martin Van Buren at the Library of Congress; in the papers of Wilson Cary Nicholas at the University of Virginia; in the papers of Otho Holland Williams and the Smith & Co. Letterbook at the Maryland Historical Society; and in records of the War and Navy departments located in the National Archives, Washington, D.C. Among other manuscript collections useful in reconstructing Samuel Smith's career are the following, listed by depositories:
Library of Congress, Washington, D.C.
James A. Bayard Papers
Stephen R. Bradley Family Papers
Breckinridge Family Papers
George W. Campbell Papers

Henry Clay Papers
Augustus Foster Papers
Alexander Hamilton Papers
Andrew Jackson Papers
James McHenry Papers
James Monroe Papers
Gouverneur Morris Papers
Robert Morris Papers
Joseph Hopper Nicholson Papers
Personal Papers Miscellaneous
Timothy Pickering Papers
William Plumer Papers
Randolph-Garnett Letterbook
John Randolph Papers
William Cabell Rives Papers
Rodney Family Papers
Massachusetts Historical Society, Boston
Adams Family Papers
Thomas Jefferson Papers in the Coolidge Collection
Maryland Historical Society, Baltimore
Bayard Papers
Elizabeth Patterson Bonaparte Papers
Harper-Pennington Papers
John Eager Howard Papers
Edward Lloyd Papers
James McHenry Papers
William Vans Murray Papers
Robert Oliver Papers
William Patterson Papers
William Pinkney Papers
Randolph-Key Letterbook
Benjamin Stoddert Papers
William Wirt Papers
New-York Historical Society, New York City
Albert Gallatin Papers
University of Virginia, Charlottesville
James Barbour Papers
Edgehill-Randolph Papers
Thomas Jefferson Papers
John Randolph Papers
Creed Taylor Papers

NEWSPAPERS

Newspapers provide much information about Samuel Smith's activities. Among other things newspapers frequently printed open letters by Smith on political issues, while notices of ship departures and arrivals revealed some information on the operations of S. Smith & Buchanan. And, of course, the newspapers add detail about such important local events as the British attack in 1814 and the bank riot in 1835. Among the more important newspapers used in this study were the following:

Annapolis
   Maryland Gazette
Baltimore
   American
   Evening Post
   Federal Gazette & Baltimore Daily Advertiser
   Federal Intelligencer and Baltimore Daily Gazette
   Federal Republican
   Gazette
   Niles' Weekly Register
   Patriot
   Sun
   Telegraphe and Daily Advertiser
   Whig
Philadelphia
   Aurora
Washington, D.C.
   National Intelligencer

GOVERNMENT DOCUMENTS

The following government documents provide a major source for Smith's activities in Congress over four decades and help illuminate local and national politics in the early national period:

American State Papers. Documents, Legislative and Executive, of the Congress of the United States. 38 vols. Washington, D.C., 1832–1861.

The Debates and Proceedings in the Congress of the United States . . . 1789–1824. 42 vols. Washington, D.C., 1834–1856.

First Records of Baltimore Town and Jones Town, 1729–1797. Baltimore, 1905.

Ford, Worthington Chauncey, ed. *Journal of the Continental Congress.* 34 vols. Washington, D.C., 1907.

Greely, A. W., ed. *Public Documents of the First Fourteen Congresses, 1789–1817.* Washington, D.C., 1900.

Hoyt, William D., Jr., ed. "Civilian Defense in Baltimore, 1814–1815." *Maryland Historical Magazine* 39 (September 1944): 199–224, 39 (December 1944): 293–309, 40 (March 1945): 7–23, 40 (June 1945): 137–232.

Journal of the Executive Proceedings of the Senate of the United States, 1789–1948. 90 vols. Washington, D.C., 1828–1948.

Miller, Hunter, ed. *Treaties and Other International Acts of the United States of America.* 8 vols. Washington, D.C., 1931–1948.

"Mayor's Messages." Baltimore City Records. City Hall, Baltimore.

"The Mayors of Baltimore." *The Baltimore Municipal Journal.* Baltimore, 1919.

Register of Debates in Congress, 1825–1837. 29 vols. Washington, D.C., 1825–1837.

Richardson, J. D., ed. *Compilation of the Messages and Papers of the Presidents, 1789–1897.* 10 vols. Washington, D.C., 1907.

Statutes at Large of the United States of America, 1789–1873. 17 vols. Boston, 1850–1873.

Steiner, B. C., et al., eds. *Archives of Maryland—Journal and Correspondence of the State Council of Maryland.* 63 vols. Baltimore, 1884–1946.

PRINTED PRIMARY SOURCES

Published letters and diaries are plentiful for this period, and this study has made extensive use of those pertinent to Smith's career. Among printed sources dealing with Samuel Smith specifically are C. I. Bushnell, ed., *Memoirs of Samuel Smith, a Soldier of the Revolution, 1776–1786* (Baltimore, 1860); and the letters written by Smith to George Washington arranged under the title "Defense of Fort Mifflin," *Maryland Historical Magazine* 5 (September 1910): 207–228.

A brief and very selective list of published papers vital to this study would include the following:

Adams, Charles Francis, ed. *Memoirs of John Quincy Adams, comprising portions of his Diary from 1795–1848.* 12 vols. Philadelphia, 1874–1877.

————. *The Works of John Adams.* 10 vols. Boston, 1850–1856.

Adams, Henry, ed. *The Writings of Albert Gallatin.* 2 vols. Philadelphia, 1879.

Ames, Seth, ed. *Works of Fisher Ames.* 2 vols. Boston, 1854.

Benton, Thomas Hart. *Thirty Years' View.* 2 vols. New York, 1886.

Brown, Everett S., ed. *William Plumer's Memorandum of Proceedings in the United States Senate, 1803–1807.* New York, 1923.

Dodd, William E., ed. "Nathaniel Macon Correspondence." *John P. Branch Historical Papers of Randolph-Macon College* 3 (June 1909): 27–93.

Donnan, Elizabeth, ed. "Papers of James A. Bayard, 1796–1815." *Annual Report for 1913 of the American Historical Association.* 2 vols. Washington, D.C., 1915.

Fitzpatrick, John C., ed. *The Autobiography of Martin Van Buren, Annual Report of the American Historical Association, 1918.* 2 vols. Washington, D.C., 1920.

Ford, Paul Leicester, ed. *The Writings of Thomas Jefferson.* 10 vols. New York, 1892–1899.

Ford, Worthington C., ed. "Letters of William Duane." Massachusetts Historical Society, *Proceedings* 2d ser., 20: 257–394.

————. *The Writings of George Washington*. 14 vols. New York, 1889–1893.

————. *Writings of John Quincy Adams*. 7 vols. New York, 1913–1917.

Haynes, George H., ed. "Letters of Samuel Taggart." American Antiquarian Society, *Proceedings* n.s., 33 (1923).

Hemphill, W. Edwin, ed. *Papers of John C. Calhoun*. 3 vols. Columbia, S.C., 1967.

Hopkins, James F., ed. *Papers of Henry Clay*. 2 vols. Lexington, Ky., 1959.

Hunt, Gaillard, ed. *The First Forty Years of Washington Society*. New York, 1906.

Lodge, Henry Cabot, ed. *The Works of Alexander Hamilton*. 9 vols. New York, 1885–1886.

McGrane, Reginald C., ed. *The Correspondence of Nicholas Biddle Dealing with National Affairs, 1807–1844*. Boston, 1966.

Morison, Samuel E., ed. *The Life and Letters of Harrison Gray Otis*. 2 vols. Boston, 1913.

Steiner, Bernard C., ed. *The Life and Correspondence of James McHenry*. Cleveland, 1907.

Index